KAYFABE

A Love Story

DAVE RUETER

Copyright © 2023
Dave Rueter
KAYFABE
A Love Story
All rights reserved.

No part of this publication may be reproduced, distributed, or transmitted in any form or by any means, including photocopying, recording, or other electronic or mechanical methods, without the prior written permission of the author, except in the case of brief quotations embodied in critical reviews and certain other non-commercial uses permitted by copyright law.

Dave Rueter
KayfabeLoveStory@gmail.com

Printed Worldwide
First Printing 2023
First Edition 2023

Paperback ISBN: 978-1-7356370-4-4
Ebook ISBN: 978-1-7356370-5-1

10 9 8 7 6 5 4 3 2 1

Cover art by Ernon Wright

In loving memory of Rupert

"This Is One of the Greatest Matches I've Ever Seen, Gorilla."

Table of Contents

Prologue 1
How Much Money on the Plastic Surgery? 4
From Parts Unknown, Weight Unknown 10
Closed Fists Are Illegal 13
Mr. Hughes, the Trendsetter..16
454 Days 19
Handicapping the 1992 Royal Rumble 25
The Conspiracy of WrestleFest '90 30
The Doctor of Ineptitude, Slick 32
The Unlikely Contender 36
With Friends Like This..40
Can We Please Get "Rugged" Ronnie Garvin a Legitimate Partner? 45
Danny Davis, You Can Go to Hell! Straight to Hell 49
David vs. Goliath 53
The Night When Skinner (Maybe) Shocked the World 56
The Colossal Collapse 59
The Wrestling Classic 62
Did the Berzerker Just Try to Kill Somebody? 66
Snake-Bitten 69
Seeing Red 76
Your Favorite Xenophobic Uncle 80
First Intermission 85
Apartment(s) Building Owner, Paul Christy 88
Open Your Eyes, Zebra 92
Get Well Soon, Hulk 96
Tito's Mid-Life Crisis 98
Quality Over Quantity 101
The 1985 Manager of the Year...104

Lust in His Eyes	107
The Blockbuster Trade	111
The Mudlick Swindler	115
Inmate #902714	119
What Was the Worst Survivor Series Team Ever Assembled?	123
This Tuesday in Texas	128
The '89 Royal Rumble	132
Where Did Bad News Go?	135
The Stars and Stripes Challenge	139
The Roast of George Wells	145
The Avenger, Ron Bass	149
Not in the Face	153
Oh, Hey, It's Scott Casey	157
Did Hogan Just Tap?	159
If You Ain't Cheating, You Ain't Trying	162
Second Intermission	166
The Other, *Other* Streak	169
Jimmy Hart	174
What I'd Like to Have Right Now …	179
No Más	183
The Barber Shop Window	186
Marty's Revenge	190
Crazy Like a Fox	193
The Destruction of "Superstar" Billy Graham	197
Canada's Greatest Athlete?	201
The Ken Patera Story	206
The U.S. Express and Their Terrible, Horrible, No Good, Very Bad Day(s)	210
The Recruit	213
Uncle Elmer's Wedding	216
The Legion of Doom and Rocco	219
The Hart Foundation	222

The Boston Bunkhouse Battle Royal	225
Third Intermission	229
Papa Shango and the Yellow Bile	232
Jim Neidhart: The Final Boss Before Hogan	235
The 1990 Survivor Series and Great Expectations	238
The 1990 Survivor Series and Great Expectations	241
"Three years to be a champion. It's a long time."	243
And Then the Rains Came	250
The Jumping Bomb Angels	253
The Unlikely Contender	256
The Miracle in Topeka	259
"I Want My Country Back"	262
Unsanctioned	266
The Insincerity of Bob Backlund	270
Hogan/Warrior	273
Talk Show Host	277
Master Fuji's Betrayal	280
The Repo Man and That One Wrestling Challenge	283
The Body Slam Challenge	287
Managerial Malpractice	291
The Kid	294
Fuji Vice	298
What's the Story, Power and Glory	301
The Coronation of King Haku	305
You Sold Out! You Sold Out!	308
Captain Lou's Swan Song	311
"This Is One of the Greatest Matches I've Ever Seen, Gorilla"	315
Good Riddance, Tunney	321
A Love Story	327
Bibliography	334

Prologue

Like most great works of literature, the idea for this book originated from the November 25th, 1989 episode of *Saturday Night's Main Event*. The Big Boss Man, managed by the fast-talking and shifty Slickster, was set to battle "The American Dream" Dusty Rhodes. Rhodes was a crafty vet; a superstar who had seen and done it all. The Slickster, too, had a well-earned reputation. He was a pro-active manager who interjected himself into his guys' matches, and Dusty knew it. Before the bell, Dream worked the official, petitioning for Slick's banishment from ringside. The Doctor of Style was now on the defensive. He tried to worm his way out of the predicament like when your mom asked you and your brother who broke the lamp in the living room.

So Slick pulled out his wallet and handed something to official Earl Hebner.

"That's his manager license – of course. He's a legal manager."

– Jesse Ventura ("Saturday Night's Main Event XXIV").

Never mind that Slick had been a manager in the World Wrestling Federation since 1986. Set aside the fact that his "manager license" looked curiously like a business card. Earl Hebner had it on good authority (Dusty Rhodes) that the Doctor of Style's license hadn't been renewed, that his paperwork wasn't up to date, and the referee had every right to cross his T's and dot those I's.

(For the record, Slick was allowed to remain at ringside).

It's why I love pro wrestling. They've always been in on the joke. There's an endearing, self-deprecating charm about the art, and everything said is accompanied with a wink and a nod. Wrestlers who were billed from

Parts Unknown but spoke perfect English. Blind as bats referees who had a better chance of finding the Fountain of Youth than catching I.R.S. holding the rope for leverage during an abdominal stretch. (Like seriously, Irwin grabbed the top rope *every time*). Wrestling's *supposed* to be fun; well, unless you witnessed Randy Savage crush your favorite wrestler's larynx. That was horrifying (more on that in a later chapter). But career-threatening throat injuries aside, wrestling's supposed to be fun.

Kayfabe: A Love Story doesn't cover the 'shoot' side of pro wrestling. I don't mention wrestlers' real names, or pushes, and backstage heat. We don't get into contract disputes, or proposed finishes, or discuss why Jacques Rougeau once brought a roll full of quarters into his place of work. There are amazing podcasts and shoot interviews dedicated to just that – I recommend them all. For the purposes of this book, Hulk Hogan wasn't a character played by Terry Bollea. Hulk Hogan was just Hulk Hogan, a dominant and charismatic (albeit a bit preachy) wrestler from Venice Beach, CA who sabotaged every friendship he ever had. The Undertaker wasn't Mark Calaway. The Undertaker was an intimidating force who got his jollies by pushing people into caskets, and the Red Rooster was – well – a rooster. You get the idea.

Paying homage to my favorite WrestleMania (1987's WrestleMania III), the book is 87 chapters of kayfabe. It covers World Wrestling Federation storylines, angles, wrestlers, and match finishes that cover the gambit from WrestleMania I through 1993.

Wait, hold up, Dave. No Attitude Era? Is this amateur hour?

Yeah – I knew you were going to hammer me for that. Do you know how many weeks are in a year? Do you know how much wrestling programming aired from '85 through '93? The fire marshal already threatened to shut us down by chapter 75. I couldn't sneak Steve Austin *and* every In Your House pay-per-view into the club. I gotta sleep sometimes, too. Besides, you always leave room for a sequel. Think of this book as the '91 Survivor Series to the not-yet-written This Tuesday in Texas.

In my research, I watched every PPV in this nine-year span, including the inaugural King of the Ring, The Wrestling Classic and The Big Event. I ran through every *Saturday Night's Main Event* and '93 *Raws*. I checked off *Tuesday Night Titans* and the Slammys. The Network was spotty in their library of *Wrestling Challenge* and *Superstars* episodes, but YouTube and Dailymotion picked up the slack. I watched *Prime Time*. Ok, I watched a lot of *Prime Time*. It became the backdrop of my life these past two years. (I swear "Iron" Mike Sharpe wrestled on every *Prime Time*). There were also the WrestleFests and the Coliseum Videos, so if you've been wandering through life in search of a chapter on *The Ken Patera Story*, you've purchased the right book. I rounded out my watch party with random episodes of *All-American*, *Championship Wrestling*, and *Mania*.

I got to relive stuff I haven't seen in years. My "research" drummed up these feelings of nostalgia, and I hope the book does the same for you. If you're here, you're willing to suspend disbelief. We're all adults. We're smart. Of course, we know there weren't two Dave Hebners, but still, between you and me, like how much did Ted DiBiase *really* pay for the plastic surgery?

It makes you think.

How Much Money on the Plastic Surgery?

> **Event:** *The Main Event* (Indianapolis, IN)
>
> **Match:** Andre the Giant (Challenger) vs. Hulk Hogan (Champion)
>
> **Date:** February 5th, 1988
>
> **Top Selling Video Game in the U.S:** *Mike Tyson's Punch-Out*

"Never in my wildest dreams, Mean Gene, would I think that I would get ripped off by a penny-pinching, two-timing referee! How much money on the plastic surgery!? How much money did he spend to pay the referee off!?"

– Hulk Hogan (*The Main Event*, February 5th, 1988).

The day after I graduated high school, my father gave me a very specific set of instructions.

"Get a job."

It was a short promo, but effective, nonetheless. I spent that morning scouring the classifieds of my local newspaper, looking to earn a little scratch and keep my pops off my back. Then I found it.

"$18/hr, no experience necessary."

Finally! Finally, someone recognized my skillset. I was the perfect fit. I both had no experience and wanted $18/hr. Considering minimum wage was $5.15 in 2002, this was the exact push my career needed. I called the number on the ad, and boy, were they excited to bring me in. It felt nice to be wanted honestly.

"Can you come in today for an interview?"

Sure can. Let me move a few things around. I'll just tape *The Price Is Right* and eat my Ellio's Pizza later. I had zero insight on the job description or even a company name, but those were just a few minor details to iron out. Fifteen or so of us crammed into a tiny office space when this flashy dude named 'Mike' (could've been a stage name) pulled out a collection of …

Knives.

I had stumbled into an interview for a sales position with Cutco Knives, perpetrator of one of the shadier business models around. We watched in awe as Mike cut a penny in half.

"Pretty cool, right?"

The coolest. Then he sliced a shoe in half, and that really brought the house down. I was 18, broke, and prepared to tap into my college fund to finance a $500 kitchenette set. I, too, wanted to cut a pair of Airwalks in half. Mike had the sales pitch down. He knew how to work the crowd. Mike could put asses in the seats.

I was hired on the spot. I had all the qualifications they were looking for in a knife salesman: Access to a car, and a list of family and friends that I could pitch. I hurried home to tell my dad. I understood the assignment: Find job. Get job. All in a day's work, pops.

"I got a job! I'm selling knives."

My dad grumbled.

"What? You told me to get a job."

"Not that job."

"These knives, you can cut a penny with 'em. You can cut a sneaker in half … You can cut your meats and your veggies … You can cut a penny with 'em … Did I mention the shoe thing?"

"Not while you're under my roof! You're not selling knives. My son isn't gonna be harassing all the neighbors. They all have knives! They don't need new ones!"

"But these are *extra sharp* knives, dad! Didn't you hear the part about the shoe?"

"Why would anyone cut a shoe!"

Ok, fair point. I put in my resignation, effective immediately. I was only a knife salesman for about an hour and a half, but what a ride it was.

~ ~ ~

Andre the Giant's championship run was over before it started. While his brief reign is officially acknowledged by the WWE – Ted DiBiase's is not – the minutes following his dubious victory over the Hulkster triggered a chaotic whirlwind that hadn't been replicated since the '72 Olympic Basketball Gold Medal game. The match had everything:

Poor officiating? Yes.

Bribery? We believe so.

Plastic surgery? There is mounting evidence.

Cloning? Can't rule it out.

Fans woke up the morning of *The Main Event* believing the sun rose in the east and there was only one Dave Hebner. By night's end, there were two. Money exchanged hands – allegedly. Plastic surgery was performed – allegedly. Hogan kicked out after a one count – allegedly.

The coup was orchestrated by DiBiase, who failed in his initial attempts to purchase the championship. While Hulk couldn't be bought, Andre understood the value of a dollar. So, the "Million Dollar Man" set his sights on the #1 contender. Buy Andre. Buy the title. It was an expensive and risky endeavor. For starters, you can't add the 8th Wonder of the World to the payroll for the league minimum. The Giant knew his worth. Then there was the *alleged* plastic surgery, where DiBiase recruited a down-on-his-luck sap to get a face transplant. Exactly how advanced was modern medicine in 1988? No, seriously. That's not rhetorical – I'm asking you. My only experience with facial plastic surgery is watching *Face/Off* on VHS. Imagine the desperation of this guinea pig, the overwhelming bills and mounting debt he must've been facing to go under the knife and wake up looking like Dave Hebner.

"Honey, sit down. I have something important to tell you. So, the good news is that we won't have to worry about the mortgage anymore. Or the car payments. Or those hospital bills ... But ... there's just one catch ... um ... so you see, this here in my hand is a picture of World Wrestling Federation referee Dave Hebner ... Handsome, right?"

"*Who's the real Dave Hebner? You tell me, Jesse Ventura!*" – Vince McMahon ("The Main Event").

The first few minutes of the title bout sailed by uninterrupted. Then the challenger tossed the Hulkster down with a modified hip toss, and all hell broke loose. Andre flopped on Hogan for the cover. The champ's shoulder appeared to lift off the mat after a one count, but Dave Hebner, or perhaps Clone Dave Hebner, didn't see it. (Or was paid not to see it). We had a new champion! Hogan protested the call, as Hogan was one to do. Meanwhile, the big man held up his end of the bargain. Andre gifted DiBiase with the World Title as boos rained down, then ... THEN ... a *second* Dave Hebner ran down the aisle.

Mass hysteria erupted, but to me it was clear: The Virtuous Dave Hebner was kidnapped and held hostage in a broom closet. The commotion from inside Market Square Arena invaded my living room. My pops wasn't overtly rooting for Andre, but he embraced the chaos. I looked to him for guidance, for a comforting hand. Surely, he would put my mind at ease; assure me that this miscarriage of justice would be overturned any second.

My dad only cackled. Fighting back tears, I screamed over and over in my Philly accent, "Hoke got his shoulder up! Hoke got his shoulder up," but Pops did nothing to lessen my rage.

"There are two Dave Hebners!" he laughed. "There are two of 'em! Where did that second one come from!"

As McMahon and Ventura tried to piece this puzzle together, I spiraled even more. If my dad had added, "Sorry, Dave, a referee's decision is final," I may have put a tiny fist through the drywall. Pops slapped his hand across his knee over and over, letting out a bellowing laugh, as both Dave Hebners accused the other of nefarious deeds. Despite my protest, the "Million Dollar Man" was your new champion. Well, that didn't work for me, brother. I ran under the dining room table and cried. I had never seen Hulk lose. The Hulkster didn't *lose*. He took every guy's best punch, then he Hulked up, and then he dropped the big leg. This was foreign territory. Yeah, Hogan had lost via count out at the '87 Survivor Series, but you think my parents sprung for a pay-per-view? On Thanksgiving no less? I probably watched a half hour of *The Wizard of Oz* until the tryptophan kicked in.

Whether by blown call or thrown call by Dave Hebner #1 or Dave Hebner #2, Andre got his WrestleMania III revenge. Save your asterisks. When you're facing the greatest force in professional wrestling, you take your breaks where you can get 'em. I doubt Don Denkinger's missed call in Game 6 of the '85 World Series tempered the celebration of Royals fans.

As for Hogan? He took Dave Hebner – seemingly the Evil one – and hurled him halfway to Muncie. My dad laughed at that, too.

FROM PARTS UNKNOWN, WEIGHT UNKNOWN

> Event: WrestleMania I (New York, NY)
>
> Match: The Executioner vs. Tito Santana
>
> Date: March 31st, 1985
>
> Attendance: 19,121
>
> #1 Movie on This Date: Police Academy 2: Their First Assignment

"Mean" Gene Okerlund interviewed the Executioner moments before the inaugural match of WrestleMania. The ring technician was candid. He pulled the curtain back on his gameplan – "I'm going after your leg" – which was as straightforward and direct as a 2 AM "U up?" text. The Executioner had a strategy. He also had complete command of the English language. He wasn't camera shy (outside of his mask anyway), and I never got the impression that he had trouble letting people in. The Executioner was, for all intents and purposes, an open book.

Moments later, however, Howard Finkel prefaced his introduction of the grappler with, "From Parts Unknown … and weight unknown …"

Wait, come again?

We don't know the place of residence and weight of *that* guy? The same guy who was minutes away from telling "Mean" Gene his thoughts on religion and the two-party political system. Didn't anybody consider just *asking* him?

"Hey, Executioner, where ya from?"

"Thanks for the question, Dave. I got family in Des Moines. I come from a long line of executioners. My father was an executioner, and his dad was an executioner. I got an uncle up the way in Cedar Falls. He's been in the executing business for years now."

"And what are you, about 250, 260?"

"Yeah, that's about right. I fluctuate a bit depending on the season. I get a real sweet tooth around the holidays."

I would say we needed a journalist to ask the tough questions (looking at you, Okerlund), but I don't think the questions were that difficult. Later that night, we were told that Brutus Beefcake also made his residence in Parts Unknown. We'd eventually discover that Brother Bruti was actually from the Bay Area. See? Was that so hard? It just took a little digging. These guys gotta live somewhere. Papa Shango and Ax and Smash – these other Parts Unknown guys – they must own or rent property somewhere. They're not commuting from Dimension X.

(After the Warlord was introduced for a 20-man over-the-top battle royal on a February 23rd, 1992 show at MSG, Monsoon ranted about this very topic).

"Parts Unknown? Where is that Parts Unknown? Do you mean to tell me you don't know where this guy's from? That he doesn't have a social security number? Or a passport?" (Championship Central 2021).

The Executioner's unknown weight was even more confounding, like it was the subject of an *Unsolved Mysteries* episode. You imagine that at some point, some pencil pusher from the New York State Athletic Commission put him on a scale. You got your permits, licenses, insurance coverage, etc, etc. A wrestler's weight is another required data point. Procedures must be followed; though, to be fair, would Gorilla have trusted the scale anyway? If the camera added ten pounds, then Monsoon tacked on fifty.

"Bundy comes into the match at 468, but from my vantage point, Jess, he's tipping the scales at around 515, maybe 530."

"Can't argue with you there, Geno."

"A condominium with legs indeed."

The Executioner never found his footing. Whether it was the mounting pressure of wrestling in front of a sold-out Madison Square Garden crowd, the unenviable task of facing a former Intercontinental Champion, or the sudden self-realization of his lonely, nomadic existence, the masked man struggled on the big stage. He didn't take advantage of Tito's bad wheel. The Executioner didn't capitalize on the prior damage inflicted by "The Hammer" Greg Valentine. Attacking Tito's leg was a sound strategy on paper, though sometimes even the best laid plans.

Our hero tapped out to the Figure-Four at 4:49.

Closed Fists Are Illegal

But are they though? All my life, I've been told that punching with a closed fist warrants an automatic disqualification, yet like jaywalking and shutting your laptop before a Windows update is complete, it seems like more a suggestion rather than law. Rules are meant to be broken, or in this case, never enforced. The 'no closed fist' is the most lax rule in wrestling outside the, "You have five seconds to leave the ring after a tag" (Looking at you, Marty and Shawn).

(The most heavily enforced rule is choking an opponent for five seconds. Wrestlers were terrified of that five count. Andre the Giant would strangle you with his singlet, sure, but he cut that shit out after 4 ½ seconds. He knew the consequences).

According to WWE official Jimmy Korderas, the closed fist was finally deemed legal in 2008 or so, but it's not like referees had been chomping at the bit to ring someone up for a left hook or a right cross (Korderas 2019). It's like waiting thirty minutes after eating before you go swimming. Yeah, it was an unwritten rule, but lifeguards didn't have a Royal Rumble-like countdown clock by the diving board. Wait twenty minutes. Wait five. Don't wait at all. Whatever. Polish off your peanut butter and jelly and work on those cannonballs (or can openers if, like me, you had to use one hand to hold your nose). Every wrestler broke the closed fist rule. Referees had no choice but to turn a blind eye. To demonstrate, I took a show from 1992 and re-created the results if officials had shown considerably less leniency:

> **Event: World Wrestling Federation Wrestling (Moline, IL)**
> **Date: January 5th, 1992**
> **Attendance: 3,000**

- Jim Brunzell def. Hercules via DQ (closed fist)
- Col. Mustafa and General Adnan def. Sgt. Slaughter via DQ in a handicap match (closed fist)
- The Undertaker def. Jim Duggan via DQ (closed fist)
- Repo Man def. Virgil via DQ (closed fist)
- I.R.S. def. The Big Boss Man via DQ (closed fist)
- The Nasty Boys def. The Bushwhackers via DQ (closed fist)
- "Macho Man" Randy Savage wrestled Jake "the Snake" Roberts to a double DQ (closed fist).

That would've been a 17-minute show, and 15 of those minutes would've been Irwin badgering people about their taxes. Leave the poor residents of Moline, IL be. It's January 5th. They got plenty of time to file.

I've never seen a match *without* the use of a closed fist. Did Duke "The Dumpster" Drose and Mantaur do their best E. Honda impression, and slap each other silly during a *Superstars* match in '95 and I just blocked it out? Every wrestler has a punch in their arsenal. What's the saying? Man can't survive on double axe handles alone? But while the rule was never enforced, it didn't stop people from lobbying for it. During the epic Intercontinental Championship match at WrestleMania III between Randy Savage and Ricky Steamboat, Jesse Ventura pointed out The Dragon's reliance on the closed fist. Bobby Heenan argued the same on the January 25th, 1993 *Monday Night Raw* when Mr. Perfect broke the rule in his Loser Leaves Town match with Ric Flair. Neither "The Body" or "The Brain" were awarded the call.

Research did discover one instance, however. There was a precedent. Perhaps to right a past wrong from his match with Mr. Perfect, Flair, while guest refereeing a December 29th, 2003 *Raw* tag contest between the Dudley Boyz and newcomers, Russell Simpson and Eddie Cramer, disqualified the Dudleys for their *illegal* use of a closed fist.

While the decision was unpopular with the San Antonio crowd, it was the correct call and one that took guts to make. Good on ya, Nature Boy.

Rules are rules after all.

Mr. Hughes, the Trendsetter

> Event: *Superstars* (Halifax, Nova Scotia)
> Match: The Undertaker vs. PJ Walker
> Date: June 12th, 1993
> Attendance: 8,000
> Highest Rated TV Show on this Date: *Dr. Quinn, Medicine Woman*

"What did I tell you? You're seeing history in the making. The Undertaker can't get up. It's the culmination of the greatest plot, hatched by the greatest mind I've ever seen, Harvey Wippleman."

– Jerry "The King" Lawler (*Superstars*, June 12th, 1993).

The Undertaker wasn't perfect. He wasn't this infallible entity. The Dead Man lost a handful of matches throughout his illustrious career. It wasn't impossible to beat Taker, just improbable. On a difficulty scale from 1 to 100, with 100 being landing that damn plane in Nintendo's *Top Gun*, beating the Dead Man was a 99. You didn't beat Taker cleanly. You couldn't beat him cleanly. Hogan blinded him. Yokozuna defeated him at Royal Rumble '94 with help from half the roster, and HBK got Taker at 1997's Badd Blood: In Your House. (All it took there was interference from the Undertaker's long-lost brother, who recovered from third-degree burns in a mental asylum). To beat the Dead Man, you needed a can-do attitude and lots and lots of luck. There was one constant, though; one strategy that seemed to be universally accepted over all others.

If you got his urn, you got the Undertaker.

To be clear, this wasn't some foolproof tactic. Stealing his most prized possession didn't guarantee Taker's annihilation, but it was a start. His urn was a source of strength, like Wonder Woman's Bracelets of Submission or Mike Sharpe's arm band. The Undertaker was the Phenom, this larger-than-life force, but maybe without his urn he became just *slightly* more human. Maybe? Opponents had to fight dirty – muck it up – and no one was better equipped to roll around in the gutter than Dr. Harvey Wippleman.

(Cue the Fink announcing, "Doctor ... Harvey Wippleman" with the biggest 'fuck you' eyeroll of all time).

Wippleman was one of the first managers who channeled his efforts towards the Dead Man's demise. He brought in guys from all walks of life. First, it was the Ugandan Headhunter, Kamala, who once ate a LIVE chicken on an episode of *Tuesday Night Titans*. Then it was an 8'0" behemoth in a (hairy) body suit. He didn't recruit grapplers with strong Greco-Roman backgrounds. He enlisted freaks and monsters. Wippleman understood that you weren't going to beat Taker with a half nelson and a victory roll. Case in point: At WrestleMania IX, Giant González suffocated the Phenom with a chloroform-soaked rag, which I don't believe is taught at wrestling schools. I credit their outside-the-box thinking. Toxin inhalation wasn't exactly a sleeper hold, just another way from Point A to B.

Leading up to their rematch at SummerSlam '93, Wippleman hatched another plan. González had proven to be formidable (losing by DQ), but there was no harm in stacking the deck. After the Undertaker disposed of up-and-comer PJ Walker on *Superstars*, Harvey and his prized protégé sauntered down to the ring. While Taker and the big man exchanged blows in the corner, Mr. Hughes, Wippleman's newest insurance policy, attacked

Paul Bearer from behind. Bearer wasn't a gatekeeper by trade. This wasn't Fort Knox. Stealing the urn from him was actually quite easy.

Even with possession of the urn, however, it was hard to imagine that the Undertaker would be undone by a guy who just finished his shift at Men's Wearhouse. But Trust the Process – don't let the suspenders fool you. Mr. Hughes was a powerhouse. He was also the only superstar who wrestled in sunglasses, and not even ones with polarized lenses. It would've been more pragmatic to rock some Rec Specs, ala Kurt Rambis, but who am I to question the big man's approach. Mr. Hughes had the urn, not me.

The crime wasn't without its punishment. Following the theft, the Undertaker had ominous funeral wreaths delivered ringside to Hughes' matches, accompanied by a note that read, "R.I.P. Mr. Hughes." He spared no expense in his psychological warfare, because those wreaths had to cost well over $100 a pop. I'm sure the Dead Man could've reclaimed his urn during any one of Hughes' matches, but where's the fun in that? He preferred emotional torture, like leaving a text message left on read.

Mr. Hughes eventually got the Dead Man in the ring. He went 0-5. (Hey, if it was easy to beat the Undertaker, then everyone would do it). But he earned points for creativity. Imitation is the sincerest form of flattery, and his methods would be studied and replicated for decades to follow. He was the first to steal Taker's urn and wouldn't be the last. Mr. Hughes walked, so Kama and CM Punk could run.

454 DAYS

"Like I said, what Honky Tonk lacks in ability, he makes up for ... the man is lucky."

– Jesse Ventura, May 7th, 1988 *Superstars*. (Monsoon Classic 2022).

I don't know how he did it. No one does. The Honky Tonk Man's success and his extraordinary Intercontinental Title reign still befuddles historians decades later. HTM survived on the bare minimum, a "C-" wrestler whose *NBA Jam* ratings would've looked something like this:

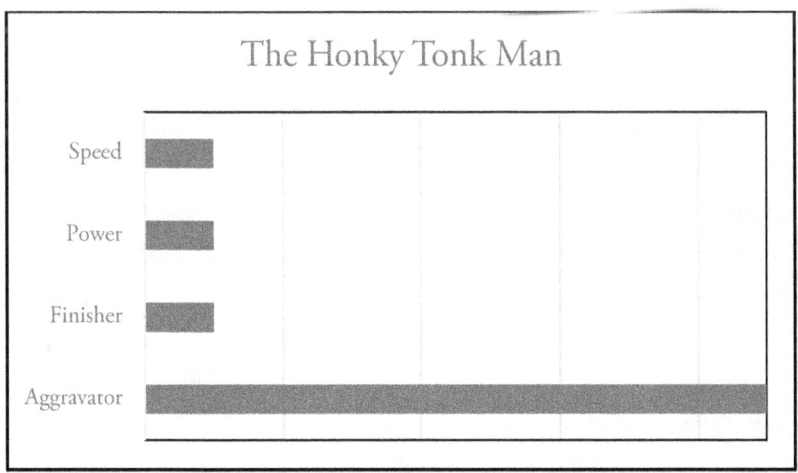

Nobody needed an ass kicking more than the Honky Tonk Man, and that includes "The Rebel" Dick Slater whose entire personality was the Confederate flag. HTM was delusional; a guy so unpopular that he was subject of a World Wrestling Federation poll that asked just one question.

"Do you like the Honky Tonk Man?"

Fans overwhelmingly voted 'no,' delivering a landslide that rivaled Franklin D. Roosevelt's win over Alf Landon in the 1936 U.S. Presidential Election. The contempt for HTM crossed international lines. On the December 11th, 1986 edition of *Prime Time*, the Honky Tonk Man wrestled Mr. X at the Maple Leaf Gardens, and you would've thought he was a goon for the Montreal Canadians. He got booed out of the building, while Mr. X, who wasn't exactly Toronto's own John Candy, earned a hero's reception. His repeated lack of self-awareness was stunning, almost unfathomable.

"People came to see the Honky Tonk Man sing."

That was unequivocally not true.

"People came to see the Honky Tonk Man dance."

SEE ABOVE.

I don't like Elvis Presley solely because of the Honky Tonk Man, which I know isn't fair, but the King of Rock and Roll is guilty by association. If there was no Elvis, there'd be no Honky, and if there was no Honky, Ricky Steamboat may still be Intercontinental Champion. On the June 13th, 1987 *Superstars*, the Honky Tonk Man stole the belt from "The Dragon." The result was deemed a major upset, because no shit. Steamboat was lightning fast, and sported the deepest arm drag in the business. Honky Tonk's offense of choice was a double axhandle. What followed was 454 days of hell, 454 days of Jimmy Hart's man clinging to his title by the skin of his teeth. I would've thrown my support behind any politician whose platform included the abolishment of the antiquated rule, "A title can only change hands via pinfall or submission." I think that "Province of Quebec Rules" stipulation has merit.

The Honky Tonk Man lost plenty between June 13th, 1987 and SummerSlam '88. The problem was, he only lost by count out or disqualification. On paper, pinning the champ seemed easy. Despite what

HTM may have had you believe in pre-match interviews; he was the underdog in just about every title defense. It takes a special person to get the shit beat out of you yet still come out smelling like roses. On that May 7th encounter with Hillbilly Jim, the Honky Tonk Man got *worked*. He looked frazzled and sluggish, and mounted next to no offense. The Man from Mudlick then missed a corner splash, and the champ rolled him up for the win (after grabbing a handful of overalls). He broke every Win Probability chart; his odds of retaining would plummet to the single digits until, yet another stroke of good fortune bailed him out. A fan's experience of an HTM title defense included this internal dialogue.

"Tonight's the night. I can feel it."

"Mess up his hair! He hates that!"

"Man, the Honky Tonk Man really stinks. How has he been champ this long?

...

...

...

"Oh, what the fuck, he retained? How!?"

We all waited for Honky Tonk to turn into a pumpkin. Shortly after his fluke win over "The Dragon," HTM wrestled the Living Legend himself.

"Joke's on you, Honky Tonk Man. Hope you enjoyed your 15 minutes of fame. Sammartino dispatched "Nature Boy" Buddy Rogers in less than a minute. This will be a walk in the park for Bruno."

Sammartino won by count out.

Steamboat then exercised his rematch clause. Surely, Ricky would right this wrong. On July 25th, 1987 at Madison Square Garden, Steamboat defeated the champion ... by count out. The next day, they wrestled again.

Steamboat won ... by DQ.

Tito Santana then beat HTM by disqualification. Jake Roberts beat him by count out. In September, "Hacksaw" Jim Duggan took his cracks. The strength advantage was glaring, and the result should've been elementary, no?

Duggan won by DQ.

On the October 3rd, 1987 edition of *Saturday Night's Main Event*, Randy Savage got his opportunity. I mean, come on. This was the "Macho Man," people. The guy had just held the belt for over a year. Surely, he'd put a stop to this.

Savage planted the paper tiger with a patented flying elbow drop.

"1 ... 2 ..."

Then the Hart Foundation interfered, forcing the disqualification. Every title defense saw Honky Tonk on his knees, hands high in the air, begging for forgiveness. Every title defense ended with him slithering away with his title. A Survivor Series team in '87 formed out of utter disdain for the Honky Tonk Man, like how the Dungeon of Doom, Flair, and Arn created the Alliance to End Hulkamania. I'd probably have toned down the rhetoric if a group of kids formed an afterschool club called, "We Hate Dave," but Honky just kept on singing and dancing. He told anyone within earshot that he was the greatest Intercontinental Champion of all time. Savage, Steamboat, Beefcake, Duggan, and Jake Roberts (two of whom were tattooed with a guitar shot) skipped Thanksgiving family dinner to pummel the champ, and you gotta really hate someone to pass on the

Turkey Day yams. On this night – overmatched and facing a 3 on 1 disadvantage – HTM took the road oft traveled.

He ran away and lost by count out.

On February 18th, 1988, Hulk Hogan challenged the Honky Tonk Man for the title in East Rutherford, NJ. Like enough already. I've played a lot of blackjack and craps. The IC champ wasn't just on a heater. This was Biff Tannen finding the Grays Sports Almanac. HTM had managed to dance through raindrops for eight months, but his luck was about to run out. Now he was in the ring with the Immortal One. Hogan pinned everybody. If I rattled off every wrestler The Hulkster beat, the list would have more lines than *Beowulf*.

Hogan won by disqualification.

At WrestleMania IV, it was Brutus Beefcake's spot in the lineup (More on him in a later chapter). "The Barber" was batshit crazy and never left home without his hedge shears. (Johnny V's success in keeping Brutus centered and focused for over two years should be studied by medical professionals). I didn't necessarily want to ride public transportation with Brutus, but he had my unwavering support on this night.

"The Barber" put HTM to sleep. The champ rested soundly in the middle of the ring, like he had just sucked down a cup of nighttime Theraflu. The ref, though, wasn't conscious to call for the bell, because Jimmy Hart had whacked him in the back of the head with his megaphone. An outside official later ruled this match a disqualification. Over 19,000 in attendance saw the Honky Tonk Man on dream street for over five minutes, yet he still left Atlantic City with the title.

Sandwiched between WrestleMania and SummerSlam '88 were more near misses. At WrestleFest in Milwaukee County Stadium, HTM again lost to Duggan by DQ. Beefcake had multiple chances, too. By late summer, we just had accepted this new reality. The sun rises in the east, sets in the west, and the Honky Tonk Man will be Intercontinental Champion for life. It was frustrating knowing his reign would somehow surpass Queen Elizabeth II's, but I had come to terms with it.

Then came Day 454. The Honky Tonk Man issued the dreaded open challenge. The man who claimed to be "cool, cocky, and bad," got *too* cocky, too overconfident. On day 454, the champ asked for an opponent – he didn't care who. Like a young player tasked with breaking up a no hitter, the Ultimate Warrior didn't understand the gravity of the situation. He didn't consider the record or the past failures of his colleagues. He just saw a chump in a jumpsuit who had been champion for far too long.

The Warrior pinned him in 31 seconds.

Handicapping the 1992 Royal Rumble

All odds courtesy of DraftKings.

Hulk Hogan (+190): Winner of the 1990 and '91 Royal Rumble, the Hulkster won't be intimidated by the big stage and even bigger stakes. He's a cut-throat competitor. Once lusted for his best friend's girl to worm his way into a championship title shot, and illegally pulled the Big Boss Man from the '89 contest after he was already eliminated. Will stoop to any level. A chalk pick, who's taking a lot of action from the casual bettor.

The Berzerker (+375): Proficient at throwing opponents over the top rope. Match is tailor-made for the young up-and-comer. Generating a lot of buzz in the gambling community (there are rumblings that he may use his sword to generate some early offense) which has dropped his opening line odds from +425.

"Hacksaw" Jim Duggan (+450): The Glens Falls native won the 1988 Royal Rumble, and his brawling style is conducive to this type of match. Can lightning strike twice for Old Glory?

The British Bulldog (+500): Has the pedigree. Won the Battle Royal at the Albert Hall in London last October, but can that success translate to the States? 65% of money on Davey Boy is from overseas and Vegas expects that number to climb.

The Undertaker (+575): The former champ is the match's biggest enigma. Taker lost the title under dubious circumstances at This Tuesday in Texas, and now must jockey with 29 other competitors. Physically has all the tools but appearing in his first Royal Rumble. Skeptics wonder if a

Dead Man can hold up for 90+ minutes, but that didn't seem to affect the plot of *Weekend at Bernie's*.

Sid Justice (+600): The 6'9" skyscraper has put the Federation on notice. Still wet behind the ears, so don't be surprised if he seeks out the counsel of his good friend, Hulk Hogan.

Sgt. Slaughter (+740): Under much different circumstances obviously, but the battle-tested veteran captured championship gold at last year's event. Should once again have the home-field advantage after shedding his Iraqi duds.

Big Boss Man (+850): The Royal Rumble is a big man's game. Remember, a combatant is not eliminated if they go through the middle ropes (that's a common misconception). Can someone lift the hefty corrections officer over the top?

"The Million Dollar Man" Ted DiBiase (+900): Purchased the #30 spot at the '89 Rumble. Is he one off the books transaction away from leaving the Knickerbocker Arena as champion? Bettors have taken notice as his odds have decreased from +1100.

Haku (+1100): Can't hit him in the head – worth a flier.

Rick Martel (+1200): Lasted a record 53 minutes in last year's contest. Conditioning won't be a problem, but there are murmurs that his in-ring work has taken a back seat to his flourishing model career.

Greg Valentine (+1500): Lasted over 44 minutes in '91. The more you strike him, the more he seems to like it so he should thrive in this setting. Monsoon says he takes fifteen minutes to warm-up. Can he avoid an early elimination while he shakes off the cobwebs?

Jake "The Snake" Roberts (+1500): High-profile star who hasn't made an impact in past Rumbles. Despite his recent sinister streak, Roberts will still be a popular pick among casual bettors, but a fade opportunity for sharps. The Snake has had a target on his scales since ruining Liz and Randy's reception.

"Macho Man" Randy Savage (+1800): One of the best to ever do it, but is winning a top priority? See above. Been seeing red after receiving the worst wedding gift ever.

The Barbarian (+2000): A golden opportunity for the big man, who doesn't take a backseat to anyone in the power department. Moderate success in singles competition (including a notable win over Tito Santana at WrestleMania VI) but has yet to put it all together. The transition from The Powers of Pain has been a bumpy one.

Ric Flair (+2000): His credentials speak for themselves, but at just 240 lb., experts don't believe this style of match suits the Nature Boy. Would benefit from a later entry number to reduce the wear and tear. Hard to imagine a deep run.

Roddy Piper (+2500): Dip in value tied to "Hot Rod" pulling double duty. Will fatigue – both physically and mentally – hamper the crowd-favorite with an Intercontinental Championship title match against the Mountie scheduled for earlier in the evening? Either way, it's hard to ignore the value here.

(Some offshore books are offering odds on potential replacements in case Piper can't compete. Jim Brunzell, the Brooklyn Brawler, and Jim Powers to name a few).

Virgil (+2800): Plenty of support for the ex-bodyguard, even after dropping the Million Dollar belt back to DiBiase last November. Rounding into form at the right time with recent victories over Kato and the venerable Bob Smedley.

I.R.S. (+3000): First few moments will be telling for the government employee. No wrestler enjoys giving Uncle Sam a cut of their winner's purse, so don't be surprised to see Schyster facing double or triple-teams early.

Texas Tornado (+3200): A deep run (24 minutes) in last year's event suggests there's value here, but the dynamic talent hasn't looked right since his lopsided loss to the Undertaker in November.

Skinner (+3500): The alligator hunter showed moxie in an Intercontinental Championship loss to Bret Hart at This Tuesday in Texas, and sharp bettors have taken notice. Trendy sleeper pick.

Jimmy "Superfly" Snuka (+3800): Will the Superfly's trademark aerial tactics be grounded with so many participants? Lack of real estate to maneuver inside the squared circle is a valid concern for potential backers.

Repo Man (+4200): The devious newcomer hopes to "re-possess" the World Championship on Sunday. Sneaky methods make him – ahem – a sneaky pick to capture gold.

Jerry Sags (+4300): Did his Nasty Boys partner, Knobbs, create the blueprint? Knobbs finished 3rd in the '91 Rumble, so expect manager Jimmy Hart to review the film from last year's event.

El Matador (+4500): Scouts have said that Tito's agility and lateral quickness has increased since adopting the Spanish bullfighting lifestyle. That theory will be put to the test Sunday. Santana has struggled on the main stage, as evidenced by his current six-match losing streak at WrestleMania.

Nikolai Volkoff (+5000): Match sets up well for the 300+ pounder, but the Russian defector has scuffled without the tutelage of the Slickster.

Hercules (+5200): Looks like a million bucks, but recent results have the former Power and Glory member's stock trending down. A two-minute *Wrestling Challenge* loss to Randy Savage last month was particularly troubling.

The Warlord (+5500): If the Warlord wants to last longer in this year's Rumble, maybe he should masturbate beforehand. Can he exorcize the Ghosts of Royal Rumbles Past? He was eliminated in only 1:35 last year and lasted a paltry two seconds in '89. If you're leery of the Warlord's prospects, you're not alone.

Shawn Michaels (+5500): The former tag team specialist has relied on quick tags and double-team tactics. You can't expect 28 superstars to wait on the ring apron while you and your partner cut the ring in half. Uber-talented, but hard to envision him ever making noise in a Rumble.

Colonel Mustafa (+10000): If you believe in momentum, Mustafa enters Sunday with none. Dating back to last year's loss in the main event at SummerSlam, the Colonel has compiled just a 6-37 record.

My Picks

Winner: The Berzerker

Exacta Box: Berzerker/British Bulldog

Trifecta Box: Berzerker/British Bulldog/The Barbarian

The Conspiracy of WrestleFest '90

To be clear, we're talking about WrestleFest, the Coliseum Video, not the trendsetting arcade game whose only rivals were *The Simpsons*, *NBA Jam*, and *Cruis'n USA*. At the top of the telecast, your host Sean Mooney explained that fans were active participants in this Coliseum feature; that they were encouraged to request their dream matches via a letter-writing campaign. We are later shown an adorable postcard from World Wrestling Federation fan, Chase Tomlinson, who campaigned for ...

Drum roll please

...

...

...

The Ultimate Warrior vs Dino Bravo.

Ok then. It wouldn't have been my first choice, but maybe the youngster missed the first 25 Warrior/Bravo matches? Mooney cut to some pre-match promos between the competitors. Before a verbal thrashing of the Warrior, Jimmy Hart acknowledged Tomlinson – a curious namedrop – and that immediately sounded the conspiracy theory alarm.

Around this time, a guy named Jerry Jacobson developed and oversaw the McDonald's Monopoly scam. The game was a sales promotion of the fast-food chain. Monopoly pieces would accompany your order, and some rare ones were worth thousands and thousands of dollars. Jacobson, or "Uncle Jerry" as he was referred to by some of his hand-picked, McDonald's Monopoly game winners, worked for a third party who was responsible for the distribution of the pieces. He pocketed the big-ticket winners and sold them to associates and close confidants for a tidy little profit. This racket continued until 2001.

The question we all have is, "Why wouldn't Chase Tomlinson want to see Hogan/Warrior?" It was the no-brainer, dream match-up that *everyone* wanted. Didn't Chase watch the 1990 Royal Rumble? Didn't he see the stare down between the two? Didn't he hear their reaction, the anticipation from the crowd as they stood toe-to-toe? Didn't his parents rent the Royal Rumble VHS from their local Hollywood Video? There's an entire world to explore outside Dino Bravo/Warrior, Chase Tomlinson. Touch some grass, kid.

Then I considered Jerry Jacobson's con. What if *every* letter written into Sean Mooney and the World Wrestling Federation requested Warrior vs. Canadian Strongman, Dino Bravo? What if Jimmy Hart rigged the system? Maybe the WrestleFest '90 card wasn't left to chance at all. This wasn't a Choose Your Own Adventure. Your path had already been long decided. Maybe every Hogan/Warrior dream match scribbled on a postcard was discarded as quickly as it arrived, because Jimmy had a friend of a friend of a friend, who knew a guy who worked the mail room at Coliseum Video. What a clever way to jump the line for a title shot, because make no mistake, Ultimate Warrior's Intercontinental Championship *was* on the line. Perhaps the Warrior defended his title against Dino Bravo at WrestleFest '90, not because of a random letter selected among thousands, but because there was no other option.

Alas, the Ultimate Warrior defeated Dino Bravo via disqualification.

The Doctor of Ineptitude, Slick

"And let me let everybody here know one thing. You are looking at a congregation ... of sophistication. Untampered by hesitation ... and totally committed to dedication."

– Slick, *All-Star Wrestling*, August 16th, 1986, after purchasing 50% interest in "Classy" Freddie Blassie's stable (WWE 2013).

I take no joy in writing this, but is the Doctor of Style's résumé a little ... lacking? Is he all sizzle, but no steak? Is Slick's reputation as one of the best managers in the business propped up by a larger-than-life personality and an impeccable sense of style?

Could he dress to the nines? You're damn right.

Could he talk you into a used car at $5K over Blue Book value? Let me grab my checkbook.

Could he lead a member of his squad to championship gold? Well, that's another story.

Slick's stable – a mass of humanity that had all the physical tools – had ZERO championships to their name, and it wasn't for a lack of opportunities. They had their chances. They had their shots, but like the Buffalo Bills of the early 90s, breaking that glass ceiling proved a tad more difficult than breaking a table at a pre-game tailgate.

Let's dive in.

Iron Sheik and Nikolai Volkoff: Under the Slickster's watchful eye, pundits assumed the former tag title holders would regain their championship form. In November of '86, the Championship Committee awarded Sheik and the big Russian with ten, count 'em, TEN title opportunities.

They lost them all.

Hercules: Always on the move, Hercules was bought and sold more than a couch on Craigslist. Slick called him, "the greatest commodity in professional wrestling," before selling Herc's contract to Bobby Heenan in late '86. If he was the 'greatest commodity in professional wrestling,' then why sell his rights? According to insiders, it was a cost-cutting move to get Slickster's stable under the luxury tax (Take that for what it's worth).

The powerhouse, along with Paul Roma, would reunite with the Slickster in 1990, but the team (more on them later) fizzled out after a lopsided loss to The Legion of Doom at WrestleMania VII.

"The Natural" Butch Reed: Squandered a golden opportunity in the Championship Tournament at WrestleMania IV. With his first-round contest against the "Macho Man" Randy Savage firmly in hand, Reed made a cardinal mistake. On his way to the top rope to finish off Savage, he paused to bark at Miss Elizabeth. The disruption provided just enough time for the "Macho Man" to complete the comeback. TV talking heads and morning radio weren't kind to the Slickster. Some critics accused him of falling asleep on the job. Others said he was out managed. One headline in the *Kansas City Star* was particularly damning.

"Fatal Distraction: Slick Silent as the Natural Falls Prey to Miss Elizabeth's Guile."

The Bolsheviks: New Year, old habits. Under Slick's guidance, the powerful Russians rang in 1988 with a tag title loss to Strike Force on *Saturday Night's Main Event*. The setbacks snowballed from there. Nikolai and Boris ended the 80s with more losses than the Columbia University football team.

One Man Gang: Fresh off a bye in the quarters, the Slickster and Gang entered their semi-final match-up of the WrestleMania IV Championship Tournament against Randy Savage rested and confident. The strategy was foolproof. Lean on a fatigued Randy, use your weight advantage, and soften "Macho Man" up for the 747 Splash.

OR…

Attempt to repeatedly hit Savage with Slick's cane until the ref disqualifies you.

These self-inflicted wounds were a common theme woven throughout the Gang's title chances. Gang compiled a 2-24-2 record against Hulk Hogan in '87 and '88. His two victories?

They were by count out and disqualification.

Akeem: Deciding that a new look, a new name, and a new heritage would rejuvenate the One Man Gang – like how all my paychecks during the summer of 2000 went to clothes from Hot Topic – Slick unveiled 'Akeem,' who now called the 'Deepest, Darkest Parts of Africa' home. Transformations like this have paid dividends before (see: Steve → Stefan Urkel) but not for the big man. Neither alias brought a title to Slick's mantle.

The Big Boss Man: No stranger to corporal punishment, the Cobb County Corrections Officer cuffed more people than your neighborhood dominatrix. Boss Man was the crown jewel of Slick's stable, and a reign atop the World Wrestling Federation seemed inevitable. He only had to beat the Hulkster, the greatest force in professional wrestling. A steel cage loss to Hogan on the May 27th, 1989 *Saturday Night's Main Event* was one they'd love to have back.

(Boss Man and the Slickster's relationship dissolved after a failed business arrangement with Ted DiBiase. More on that in a later chapter).

Rick Martel: The former three-time tag team champion had a brief partnership with Slick but bailed before the stench of mediocrity rubbed off on him. Can't blame 'em.

Martel had already put up with that loser Tito Santana riding his coattails.

The Warlord: *"You know, Mr. Fuji, you drive a haaaaaaard bargain, brother. I had to dig deep, deep I say, into my pockets to purchase the Warlord's contract."* – The Slickster, *Superstars*, March 10th, 1990 (Old School Wrestling TV 2019).

Fuji fleeced him.

Kamala: No titles either for the Ugandan Giant, but in Reverend Slick's defense, he was dealt a difficult hand. The reformed Slickster inherited a big man, who after years of terrorizing the Federation, suddenly forgot the most basic rule of wrestling:

HE FORGOT HOW TO PIN AN OPPONENT.

Kamala flopped on the *back* of his fallen competitor and waited for a referee's count that never came. Whether this mental block was due to years of mistreatment and abuse from his handler, Kim Chee, or some sort of Steve Sax Syndrome, most of Slick's efforts with the Ugandan Giant focused on the basics.

He also taught Kamala how to bowl, so I guess that's something.

THE UNLIKELY CONTENDER

> Event: Saturday Night's Main Event (Sacramento, CA)
>
> Match: Super Ninja (Challenger) vs. The Ultimate Warrior (Champion)
>
> Date: November 26th, 1988
>
> Attendance: 15,900
>
> #1 Movie on This Date: The Land Before Time

"Where on the face of the globe did you find this world class athlete? Combining a blend of the best of martial arts and Western scientific wrestling? He is the Super Ninja."

– "Mean" Gene Okerlund ("Saturday Night's Main Event XVIII").

Mr. Fuji was a tireless recruiter. He scoured the globe looking for talent. No rock was left unturned; no country was too far, and no continent out of reach. He managed multiple wrestlers who hailed from Parts Unknown, so I asked a friend of mine who works at Delta, and he confirmed my suspicions. There are no direct flights to Parts Unknown. The trek involves planes, trains, and automobiles, and even then, you need to get lucky and bump into someone who grew up with the Missing Link. It's a testament to the Devious One's commitment – and his Frequent Flier status. Despite his recruiting chops, however, Fuji's reputation remains spotty. He made some mistakes (more on those in later chapters), but once you sift through the brain farts and the salt throwing (and there was a lot of salt throwing), you see the appeal. Consider this:

What other manager could've gotten Super Ninja an Intercontinental Title shot?

How did he do it? Whose phone number did he dial? Fuji was always one to massage the rules, and I had a hunch that his underhanded tactics weren't relegated to only the squared circle. Did the Devious One do some politicking? Did he grease the pockets of some members of the Championship Committee board? Did Chief Jay Strongbow get a cut? George Scott? How much did President Jack Tunney bank after Super Ninja – sight unseen – vaulted overnight to #1 contender for the Intercontinental Championship?

So I did my homework. This is a non-fiction book, mind you. I struck gold at an estate sale outside Stamford, which spared me from anymore dumpster diving outside WWE Headquarters. I present to you the Championship Committee's Intercontinental Championship Contender Rankings (The ol' CCICCR,) which were distributed daily via internal memo.

Committee's Official Rankings: Intercontinental Championship (11/25/88)

(c) The Ultimate Warrior

1. Honky Tonk Man
2. "Outlaw" Ron Bass
3. Brutus "The Barber" Beefcake
4. "Ravishing" Rick Rude
5. King Haku
6. Greg "The Hammer" Valentine
7. Dino Bravo
8. Koko B. Ware
9. The Red Rooster
10. Scott Casey

Now, spot the difference.

Committee's Official Rankings: Intercontinental Championship (11/26/88)

(c) The Ultimate Warrior

1. Super Ninja
2. Honky Tonk Man
3. "Outlaw" Ron Bass
4. Brutus "The Barber" Beefcake
5. "Ravishing" Rick Rude
6. King Haku
7. Greg "The Hammer" Valentine
8. Dino Bravo
9. Koko B. Ware
10. The Red Rooster

I'm not here to change your mind, only to present the facts.

It was a meteoric rise for the man cloaked in secrecy. He entered his title match against the Ultimate Warrior with a blank slate, a 0-0 record. On one hand, Super Ninja had zero match experience. On the other, there was no game film on him. Any preconceived notion about the challenger was pure conjecture, like when I sat down to watch *Human Centipede* expecting an adaptation of Kafka's *Metamorphosis*. (SPOILER: it was *not* an adaptation). Fuji never tipped his hand. He understood that you can't prepare for an unknown quantity, especially one who "combined a blend of the best of martial arts and Western scientific wrestling."

"Mean Gene, Super Ninja has trained totally in secrecy for seven years, in seven continents, and in seven arts."

When pressed by Okerlund about the 'seven arts,' Fuji didn't flinch.

"Foolish question from a foolish man." ("Saturday Night's Main Event XVIII").

Well, either the Super Ninja had an off night, or the Championship Committee has some explaining to do. The challenger's martial arts had no effect on the champ. His Western scientific wrestling didn't fare much better. Super Ninja was a complete stiff.

The Ultimate Warrior dismantled the #1 contender in a crisp 2:11.

With Friends Like This

> **Event:** *Championship Wrestling* (Poughkeepsie, NY)
>
> **Match:** Hulk Hogan and "Mr. Wonderful" Paul Orndorff vs. Big John Studd and King Kong Bundy
>
> **Date:** July 19th, 1986
>
> **#1 Movie on This Date:** *The Karate Kid Part II*

Bruno: *"I don't believe this! What in the world is wrong with Orndorff!"*

Vince: *"He's waving Studd in. He's waving Bundy in. Heenan coming in."* – *Championship Wrestling*, July 19th, 1986 (The Hulk Hogan Archive 2019).

My college roommate was from Cleveland, and by proxy, a huge LeBron James fan. He was out at the bar one night in his Cavs jersey, when a bunch of Syracuse bros picked a fight over who was the better player: Lebron or the Denver Nuggets' young sensation, Carmelo Anthony. I'm not condoning it. It was incredibly dumb, but in their defense, it was 2005 and you had to pass the time somehow while waiting for songs to download on LimeWire. Both parties held their ground, regurgitating statistics back and forth. As the pitchers of beer flowed, so did the personal insults. That's when my phone rang.

"Dave, I need you to come down to the Tap Room now! I'm about to get in a fight with six guys."

I had been asleep for hours, so please excuse my reply.

"The fuck?"

"These guys think Carmelo is better than LeBron, and I'm about to fight them all. I need back-up."

After mumbling something about Anthony being one-dimensional, I hung up. It wasn't my fight, I figured. Besides, I was an Allen Iverson fan. I didn't go to the Tap Room. I didn't even get out of bed. Cooler heads fortunately prevailed. There was no scrap, no blows exchanged, but I woke up riddled with guilt. I had this nagging feeling I couldn't shake. My boy needed a hot tag, and I left him to rot like Tito Santana at WrestleMania V. Whether or not I was bearish on Carmelo Anthony's long-term potential was beside the point. I messed up. When my buddy needed help, I turned my back on him. When he called me, I became the person I detest the most.

I turned into 1986 Hulk Hogan.

~ ~ ~

Paul Orndorff spent the better part of the 1980s being used and discarded by his closest friends. He's arguably the most sympathetic figure from my childhood; even after accounting for that *Fresh Prince of Bel-Air* episode where Will asked Uncle Phil, "How come he don't want me, man?" Paul's blind loyalty to his 'friends' was never reciprocated. "Mr. Wonderful" acted out in the summer of '86, not out of jealousy or anger, but because he was hurt. I can't blame him. What other choice did he have?

"Rowdy" Roddy Piper and "Cowboy" Bob Orton

In the main event of WrestleMania I, Piper and Orndorff teamed up to rid the World Wrestling Federation of the attention-starved glory hogs, Hulk Hogan and Mr. T. It was a noble yet lofty endeavor, so they enlisted the help of Bob Orton to supervise the proceedings. In the final moments of the contest, Paul locked Hulk in a full nelson square in the middle of the ring. From my vantage point, Orndorff's fingers were locked, his technique sound. Kid tested; Billy Jack Haynes approved. With special guest referee Pat Patterson tied up with Piper and Mr. T, Orton climbed to the top rope. Hogan slipped from Mr. Wonderful's grasp, and Orton knocked our protagonist into the middle of next week with a cast-aided single-axhandle to the back of the head (Or the 'external occipital protuberance area,' if you want to be exact).

Lost in the aftermath of Hogan and Mr. T's celebration was an injured Orndorff. Roddy and Bob had their scapegoat. It was like a team committing five turnovers and 12 penalties but blaming the kicker for missing a 35-yarder before halftime. Piper and Orton walked out of Madison Square Garden in defiance, Irish exiting their way out of Mr. Wonderful's friend circle as Paul laid unconscious in the middle of the ring. Orton shouldered none of the blame, even though it was *his* arm that knocked Orndorff out. It was *his* cast. It was *his* doctor, who failed to properly fix the finicky bone in his left arm*. How was Orndorff the fall guy? Did Mr. Fuji blame Yokozuna when Hogan ducked his salt at WrestleMania IX? Of course not. Fuji's a pro's pro. He and Yoko watched some film, made some adjustments, and got their revenge at that year's *King of the Ring*.

*A quick note on Orton's injured arm: During a *Piper's Pit* on the December 21st, 1985 *WWF Championship Wrestling*, Hot Rod invited a doctor to discuss the recovery time of a hairline fracture. The accredited physician said patients are looking at a four-week timetable for an arm to fully heal. Piper interjected – he was skeptical – and explained to the doctor that Orton's been wearing a cast for nine months.

Piper: *"Is it possible for an arm to be fractured for nine months?"*

Doctor: *"No."*

Piper: *"Yes, it is possible."* (All Out of Bubblegum 2016).

Gotta hear both sides, I guess.

On May 11th, 1985, Orndorff appeared as a guest on *Piper's Pit*.

Piper: *"At WrestleMania, it wasn't my shoulders who were pinned to the ground. It was your shoulders."*

Orndorff: *"You left me there flat."*

Piper then called him "a piece of garbage," and a friendship doesn't survive that (*Saturday Night's Main Event I*).

Hulk Hogan

Later that night, Hogan defended his championship against Orton. Post-match, Piper and Cowboy Bob cornered the champ, and the odds appeared insurmountable. Hulk looked resigned to an NBC ass kicking before a charging Mr. Wonderful ran to his defense, because an enemy of your enemy is a friend. That night sparked a budding friendship. Orndorff and Hulk. Hulk and Orndorff, just two guys being dudes. Slap a New York Jets jacket and a pair of black-rimmed glasses on the pair, and they were Kevin Arnold and Paul Pfeiffer. On *The Flower Shop*, Adrian Adonis needled Paul. He called him "Hulk Jr," both a slanderous and scandalous jab. Orndorff shrugged it off, but the dig affected him. How could it not? I could imagine his thinking.

That's the perception people have? I'm just Hulk's sidekick?

No one wants to live in another person's shadow. It's why Kit Keller got traded to the Racine Belles.

Orndorff would again appear on the June 28th, 1986 *Flower Shop*. This time, Bobby Heenan joined and issued a challenge. His mammoth tag team, Big John Studd and King Kong Bundy, against Orndorff and a partner of his choosing. Heenan didn't want "Mr. Wonderful" to choose some ham and egger, though. Bobby wanted the best. He wanted Hogan.

Our hero gladly accepted, no, *proudly* accepted. In fact, Paul promised to call his friend right then and there.

AND THAT MOTHER FUCKER NEVER TOOK ORNDORFF'S CALL.

Hulk couldn't be bothered. (Excuse me while I go hock a loogie in this here spittoon). The Hulkster was home for the record. Some assistant or receptionist told Paul that Hogan was tied up. He was too busy clangin' and bangin' in the gym to take his call.

Pathetic.

At least *I* was sleeping, Hulk, *and* had an 8:00 class in the morning. What's your excuse?

Hogan eventually finished his workout, and the match took place on the July 19th *Championship Wrestling*. Their chemistry was off, though. Think Brandon Walsh and Kelly Taylor after the latter was burned in a fire and joined a cult. Before the big match, Hulk and Orndorff had a tune-up against the Moondogs. Orndorff did most of the heavy lifting, generously giving Hulk a breather after his rigorous leg day. Hogan seemed uneasy with the arrangement, uncomfortable with taking a backseat. The champion was used to sucking all the air out of the room, not holding a tag rope.

Orndorff and Hogan's partnership ended the following week. Bundy and Studd looked on while "Mr. Wonderful" engaged in a little self-care. Paul picked up a battered Hulkster and decapitated him with a well-deserved clothesline.

He then piledrove his former friend into oblivion.

Can We Please Get "Rugged" Ronnie Garvin a Legitimate Partner?

I went on summer vacation in 1991, and by 'summer vacation,' I mean my family went to my sister's softball tournament.

"Dave, pack your bags! We're leaving Thursday!"

"We're going to Disney World, dad!?"

"No, son. Harrisburg."

"Oh."

I was watching *Superstars* in the hotel room when Jimmy Hart's dangerous Natural Disasters made their way down the aisle. It was an uphill climb for whomever they faced, a real test for their oppo – hey, it's Koko! Koko's here! The Bird Man! I *loved* me some Koko B. Ware. He had the speed to give Earthquake and Typhoon fits. He had the agility. I perked up. We're in for a good one here, I thought, a true contrast of styles. This was anyone's contest. The Natural Disasters versus Koko B. Ware and ...

Bob Frazier?

Bob Frazier?

Who the fuck is Bob Frazier?

"Bob Frazier! Ugh! Who's this guy!?"

"Maybe he'll surprise you, honey," my mom said, looking up from her crossword puzzle. I rolled my eyes. I didn't have time for my mother's glass-half-full outlook.

"Bob Frazier stinks."

Turns out, moms don't know everything. After Koko wrestled the duo to a stalemate, Frazier rolled over. They needed a spatula to scrape up poor Bob after a Typhoon splash. Now, Koko wasn't alone here. This epidemic – teaming with some average Joe (or Bob in this case) – wasn't isolated to just the Bird Man. It was widespread; it was everywhere. In fact, Koko wasn't even your biggest offender.

Prime Time Wrestling **(July 23rd, 1990):** Rhythm and Blues def. "Rugged" Ronnie Garvin and George Anderson.

Wrestling Challenge **(August 19th, 1990):** Demolition def. "Rugged" Ronnie Garvin and Troy Williams.

Wrestling Challenge **(September 2nd, 1990):** Rhythm and Blues def. "Rugged" Ronnie Garvin and Glen Ruth.

Superstars **(October 13th, 1990):** Orient Express def. "Rugged" Ronnie Garvin and Major Yates.

What's the opposite of outkicking your coverage, because Ron Garvin swiped right on everyone? If you had a pulse and could hold a tag rope, "Rugged" Ronnie would take you for a spin.

Small?

"No matter."

Slow?

"No problem."

No talent?

"Perfect, you can team with me."

It was like Danny O'Shea recruiting players for the Little Giants. The best 'ability' was availability. Ronnie Garvin was either the worst talent evaluator this side of Mel Kiper, or "Rugged" Ron just didn't want to let people down. Were these Glass Joes trying to level up – teaming with Garvin to improve their stock – or was "The Man with Hands of Stone" *proactively* courting the Glen Ruths of the world? Like Glen Ruth? GLEN RUTH? Come on, Ronnie. Why settle on those guys when Jim Powers was RIGHT THERE.

George Anderson: His trunks, knee pads, and boots were all different colors – a major red flag. May as well wrestle in pajamas. He managed two overhand rights before succumbing to a devastating double team maneuver.

Troy Williams: Looked like a villain from *3 Ninjas*. If you can't keep Rocky, Colt, and Tum Tum at bay, then you're gonna have your hands full with Ax, Smash, and Crush. Williams was quickly discarded.

Glen Ruth: Ruth and Garvin showed some brief chemistry. A beautifully executed double Irish whip sent the Honky Tonk Man and "The Hammer" crashing into each other. Ruth then leapt on Valentine for the pin attempt but *didn't hook the leg.*

Good grief. You're never going to pin "The Hammer" that way, Glen. A minute later, it was over.

Major Yates: I was more offended by his *inaction.* After delivering the Garvin Stomp to Tanaka, "Rugged" Ron grabbed his opponent's legs for his finishing hold. We had an upset in the making! Tanaka's partner, Sato, (illegally I might add) then leapt off the top rope and slammed a forearm into Garvin's back. No heads up, no warning. Garvin never saw it coming.

Major, have you ever taken the subway? If you see something, say something. Yates stared blankly at the in-ring action, like it was one of those Magic Eye puzzles. Not even a half-assed complaint to the referee about the illegal double team. It was inept on all accounts. I would say Garvin deserved better, but maybe this was exactly what "Rugged" Ron deserved.

Seriously, Jim Powers was right there.

Brunzell, too, for that matter.

Danny Davis, You Can Go to Hell! Straight to Hell

> **Event:** *Wrestling Challenge* (Hershey, PA)
>
> **Match:** The Dream Team & Dino Bravo vs. Tito Santana, Pedro Morales, & Hillbilly Jim
>
> **Date:** January 17th, 1987
>
> **Attendance:** 9,500
>
> **Highest Rated TV Show on this Date:** *The Golden Girls*

Jack Tunney: *"Referee Danny Davis has a statement to make to us at this time."*

Danny Davis: *"To all those people, who think that I owe them an apology for the way I officiated, well, I'm sorry.*

Even though I don't mean it."

Jesse Ventura: *"I cannot believe that Tunney would do a humiliating thing like that to one of his own referees."* (*Superstars*, November 8th, 1986).

I hated Danny Davis. Whether you feel that Vince screwed Bret or Bret screwed Bret, we can all agree that Danny Davis screwed everyone. In '86 and '87, Davis headlined a Tour of Incompetence that fucked over every one of my favorite wrestlers. Some people are bad referees. Some are smarmy assholes. Davis was both. I collected those 1987 Topps wrestling cards (You know the ones – they had the blue backgrounds with the red and white stripes), and the set contained a Davis card that read, "Ref Turned Wrestler." I gave mine devil horns and poked holes through it with a pencil. I purposely left it on our driveway so mom would run over it with her station wagon. Danny Davis defenders – AND THERE ARE A FEW – always fall back on their same tired excuses.

"Any ref would've missed Savage using a foreign object against Tito Santana. That Boston Garden lighting was always tricky."

"What did he do wrong? Davis correctly checked in on the Dynamite Kid's condition during the Bulldogs/Hart Foundation title match."

"Depending on the camera angle, it was reasonable to conclude that Orndorff's feet touched down before Hogan's."

That was just scratching the surface. On the November 1st, 1986 *Wrestling Challenge,* Randy Savage's Intercontinental Title reign was hanging on by a thread. Billy Jack Haynes slapped the champ in a full nelson, and those fingers were locked tighter than the lid of a pickle jar (take notes, Hercules). Davis looked unsure, hesitant of the next steps in the referee handbook. A competent official would've asked the champion if they gave up, but this piece of garbage was anything but.

"Danny Davis, what is he doing? Why doesn't he ask him? He's checking the arm ... you don't go to sleep with this hold! What is this? The bell has rung. We may have a new champion. We could have history made here on Wrestling Challenge with a new Intercontinental champion!"

– **Gorilla Monsoon (*Wrestling Challenge*, November 1st, 1986).**

While flailing his arms in a last gasp to free himself, Savage contacted Davis. Danny disqualified Billy Jack for "swinging his opponent into an official" and ...

Give.

Me.

A.

Break.

The fix was in. Monsoon called out this bullshit right away.

Following the decision, did Gorilla say:

    A. "A miscarriage of justice"
    B. "Highly unlikely"
    C. "You gotta be kidding."
    D. "This is indeed a happening"

(Tune into the end of this chapter for the answer).

Danny Davis was the absolute pits. He truly was one of the worst referees to disgrace this sport, or any sport for that matter. A 1990 college football game between #12 ranked Colorado and Missouri was decided because official J.C. Louderback and his crew forgot how to count. They inadvertently gave Colorado five downs. On the hardwood, NBA ref Tim Donaghy influenced, and bet on games he officiated. Neither holds a candle to Danny Davis.

On January 17th, three superstars reached their wits end. Frustrated with continuous missed calls and one-sided slow counts, the six-man team of Santana, Morales, and Hillbilly Jim walked off. Tasked with either a fight or flight response, wrestlers who choose the latter are usually serenaded with a chorus of boos. Heaven knows Money Inc. never got the benefit of the doubt. But the crowd in this case stood firmly behind the trio. Though the match ended abruptly, and Davis awarded the Dream Team and Bravo with a count out victory (then shook their hands afterwards), the fans cheered the losers' moral stand. Their protest was more significant than the match result. Their actions were an act of defiance and a matter of principle.

Before he became "Dangerous," his sloppy and biased officiating wreaked havoc across the Federation for almost a year. On his watch, titles changed hands. Winners became losers, and losers fell backwards into tainted victories. Why Davis was assigned so many marquee matches around this time is anyone's guess, and as soon as someone pulls that donkey Jack Tunney off his yacht, I'll ask him myself. The president finally showed his face in February of '87. On the Valentine's Day edition of *Superstars*, two weeks after Davis hosed Davey Boy Smith and the Dynamite Kid out of the tag titles, Tunney suspended Danny Davis for life, plus ten years. It wasn't a moment too soon.*

*Jack, of course, quietly reinstated him in 1989 – fuckin' Tunney.

(The answer was "C," *You gotta be kidding*. The more you know).

DAVID VS. GOLIATH

> Event: World Wrestling Federation at the Spectrum (Philadelphia, PA)
>
> Match: Ron Shaw vs. David Sammartino
>
> Date: November 22nd, 1985
>
> Attendance: 13,500
>
> #1 Song on This Date: "We Built This City" by Starship

"David Sammartino never gave up in his life. Even if he had broken a rib on any of those slams, or cracked a rib, this youngster has got too much guts to ever give up."

– Gorilla Monsoon, shortly after David Sammartino gave up (Randall G 2016).

In hindsight, we should've seen this coming. We're all guilty of complacency here. You, me, Monsoon, we all got caught napping. We swooned over the lineage. Bruno, David, Grandma Sammartino, any of them would mop the floor with the young up-and-comer, Ron Shaw, right? *Right?* Never mind that Big Ron Shaw was, per Gorilla, "6'5", 6'6", and close to that 300 lb mark." Set aside the lack of respect, too. Ron Shaw, Philly's own Ron Shaw, was booed out of the Spectrum by the hometown crowd, and there is no greater motivator in this world than disrespect. Shaw entered this contest with a chip on his shoulder. He entered the ring as the bigger man, the stronger man, and held a sizeable reach advantage over David Sammartino.

But Shaw's father wasn't World Champion for over 11 years. *David* was the heir apparent. David was the future. This match with the local scrapper was just a tune-up for junior, another small step in the steady climb up wrestling's hierarchy. The result of the contest was never in doubt; the only variables were the events that would lead to Sammartino's inevitable pinfall victory.

EXCEPT NO ONE TOLD BIG RON SHAW.

To quote Duke from *Rocky*: "He doesn't know it's a damn show! He thinks it's a damn fight!"

Sammartino extended a hand after the bell – a gesture of goodwill and good sportsmanship – but Ron Shaw had zero interest in winning a Lady Byng Award. He attacked David early, and hit Sammartino with seven, yes, seven body slams. Play the hits, Big Ron. Nobody came to hear your B-side tracks. I feared Shaw went to the well one too many times, but the local boy expertly softened up Sammartino's lower back with each crashing thud to the mat. See body part, isolate body part. It was Wrestling 101.

After the third slam, Shaw went for the quick cover. But deciding to test fate, and not wanting to collect that winner's purse quite yet, Ron picked David's shoulders off the mat after a two-count. It was a cardinal mistake, no doubt, a glaring example of the big man's inexperience, and most expected that the misstep would be the opening David needed. Gorilla sure did.

"If you have a chance to beat David Sammartino, you best take it."

There was no comeback, however – no second wind. Body slam after body slam after body slam left Sammartino's back more crooked than Boss Tweed's business deals. He was cooked. After four more slams, Ron hooked his injured opponent in an airtight bear hug, and it was elementary from there. Young Sammartino had no choice but to either quit, or risk permanent injury.

The lopsided victory left Monsoon incredulous. He called ring announcer Mel Phillips' official decision, "Highly unlikely." Chants of "Bullshit! Bullshit!" cascaded down after the submission. Witnesses scrambled for a reason to explain how Sammartino lost, but truth was, the answer was right there in the center of the ring. David ran into an immovable object. This was no upset. This was no fluke.

The better man won.

The Night When Skinner (Maybe) Shocked the World

> **Event:** *Monday Night Raw* (Manhattan, NY)
> **Match:** The Undertaker vs. Skinner
> **Date:** February 22nd, 1993
> **Attendance:** 1,000
> **#1 Movie on This Date:** *Groundhog Day*

I have a healthy suspicion that Skinner pinned the Undertaker clean in the middle of the ring. Call it a gut feeling.

Can you prove it, Dave?

Not exactly.

Do you have visual evidence?

Well, no.

But Skinner passed the eye test. In the two minutes of action we saw on the February 22nd *Raw*, the gator hunter controlled the pace. He dictated the tempo. Even the biggest Taker apologists concede that. The Phenom was looking over his shoulder. He wasn't in the right headspace. At the previous month's Royal Rumble, Taker was humbled by Harvey Wippleman's newest protégé, the 8'0" Giant González. We were now witnessing a systematic dismantling of the Dead Man before the inevitable

Gatorbreaker (inverted DDT) finisher, and *no one* kicked out of the Gatorbreaker. Nobody.

(Ok, to be fair, Bret Hart kicked out of the Gatorbreaker at This Tuesday in Texas. And, for transparency's sake, Owen Hart did also at WrestleMania VIII. Those were anomalies, however; byproducts of Skinner not hooking the leg on the cover, and he wasn't about to make that mistake again).

Skinner was choking Taker with a gator claw (nothing to see here, ref) when Vince McMahon suddenly signed off the broadcast. One minute, I'm watching the biggest upset since NC State beat Houston in the '83 NCAA tournament. The next, a crime of passion from a Palm Beach hotel room in the opening scene of *Silk Stalkings*.

"Looks like we're about out of time here on Monday Night Raw. We'll give you the conclusion of this match next week ..." (*Monday Night* Raw, February 22nd, 1993).

Next week never came. The finish wasn't shown on *Raw, Superstars, WWF Mania*, or *Wrestling Challenge*. We couldn't even get an update from Lord Alfred Hayes on *Wrestling Spotlight*. The Skinner/Taker finish remains in purgatory. Only the 1,000 or so fans in attendance know the result, AND THEY'RE NOT TALKING. Did everyone in the Manhattan Center sign an NDA? Have we stumbled upon one of the greatest conspiracies in history? Did Skinner handle his business, but the higher-ups realized that an Undertaker loss ahead of his WrestleMania IX match with Giant González wouldn't be "best for business?" Every piece of evidence is seemingly buried with Jimmy Hoffa's body. That following morning, I told my mom, "I think Skinner beat The Undertaker!"

"That's nice, Dave. Did you empty the dishwasher?"

Good thing she never asked me any follow-up questions, because thirty years later, I'm no closer to solving this puzzle (But seriously, why didn't a Skinner upset pique mom's interest?). *Monday Night Raw* has long been a vehicle for underdog stories, but a Dead Man defeat would've trumped them all. Remember, a locker room of wrestlers *slayed* the Undertaker at the 1994 Rumble, yet he was still back in time for SummerSlam.

Skinner's career was the ultimate "what if?" What doors would've opened if the match's conclusion aired? The Championship Committee would've assuredly taken notice. So would have sponsors. Skinner's Gator Meat would've been lined up right next to Tyson's Chicken at your local grocer. Unfortunately, not all stories have a happy ending. Skinner quietly left the World Wrestling Federation a month later.

He finished on a high note, defeating Koko B. Ware.

The Colossal Collapse

> **Event: WrestleMania VI (Toronto, ON)**
>
> **Match: The Colossal Connection (Champions) vs. Demolition (Challengers)**
>
> **Date: April 1, 1990**
>
> **Attendance: 67,678**
>
> **Highest Rated TV Show on this Date:** *America's Funniest Home Videos*

There are plenty of things in this world that appear impossible (time travel, swimming across the Pacific, etc), but I've watched enough wrestling to know that restraining someone for three seconds tops the list. You'd have better luck headbutting a Samoan. The success rate doesn't sniff the Mendoza Line, yet it hasn't stopped countless teams from trying. In '83, the Wild Samoans became another statistic when the Soul Patrol's Tony Atlas ducked a chair shot from "Captain" Lou Albano, and that mishap cost Afa and Sika the Tag Team Championships. There are countless examples, too many to cite. Now here was the Colossal Connection's attempt to defy the odds. Andre the Giant held Smash from behind, serving him up to Haku for one of his patented crescent kicks. Smash moved. They *always* moved. Andre took Haku's foot square in the jaw. The big Redwood collapsed backwards and got tied up in the ropes. As Bobby Heenan desperately tried to unknot his meal ticket, Ax and Smash lined up Haku for their Demolition Decapitation. Moments later, history was made.

Demolition caught a break. They didn't beat Andre and Haku, as we know them. Ax and Smash beat a team on the fritz, a malcontent, watered-down version of the Colossal Connection, like beating the 90s Bulls, but later admitting it was the Pete Myers-led outfit. The champs didn't bring their "A" Game. Their undoing was their own. These were self-inflicted wounds; careless, sloppy mistakes that were magnified by one, gigantic schematic oversight.

Where was Andre?

"I would have to say in my professional opinion, Gorilla, it's about time for Haku to tag in the big man." – Jesse Ventura (WrestleMania VI, April 1, 1990).

A quick aside.

The original Nintendo came with *Super Mario Bros.* and *Duck Hunt*, two separate games that were connected to one cartridge. The entire package – the system, the game, etc – included two controllers and a 'zapper' gun. My siblings played *Super Mario Bros.* incessantly. I was the youngest and begged and pleaded and cried (I cried a lot) to let me play. My sister finally got fed up with the whining. One day, she handed me the Nintendo gun and told me to "Shoot the mushrooms, Dave. That'll be a big help." I was ecstatic. It was about time she recognized my worth. For months, I thought I was helping the cause, ridden the world of King Koopa's hired muscle through an endless supply of bullets. Turns out, I wasn't doing shit. That gun only worked for *Duck Hunt*.

In a world full of Hakus, I was an Andre.

What's the point in having a Lamborghini if you never take it out of the garage? Haku didn't tag his partner once. He wrestled the entire match. Listen, the Tongan powerhouse was royalty, and I'll be the first to bend the knee, but icing out the 8th Wonder of the World subjects even the former King of Wrestling to second-guessing. Hell, even Jay Leno got a little playing time at Road Wild. The World Wrestling Federation tag division wasn't Little League. Not everyone has to play (I get that), but Haku's partner was 7'4", over 500 lb. That's like playing the *X-Men* arcade game and not picking Storm. Besides, do you think the COLOSSAL Connection got their name because of the size of Haku's thighs?

There was a lot of post-match finger pointing. The team was big on passing the blame, but short on accountability. Heenan admonished Andre, chastising him for his passive approach. Giant protested (Haku never tagged him!) and pleaded his case while fighting the lingering effects of a beautifully executed crescent kick. Meanwhile, Haku skated by scot-free. "The Brain" had his scapegoat.

Bobby got more and more animated. He reminded Andre that, "I'm the fucking boss." Then he slapped him. He slapped the Giant. It was disgusting and pathetic, and a sad end to a 3 ½ year friendship. Make no mistake about it. Heenan and Andre *were* friends. Bobby lobbied for his reinstatement in late '86. "The Brain" helped secure his first-ever World Championship opportunity in '87. It wasn't strictly business. It's never *strictly* business.

Andre retaliated, slapping the taste out of Heenan's mouth to a monstrous ovation. He followed that up with a big overhand right. He cleared Haku from the ring and furthered the humiliation by tossing them both out of the motorized cart. Let 'em walk, Andre figured. (All proceeds of this book will be going towards my purchase of a WrestleMania VI wrestling cart. Tell your friends).

It was the Colossal Connection's final match together. There was no official statement, no penned letter from a PR firm citing 'irreconcilable differences.' The break-up was ugly and public, and occurred on the grandest stage of all. It was hard to watch. The only thing missing from the split was a broken barbershop window.

(And we'll get to that soon enough).

The Wrestling Classic

Rules? What Rules?

> Event: The Wrestling Classic (Rosemont, IL)
>
> Match(es): The Prestigious 16-Man Tournament
>
> Date: November 7th, 1985
>
> Attendance: 14,000
>
> Highest Rated TV Show on this Date: *The Cosby Show*

"The only rule actually you have to follow ... is you have to win your match to proceed along in the tournament."

– Jack Tunney (The Wrestling Classic, November 7th, 1985).

Thank you for clearing that up, Mr. President. I wasn't aware of how tournaments work. When I heard the above – it occurred during a brief interview with Okerlund before the night's proceedings – I laughed. It was silly and nonsensical, and I don't think the viewing audience expected The Wrestling Classic to follow the same format of a curling bonspiel, where there is a three-game guarantee, win or lose. I later realized that I had focused on the wrong part of Tunney's explanation. The hapless dope's words proved to be ominous. Anarchy reigned on that November night. Fair play was discarded, and wrestlers stooped to any level. Tournament participants took President Jack's words to heart: Winning was the only rule that was followed.

Dynamite Kid vs. Nikolai Volkoff (First Round)

People *really* didn't like Volkoff singing the Soviet National Anthem. I've butchered Wheatus' "Teenage Dirtbag" at karaoke once or twice, but never dealt with an audience reaction as harsh as what Nikolai faced on a nightly basis. It was a minor miracle if Volkoff ever got through the second verse.

Dynamite allowed the big Russian to serenade the crowd (a classy gesture) but blindsided him with a missile dropkick seconds later for the victory. The finish of the match (nine seconds) was the same time as King Kong Bundy's WrestleMania win over Special Delivery Jones, but this pinfall was much, much quicker than S.D.'s annihilation. As Jesse Ventura pointed out, "Nikolai didn't even get a chance to take his jersey off."

(A moot point obviously, but if he had advanced through, would Nikolai have sung the same song before each one of his matches? Wouldn't have minded him mixing in a little Tears for Fears).

"Macho Man" Randy Savage vs. Ivan Putski (First Round)

"Look at Elizabeth. She knows what went down." – Gorilla Monsoon.

Even Miss Elizabeth, the epitome of grace, turned a blind eye to the night's debauchery. I expected the shiftiness from Randy, but damn, *et tu*, Liz? Savage vs. Putski was a contrast in styles. "Macho Man" struggled to withstand the onslaught from the Polish Power, seemingly on his heels from the opening bell. Ivan worked Savage over in the corner, chopping Randy down with a series of boots. An early round exit appeared a given until Savage managed a double leg takedown. He then *illegally* draped both his legs over the middle rope for added leverage and got the pinfall.

Savage and Liz fled the scene like they had just stolen something. They did. They robbed the veteran Putski and slithered into the quarterfinals.

The Junkyard Dog vs. Moondog Spot (Quarterfinals)

"The Dog counted him out himself. I don't think that's going to be official. The Dog's leaving. He's saying, 'I won this one.'" – Gorilla Monsoon.

Spot's run in The Wrestling Classic was littered with shenanigans. In the opening round, he and Terry Funk agreed to *not* wrestle. Taking a page from Joshua Waitzkin's playbook in *Searching for Bobby Fischer*, Funk offered his opponent a draw, or more specifically, a double count out, and I found the pacifism within the cutthroat tournament construct oddly refreshing. Both superstars walked up the aisle in solidarity, but you don't microwave fish in the office break room, and you never trust a man from Double Cross Ranch. Funk hit Spot from behind and made a mad dash back towards the ring. Moondog, though, was a wily veteran, a former tag team champion. He chased down Funk and yanked him from the apron. A poorly placed backdrop from Terry catapulted Spot back inside before the ref's ten count. Survive and advance, Spot. Survive and advance.

In the quarters, the Junkyard Dog defeated Spot with a devastating headbutt. It's a sentence that seems tame and mundane on the surface. Then you dig deeper. You study the tape. You realize that JYD and Moondog Spot wrestled *without a referee*. You comb through the footage, watching and rewinding, watching and rewinding, and you listen closely for the bell – a bell indicating the start of the match. You never heard that bell. You scribble in your notepad, right under your grocery list and cursory ranking of the top-25 Greatest Intercontinental Champions of all time.

"Where was the bell? Match not official??? Moondog Spot screwed???"

So few answers, so many questions. After the headbutt, Dog flopped on Spot for the cover. With no official on site, he improvised. He made his own rules. JYD slapped his hand on the canvas for the 1-2-3, and that was that. The Junkyard Dog moved on. Life moved on. Everyone accepted Referee JYD's decision as final. Moondog Spot was eliminated via an unsanctioned, unsupervised, and unofficial* match in the most prestigious wrestling tournament of all time, and everyone merely grabbed a pen and updated their brackets.

*Monsoon and tournament officials would later cover their tracks by saying, "A judge was at ringside, and he gave the nod." I take no joy in saying this, Gorilla, but ... *highly unlikely.*

Ricky "The Dragon" Steamboat vs. "Macho Man" Randy Savage (Quarterfinals)

Is that a foreign object in your pants, or are you just happy to see me? Savage was the only wrestler who had more hidden pockets than a pair of cargo shorts. He had an unidentified weapon for every occasion; a guy who reached into his trunks more than a teenager left alone for the weekend. Steamboat had "Macho Man" up for an atomic drop, but Savage pulled a foreign object from his pants and decked him. The official was none the wiser. (Randy would defeat Tito Santana in Boston for the Intercontinental Champion via the same reprehensible methods).

Cheaters do prosper. JYD and Savage, two of the tournament's most egregious offenders, met in the championship. Integrity, it turns out, only gets you to the quarters. JYD had a fortuitous draw. He coasted through the semis after Paul Orndorff and Tito Santana were both eliminated via double count out.

A count out victory also decided The Wrestling Classic. JYD backdropped "Macho Man" out on to the concrete floor, and Savage never beat the ref's ten count. Now, there has been a long standing, rarely enforced rule, which states that intentionally tossing someone over the top rope warrants a disqualification. Jesse Ventura argued this point at WrestleMania III when "The Dragon" backdropped "Macho Man" at the Pontiac Silverdome. The rule was overlooked then, and it wasn't enforced here.

Not much was enforced on this night.

DID THE BERZERKER JUST TRY TO KILL SOMEBODY?

> **Event:** *Superstars* (Kalamazoo, MI)
> **Match:** The Berzerker (with Mr. Fuji) vs. The Undertaker (with Paul Bearer)
> **Date:** April 25th, 1992
> **#1 Song on This Date:** "Jump" By Kris Kross

"Finally, someone has destroyed The Undertaker!"

– Mr. Perfect (*Superstars*, April 25, 1992).

Just your run-of-the-mill murder attempt on this edition of *Superstars*. Led by the Devious One, the unpredictable and impulsive Berzerker squared off against the Phenom. The Berzerker had the size to match the Undertaker. He had the strength. His biggest weakness, critics cited, was an elevator that didn't quite reach the top floor, but that's why he had Fuji, the brains to the Berzerker's brawn. Oh yeah, I almost forgot: He also carried a sword and shield to the ring, like someone really into Zelda cosplay.

We assumed the weaponry was only for show. It was just part of the presentation and the ambiance, like a pianist playing Frank Sinatra at an Italian restaurant. Besides, there was arguably no bigger pacifist in the World Wrestling Federation than the Berzerker. His preferred method of victory was via count out, the softest of all decisions outside the time limit draw. He had no finishing maneuver, no submission lock or devastating backbreaker in his arsenal. He tossed his opponents over the top rope and sent them on their way, a classic catch and release technique, which made the night's proceedings all the more shocking.

Every time a serial killer is arrested, a local story always interviews the suspect's neighbors.

"Todd seemed like such a nice guy. He was quiet. Always kept his lawn cut and had his Christmas lights down right after New Year's. It's hard to imagine he did something like this."

That was the Berzerker. Licking his hand, holding his wrist, shouting, "Huss! Huss!" They were weird ticks no doubt, but harmless idiosyncrasies. For context, the Undertaker, his opponent on this day, tried to bury multiple people alive, once hung the Big Boss Man, and crucified "Stone Cold" Steve Austin. He also tried to embalm Stone Cold, which was a nice gesture – preserving a corpse from decay – but the problem was that Austin was very much alive at the time.

Before the bell, Fuji's man blindsided Paul Bearer with a shield shot to the back. He then delivered one to the Dead Man. With the Undertaker reeling, Berzerker grabbed his sword and drilled Taker with the flat side of his blade. The official, who had jumped outside to check on Paul Bearer, took one look at the sword-wielding powerhouse from Parts Unknown, and said, and I'm paraphrasing here, "Fuck this. I'm a referee, not a member of Kalamazoo S.W.A.T." No officials or security intervened. With Taker lying on his back, Berzerker went for the jugular. He raised his sword over his head and the good people of Michigan were about to witness a real, live murder. Thankfully, Taker dodged decapitation. Berzerker then delivered a piledriver outside the ring. It was impactful – a devastating maneuver – just not quite homicide.

Still, crimes were committed.

KALAMAZOO, MI – *A Parts Unknown man was arraigned at 8th District Court Monday after attempted murder allegations.*

The Berzerker, age unknown, appeared in court with his attorney, Clarence Thomas, and entered a not guilty plea to three felony accounts of attempted homicide. The affidavit filed in court alleges that on the afternoon of Saturday, April 25th, the Berzerker attempted to stab the victim with a Viking (or Carolingian) Sword.

The affidavit states that the victim was repeatedly hit with a thousand-year-old shield with origins back to the Iron Age. The report alleges that the accused then grabbed a sword and attempted to drive it through the torso of his fallen victim.

The incident took place at Wings Stadium and was captured by a video recording and broadcast worldwide. Outside the Kalamazoo Court House, Thomas, the attorney for the defense, addressed reporters and denied all allegations.

"This is a clear case of mistaken identity. My client wasn't even in Kalamazoo at the time, and we have a witness, Mr. Fuji, prepared to testify about my client's true whereabouts. We look forward for our day in court, and we will take no further questions at this time."

SNAKE-BITTEN

> Event: *Superstars* (Fort Wayne, IN)
>
> Match: Jake "The Snake" Roberts vs. Bob Werner
>
> Date: November 23rd, 1991
>
> Attendance: 6,000
>
> #1 Song on This Date: "When a Man Loves a Woman," by Michael Bolton

"The snake is biting him! The snake is biting him! Roddy Piper on his way ... to get some help. The snake is gnawing on the arm of Randy Savage ... who's helpless, tied in the ropes. All I can say is ... that snake better be de-venomized ... it better be!"

– **Vince McMahon (WWE 2010).**

I found a snake in my basement. It was black, about two feet long, and had a menacing face – the kind of face that you just knew was looking for trouble. I wish I could tell you I calmly grabbed it by the head and escorted it off the premises, but truth is, I got a legit phobia. I morphed into Andre the Giant at the 1989 Royal Rumble.

After the paralysis wore off, I sprinted upstairs and locked the door behind me (I didn't think the demon could pick a lock, but I wasn't about to take that chance). I then called my buddies. I filled them in on my newest houseguest, and suddenly everyone was a zoologist with a concentration in North American reptiles.

"It's probably just a garter snake. They're harmless."

How do we know it wasn't an underdeveloped cobra or boa? Also, I didn't hear a rattle, but I couldn't rule it out. It's easy to make sweeping assumptions when the snake isn't in *your* basement. My friends thought they had all the answers, but I, too, was an expert you see. I owned WrestleMania 2 on VHS. I saw what happened to poor George Wells. I couldn't recruit the services of a local mongoose, so I secured the next best thing: 'Hank' the Snake Man (Not his real name). Hank the Snake Man was from Wildlife Control and dressed like Outback Jack but looked like Al Snow. He rolled in with a truck covered in snake decal and called you, "brother." I loved Hank.

"Heard you got an uninvited visitor, brother?"

Sure do, Hank. I had worked up the courage to place a bin over the snake before Hank's arrival and weighed it down with gallon water jugs (It's my most courageous feat to date). The Snake Man didn't have gloves or any protective gear. Didn't need 'em. I, on the other hand, had rummaged through my garage looking for a hazmat suit and the coal miner's glove from Halloween Havoc '92, because you couldn't be too careful. Hank circled the perimeter of the bin, buying time while he finished his thoughts on the current housing market. Then, before lifting the bin, he made a confession.

"Can I tell you something, brother?"

Of course you can, Hank. We're kindred spirits now. In our short three minutes together, Hank and I had also discussed the weather, raccoon infestations, and football. We've only scratched the surface of our friendship. Whatever you have to tell me, I can handle it.

Well, I wasn't prepared for this.

"I don't really like snakes either, brother."

…

...

...

Huh.

I admit – that caught me off-guard. I was standing on the third step of the stairway at the time (I had sought higher ground) and gave Hank a pep talk.

"Hank, you are literally the only person in this basement equipped to pick up this snake. I certainly can't do it. You can do this, Hank. I believe in you." My positive reinforcement was well-received.

"Thanks, brother, you're right. I can do this."

That's the spirit, Hank. Give it hell. He then lifted the bin.

There was no snake.

CODE RED! CODE RED!

There was a hole in the bin, about the size of the quarter, and this crafty SOB had slithered to its freedom.

"We got a jailbreak, Hank! Call it in! Call it in!" Hank turned on his flashlight.

"We gotta find this snake, brother."

Couldn't agree more. Now, I have a phobia, but my wife – my lovely, amazing wife – can't even be within one mile of a spider without losing her mind. If she saw a snake, an honest to God rattlesnake (?), she'd cash in every single one of her Marriot Rewards points. On the plus side, Hank had a plan. It just wasn't a good one. He had me lift the couch on the count of three, which was just about the worst plan one could draw up. If I lifted the couch and saw this copperhead (?), I'd drop the sectional on Hank's head. He and I were boys, sure, but if Shawn could throw his longtime friend through a barbershop window, then don't assume my loyalty while a snake crawls up my pant leg.

We never found the cobra (?). Whether it was for utility or just his amusement, Hank sprayed coyote urine around my property (a natural predator, I guess). He then flung snake traps around my basement like they were Lanny Poffo's frisbees.

"I'm sure it's a friendly snake, brother."

Right. Like Casper, but venomous. I like to think the snake found greener pastures, but who knows. Maybe we've been living in harmony all this time. I re-watched WrestleMania 2 for the purposes of this book – out of necessity more than enjoyment – and you're damn right I skipped past that Jake Roberts/George Wells match.

Some things hit too close to home.

~ ~ ~

"Macho Man" and Miss Elizabeth tied the knot at SummerSlam '91. It was a beautiful ceremony, and guests were later treated to an elegant reception with the smooth sounds of the Fast Fingers Orchestra serenading those in attendance. It was breathtaking, a 5-star affair, but the turnout was … lackluster? There weren't many people there. Like 60? 75? I didn't get it. They were wrestling's "It" couple, so it got me thinking. Where was everyone?

August 26th, 1991 was a Monday. No wonder nobody showed. Randy saved a few bucks and got the weeknight discount at the banquet hall, but at what cost? Uncle Elmer at least had the decency to get married on a Saturday. After the first dance and cake cutting, Savage made the curious decision to open the gifts *during* the reception. Kinda tacky. It grinds the evening to a halt. Guests want to maximize the open bar and dance to Color

Me Badd. They only have the sitter 'till 11, and most of them have work the next day since tomorrow is, ya know, a Tuesday.

Proper wedding decorum aside, the unwrapping was going well, nothing out of the ordinary. The couple received a blender, some stunning candlesticks, a serving dish, all the necessities. Then Miss Elizabeth opened a pink box – maybe some fine china? Silverware? An '87 Survivor Series t-shirt?

Nope. It was a fucking cobra, which I assume was NOT on the registry. Everyone lost their shit. Guests scattered for the exits; blood-curdling screams ricocheted off the banquet hall walls. I would've already been halfway across the George Washington, knocking over any feeble guest that stood between me and my Chevy Cavalier. Sorry, Grandma Savage. It's every guest for himself. Jake Roberts and the Undertaker then crashed the party. Taker hammered away on the groom and Roberts terrorized Liz with the cobra until, thankfully, Sid Justice, who attended the wedding in a pair of jeans like that one cousin everyone has, chased the duo away with a folding chair.

Savage lost a Retirement Match to the Ultimate Warrior at WrestleMania VII. Five months later, his wedding day was ruined. His wife suffered an unthinkable ordeal. You can't let that slide. Randy's hands were tied, though. He wanted Roberts – he wanted retribution – but couldn't get reinstated because the incompetent Jack Tunney (more on him later) was less flexible than a dumbbell. He pleaded his case to the World Wrestling Federation president, but Tunney I guess felt that defending your wife's honor wasn't a noble enough cause. "Macho Man," in turn, trashed the president's office and got placed on probation.

Dave, sorry to interject. Roberts terrorized opponents with a snake for years, but Savage got the book thrown at him for some light vandalism?

Yes, that's right, reader. That's Tunney for ya.

"Reinstate 'Macho Man'" gained a groundswell of support. At $.79 a pop, the Federation offered a 900-number to voice your opinion, but you needed a parent's permission before calling. Mom shrugged me off when I broached the subject ("That's a waste of money, Dave") which was rich coming from the same woman who sprung for my brother's trumpet lessons. The guy couldn't play a lick, while Savage was a former Intercontinental and World champion. What's the better investment?

On the November 23rd, 1991 *Superstars*, Roberts quickly disposed of an outmatched Bob Werner. After the victory, the Snake goaded Savage on the mic.

> *"There are two things, ladies and gentlemen, stopping him from coming in here. One is common sense. And the other is fear."*
>
> **– Jake Roberts (WWE 2010).**

There's only so much a man can take. "Macho Man" stood up from the announcers' table and approached the ring. An official pleaded with Randy, knowing that any encounter would be a violation of his probation. Savage jumped on the apron as Roberts lobbed more and more insults. The official grabbed Randy's leg, trying to restrain him. Jake used the opening to clobber the "Macho Man" with a clothesline. He dished out more punishment before tying him up in the ropes.

Then the cobra came out. There are 30-something-year-olds today who still can't sleep through the night; grown adults who can trace the onset of their trauma back to this day. With Roberts' prodding, the predator sank its fangs into Savage's arm AND THE SNAKE WOULDN'T LET GO. The cobra gnawed on "Macho Man" for close to 30 seconds (I timed it), but it may as well have been a month. Fans gasped. Others screamed in horror. I slept on the floor of my parents' room for a week. I saw cobras everywhere. Sticks in the front yard, garden hoses, Stretch Armstrongs underneath the living room couch all looked like cobras. I didn't ask for this. I was a youngster watching *Superstars*, not a Wes Craven movie. I had only tuned in the first place because of El Matador.

Finally untied from the ropes by Piper and officials, Savage tried to fight back. With blood on his arm and poison in his veins, a badly injured "Macho Man" flailed helplessly at Roberts. Liz joined Piper and personnel outside the ring – frantically looking for an opening to save Randy – but when there is a pissed off cobra in the ring, the list of volunteers ready to make that rescue mission was nil.

"Everyone out at ringside doesn't know what to do! Get him out of there! For god's sakes, get Randy Savage out of there!"

– Vince McMahon (WWE 2010).

Piper eventually pulled Savage to the outside as the snake, in a periscope position, admired its handiwork. In the aftermath of the assault, and under mounting pressure from critics, President Jack Tunney stepped out from his ivory tower and finally reinstated the "Macho Man."

He also banned snakes from ringside, but a little late on that one, Jack.

SEEING RED

> **Event: Prime Time Wrestling**
>
> **Date: January 16th, 1989**
>
> **On This Day: Cincinnati Bengals running back, Ickey Woods, graces the cover of Sports Illustrated**

"As far as Gorilla Monsoon is concerned, he just got in the way. I never meant nothing to happen to him. Brawler never meant nothing to happen to him. But Taylor, it was planned for you."

– Bobby Heenan (*Prime Time*, January 16th, 1989).

The fallout occurred on *Saturday Night's Main Event*. It was an ugly one, too, the kind of break-up that has everyone in the dining hall talking the next morning. The partnership of Bobby Heenan and his newest protégé, the Red Rooster, ended abruptly after a nationally televised defeat at the hands of Tito Santana. On top of the 15% he was skimming from the Rooster's earnings (which did not seem to be industry standard at that time), the Brain micromanaged his pupil – displaying a case of backseat driving usually reserved for mothers-in-law. Rick Rude, Andre, the Brain Busters, these guys were awarded a certain amount of *carte blanche* that Terry Taylor was not, and I don't fault the young upstart's resentment. I get it. I can't count the number of times I've threatened to 'turn this car right around' when a passenger asked, "Why did you get in this lane?"

Heenan had a short fuse. Mic'd up at ringside, he displayed the patience and poise of someone demanding to speak to your manager. The youngster was holding his own, too. I didn't get the Brain's frustration.

Rooster was undefeated. He had notched big wins over savvy technicians like Koko B. Ware, Jim Brunzell, and Reno Riggins. At one point, Tito tried to lock Heenan's man in his trademark Figure-Four, but a beautiful counter led to his escape. I expected a pat on the back from his manager, a little Barry Horowitz-like love. Instead, Bobby yanked him out of the ring and delivered a tongue-lashing. Later, after the Rooster was clotheslined over the top rope, Heenan gave another verbal onslaught. Then he shoved his man back into the ring. Whether to prove a point, or mistakenly thinking this was a Lumberjack Match, Heenan's misstep was costly. A confused Red Rooster looked back at his manager and Santana rolled him up for the surprise win. Fair or not, Heenan's criticism continued post-match. The loss, he felt, was a direct result of the Rooster's insubordination. The setback embarrassed Bobby – and on national TV no less. (Though, it should be noted, that the Heenan Family lost *a lot* on *Saturday Night's Main Event*).

Bobby then slapped his protégé.

The Red Rooster, in turn, beat him senseless.

So, with the wounds from last *Saturday Night's Main Event* still fresh, Rooster appeared as an invited *Prime Time* guest of apparent shit-starter, Gorilla Monsoon. Read the room, Gorilla. The reunion gave off *Vanderpump Rules* vibes. The tense interaction between Heenan and the Rooster was compounded by ~~Andy Cohen~~ Monsoon, who played more the role of instigator, rather than mediator.

I didn't like the Red Rooster's outfit. Forget the fact that he usually dressed like poultry. I'm not talking about that. The Red Rooster donned a blue blazer for the occasion, like this guest appearance was just a pit stop before the Harvard/Yale Regatta. I need a little more edge from my up-and-comers. I need him to look the part. Wear the tights. Flaunt the ring jacket. Show off the guns. Even outside the ring, you saw wrestlers in their gear –

or at the very least – rocking a muscle shirt (Andre and his sport coat was the exception). You never saw the Barbarian interviewed in a sweater vest, did you? Or Damien Demento, who hailed from The Outer Reaches of Your Mind, you think he picked up some groceries in a tracksuit? Hell, Hulk Hogan was a groomsman for Uncle Elmer's wedding (a formal occasion!) and CUT THE SLEEVES off his dress shirt. If he rented that tux, self-tailoring carries a hefty fine but you gotta show off those pythons. We were supposed to believe that this extra from *Dead Poets Society* – that the guy in Sperry's – could scrap? Maybe Heenan was right all along.

After a prolonged bathroom break, Bobby reentered the studio and offered the Red Rooster an apology and a handshake. I dug it. Hey, sometimes personalities and styles just clash. It's nothing personal; there's no reason to carry that venom with you. Disagreements happen, but it's how you respond in the aftermath that reveals one's true character. Here were two adults ready to leave the past behind and kudos to them both.

Then Heenan slapped him.

Fuck. How did I not see that coming?

There was no Red Rooster counterpunch this time. Journeyman Steve Lombardi, wearing a torn-up Yankees shirt (and later dubbed the Brooklyn Brawler), burst onto the scene wielding a friggin' barstool, and which TED Talk panel did he grab that from? Lombardi was ruthless. After drilling Rooster in the back, he then vaulted to public enemy #1 and TOOK OUT MONSOON, like some twisted piece of gutter trash.

I will only say this once. Get. Your. Fucking. Hands. Off. Gorilla. Were you raised by wolves, Lombardi? Here me loud and clear: Gorilla Monsoon is an institution and a national treasure. He's off-limits. If you're gonna ambush anyone, ambush Craig DeGeorge.

It took time, but the Red Rooster would exact his revenge. After racking up – let me check my math here – 26 wins against the Brawler over the next few months (Lombardi had a short memory), Rooster would defeat Bobby Heenan at WrestleMania V. This certainly wasn't the first manager/wrestler break-up in history, but it's the only split that dragged poor Gorilla into the muck. Monsoon was rightly pissed. He returned the following week with a 2x4 by his side and laid down the gauntlet.

"That's the last time you will ever flim-flam me." (*Prime* Time, January 23rd, 1989).

You tell 'em, Gorilla.

Your Favorite Xenophobic Uncle

> **Event:** *Superstars* (San Antonio, TX)
>
> **Match:** "Hacksaw" Jim Duggan vs. Yokozuna ("The Knockdown Challenge")
>
> **Date:** February 6th, 1993
>
> **#1 Song on This Date:** "I Will Always Love You" by Whitney Houston

Raymond Rougeau: *"Hacksaw, do you know as of yet, no one here in the World Wrestling Federation has been able to knock Yokozuna off his feet?"*

Jim Duggan: *"Yes, yes, I'm aware of that. I'm aware that big Yokozuma (sic) has not been knocked off his feet. But right now, I am going to challenge him. 'Hacksaw' Jim Duggan, this American, is going to challenge this large Japanese man to bring his Japanese flag to the ring. To bring his Japanese manager to the ring. I will not only knock him off his feet, but I will stand over him with the Stars and Stripes and wave it proudly."* (*Superstars*, January 30th, 1993).

Years ago, I played in a basketball game and my jersey of choice was a "Hacksaw" Jim Duggan t-shirt. (What? What would you have worn?). After knocking down a corner three (old hat), I ran down the court and gave a thunderous "OHHHHHHH!" My intentions were pure – I was paying homage to ol' "Hacksaw" – but in retrospect, was I inadvertently celebrating one of the most close-minded, bigoted poor sports to ever step foot in the squared circle?

The following is a list of superstars "Hacksaw" Jim Duggan either feuded with or wrestled on a major pay-per-view.

- The Iron Sheik (Tehran, Iran)
- Nikolai Volkoff (Moscow, Russia)
- Harley Race (Kansas City, but believed in a monarchy)
- Andre the Giant (Grenoble, in the French Alps)
- Ted DiBiase (Made his winter residence in Netherlands Antilles)
- Boris Zhukov (The Soviet Union)
- Dino Bravo (Canada, but the French part)
- The Fabulous Rougeau Brothers (Memphis, TN, but immigrants)
- King Haku (Tonga)
- Akeem (The Deepest, Darkest Africa)
- Randy Savage (Sarasota, but believed in a monarchy)
- The Orient Express (Tokyo, Japan)
- Sgt. Slaughter (Iraqi sympathizer)
- The Mountie (Canada, but the French part)
- Yokozuna (Land of the Rising Sun)

Hacksaw had a type. He dismissed anyone who didn't look or talk like him. I'm surprised Uncle Jim never teamed with the pirate, Jean-Pierre LaFitte, because you just know he was dying to use a hard 'R.' If any international wrestler had the *gall* to seek out the Land of Opportunity, you could expect "Hacksaw" to not be far behind. Every Duggan promo was a roundabout way of asking, "Where are your papers?" Looking back, I have no idea how the Bushwhackers or Outback Jack escaped his wrath.

"Hey, Outback Jack, you talk funny."

Jim loved his country. At WrestleMania VI – in Canada, mind you – he started a "U.S.A" chant without the slightest hint of self-awareness.

According to the Elias Sports Bureau, he led the league in "U.S.A." chants from '87 through '93.

1. Duggan (326,827 "U.S.A." chants)
2. Hulk Hogan (324)
3. Lex Luger (285)
4. Corporal Kirchner (16)

(He also recited the Pledge of Allegiance on the May 31st, 1993 *Raw*, showing his versatility). Nothing got Duggan's rocks off more than reminding a foreign adversary where they were.

"This is the U.S.A."

I know, Jim. I know where I am. I flew into LaGuardia.

Most of the time, these guys were minding their own business, just trying to earn a living. Consider the Iron Sheik. At WrestleMania III, he had B. Brian Blair in the camel clutch, bent like a piece of licorice, when Hacksaw, who, according to my research, was NOT a member of the Killer Bees, charged into the ring and popped Sheiky Baby to Kingdom Come with a 2x4. Like, we're cool with that Jumpin' Jim? You know you and B. Brian aren't getting the winner's purse now, right? Maybe Blair could've powered out, or grabbed a rope, or made a tag, I don't know. The camel clutch is a devastating maneuver, but I'd be willing to roll the dice on the newcomer's resolve. Instead, Duggan saw a foreigner in a compromising position, looked down at his 2x4, and said, "Eh, fuck it."

(Or "OHHHHHHH!" Either way).

Wait, why was he at ringside, Dave? He didn't have a manager's license, did he?

That's a GREAT QUESTION, reader. I have no idea. I watched Slick get accosted on *Saturday Night's Main Event* so I can't explain the double-standard; though, I'm sure we could drum up a theory. Duggan fifth wheeled his way into the proceedings. No invite, no nothing, but I have a sneaky suspicion that ol' "Hacksaw" would've minded his own business if the Bees wrestled the U.S. Express.

Jimmy Hart petitioned to ban the DDT, yet Hacksaw's 2x4 always got a free pass. "The Mouth of the South" barked up the wrong tree. Jake Roberts' DDT was a legitimate finishing move. The 2x4 was a foreign object. Ok, it was probably American made, but still. Jim pulled out his lumber time and time again while sarcastically referring to his foes as "tough guy," and the irony wasn't lost on me. It takes a big man to talk shit while holding a giant piece of wood. It had no place at ringside. The 2x4 wasn't a manager. It wasn't a mascot or an emotional-support animal like Matilda, or Frankie, or Ricky Steamboat's Komodo Dragon. If a match didn't go his way, or an official result wasn't to Duggan's liking, Jim got dirty. "Hacksaw" didn't lose gracefully. Every victory over Duggan turned into a fire drill. You had fifteen seconds to clear the ring, or you'd be picking splinters from the side of your head for the next month.

"What happened to Frenchy Martin? He looks like hell."

"Oh, Dino Bravo beat Duggan in Sioux Falls. Hacksaw caught him with one."

Duggan was a brawler. He also was an instigator. He started most of these fights, and maybe that was his problem. Maybe a little more tolerance and acceptance of others would've saved him from a few scraps, saved him from a few rough nights at the office. On the February 6th, 1993 *Superstars*, one week after his above interview with Raymond Rougeau, Hacksaw and Yokozuna participated in a "Knockdown Challenge." This wasn't playing the computer on "All-Madden" level. "Hacksaw" didn't have to pin the '93 Royal Rumble winner, just get him off his feet. Duggan "won" and then celebrated, waving Old Glory to the high heavens just as he'd predicted.

The San Antonio crowd erupted in tow. He had vanquished yet another foreign threat, repelled another enemy abroad.

Not quite. Yokozuna was a different beast entirely. Years of bullying Boris Zhukov couldn't prepare Duggan for a challenge of this magnitude. Yoko recovered and obliterated Duggan with four, count 'em four, Banzai Drops – each finisher more punishing than the last (To add insult, Mr. Fuji draped the U.S flag over Hacksaw for the final blow).

The cheers from the hometown crowd evaporated; replaced with audible gasps as officials and medical personnel carried the American hero away on a stretcher.

First Intermission

The King Kong Bundy LJN Action Figure

(We interrupt this program to discuss LJN Action Figures).

I'm not a collector. I've never kept a toy in its original packaging or taken any basic steps to preserve its condition. I put my toys through hell. I used to play "football" with my 1988 Topps NFL cards and ran my Bo Jackson rookie into a hungry defensive line composed of G.I. Joes. A Beckett's Pricing Guide would've valued my cards in "Poor" condition, which was accurate, though still hurtful. (I prefer the gentler terms, "used" or "played with"). But go hard or go home, right? That applied to my toys, too. Never ask me to babysit your T206 Honus Wagner. He'd end up in a 20-man battle royal with Skeletor and Casey Jones.

The LJN guys were the gold standard of wrestling figures. Compared to the Hasbro figures of later years, whose stiff design limited you to punches, dropkicks, and one-star matches, LJN wrestlers offered much more creativity. It wasn't suggested, but you could also color them, so I kept a red crayon nearby.

"Need a little color from you tonight, Brutus. Kamala has to go over strong."

My pops would take me to a Lionel Kiddie City (R.I.P) and let me pick a figure. I bought my favorites at first – Hogan, Ricky Steamboat, George Steele, etc – but I then realized the positioning of their hands was even more important than the wrestler itself. Bruno Sammartino was "The Living Legend" no doubt, but Action Figure Bruno's arms were down at his sides like he was about to bear hug a refrigerator. Completely useless. Paul Orndorff's figure, on the other hand, is positioned in a double bicep flex pose, which was optimal for both punching and suplexes. Terry Funk had his left arm by his side which allowed for a textbook DDT. Tito Santana's figure could execute a perfect arm drag. Every figure had their pros and cons.

Then there was King Kong Bundy. If the average LJN action figure weighed 2 lb, then King Kong Bundy weighed 75. LJN Bundy wasn't a toy. It was a fire hydrant. I haven't tried to fly with one, but it'd probably get flagged at a TSA screening. I attacked my brother with Bundy on multiple occasions, hurling the Condominium with Legs at his exposed shins. When you're five years younger, you fight dirty. It got Bundy and me a lot of heat in both the territory and with my mom. Like everyone else, I reckon, my LJN Sling 'Em Fling 'Em wrestling ring cracked down the middle. Was it because I accidentally ran over it in the garage with my Huffy? Maybe, but my money is on one too many Bundy splashes. I gave him the strap and let the babyfaces chase. His standard five count didn't provide enough humiliation. He wanted to permanently end careers. Bundy would drape a steel chair over his fallen opponent and bludgeon them with another post-match splash – and by 'steel chair,' I mean an empty Tic-Tac container (obviously). Art imitated life. Bundy squashed S.D. Jones in nine seconds on my living room floor. Captain Lou Albano came out to save poor Special Delivery, and he got an avalanche for his troubles. (The next time I saw Action Figure Lou was 25 years later at my parents' yard sale. It sold quickly, but S.D. is still missing.).

LJN Bundy was a fighting champion. He ducked no one, not even the immortal Hulk Hogan. The Hulkster kicked out of a Bundy avalanche – naturally – so our champ amped up the devastation. A second splash? Nah. A splash from the top rope? Getting warmer. Bundy channeled his inner-Jimmy Snuka and climbed, but not to the top of the cage, oh no no no. He climbed to the top of my parents' TV stand. Hogan sat helpless in the middle of the (cracked) ring, as Hulkamania clung to its final breaths. I stood up. I saw the twinkle in Bundy's eye, before he catapulted off a television five feet above.

And landed right on my bare foot.

OWWWWWWWWWWWWW!

OWWWWWWWWWWWWW!

MOM! MY FOOT! MY FOOT!

I got double-crossed. Bundy Screwed Dave, or as my critics would claim, "Dave Screwed Dave." Also, I don't buy the explanation that, "Well, Bundy turned heel," because HE WAS ALREADY A HEEL. (And speaking of heels, I expected my foot to be amputated). I rolled on the carpet screaming while my mom finished up her crossword puzzle. Where was her concern? Was she in on the swerve too? Monsoon always called aerial tactics "high risk, high reward," and Gorilla rarely missed. LJN Bundy tried to end Hulkamania. Instead, I iced my foot every two to three hours until the swelling went down.

(Hogan won via count out. The title did not change hands).

We now return to our regularly scheduled programming.

APARTMENT(S) BUILDING OWNER, PAUL CHRISTY

> **Event: TNT (Tuesday Night Titans)**
>
> **Guest: Paul Christy, Apartment Building Owner**
>
> **Date: May 21st, 1986**
>
> **#1 Movie on This Date: Top Gun**
>
> "I'll give you 'boo.' I'll come out and break your neck, you jerk, you turkey."
>
> - Paul Christy (Tuesday Night Titans, May 21st, 1986).

Not much shocks me anymore. I've been through the gamut. I saw James "Buster" Douglas knock out the invincible Mike Tyson. I went to a Goldfinger concert and watched a fan eat a Twinkie from the drummer's ass. I witnessed the O.J. car chase and recall the tragic passing of Katie Vick (God rest her soul). There is a lot of tread on these tires. Nothing, however, prepared me for the May 21st, 1986 episode of *TNT*.

Of the book's 87 essays, I had prior knowledge of every protagonist but one. I don't remember Paul Christy. I had never heard of Paul Christy, and, as far as I can recall, he has never been in my kitchen. Host Gene Okerlund introduced Christy, the newest up-and-comer in the World Wrestling Federation, and what transpired was a mind-blowing eight minutes that left me with more questions than answers. But I'll condense my many, *many* questions down to one:

Just who was Paul Christy?

Beats me. I watched this segment five consecutive times, and I'm still not sure. Here's what we do know:

He was a wrestler.

And a magician.

And a hypnotist.

And a womanizer.

And owned many apartment buildings?

And also shopping centers?

Actually, I guess we know a lot about the mysterious Paul Christy. He was a Renaissance Man. He was both a landlord and a businessman. He was also Phantasio? Christy knew how to make an entrance, arriving on set dressed to the nines with a red gift box in hand. His magic was immediately on display. He sailed red flares over the head of Lord Alfred Hayes like his arm doubled as one of those Assault missile launchers from *American Gladiators*. He had a presence about him; he was a showman. His sleight of hand wasn't quite David Copperfield making the Statue of Liberty disappear, but I was still intrigued.

Things then went off the rails. Okerlund offered Christy a seat and he refused, like the chair was literally *and* figuratively beneath him. He did the entire interview standing up, and I'm using 'interview' loosely here. "Mean" Gene never asked him a question. After rattling off his diversified portfolio, Christy outlined that the three greatest drives in this world were sex, power, and money. Blessed with a beautiful pair of baby blues, Paul had no problem with the ladies. Money? He had an endless supply. You don't live paycheck to paycheck when your name is on the marquee of multiple apartment buildings *and* shopping centers. Power, though, that's what Christy craved. That was the final piece on his vision board – that's why he was here in the World Wrestling Federation – and the quickest point from A to B was through … hypnosis?

As an appetizer, Christy promised to program the minds of the studio audience, a little hypnotism 101. I didn't know if his powers extended through my television, but I wanted to tag along for the ride. First, though, I apologized to my wife and kid. Then I popped a gummy.

"I won't be around for bath and bedtime. Daddy is dabbling in some mind control."

Hypnotic bliss, though, eluded us. "Mean" Gene, that good-for-nothing *motormouth*, kept interrupting Paul. Anyone with half a brain knows you need pristine conditions for mind control. It's like a NASA space launch. Okerlund was a nuisance. At one point, he pushed a pencil against Christy's backside, and how is someone supposed to execute a proper hypnosis with a Ticonderoga #2 up your butt hole? And it wasn't just "Mean" Gene. Paul faced a tough crowd. The live studio audience was cynical, and a disruptive production crew mic'd in toilet flushing sound effects. This infuriated Christy. His ranting and raving triggered a lot of stopping and starting, until mercifully, we got a commercial break.

Christy righted the ship. He expertly blended both disciplines. After a card trick, he asked Lord Alfred to pick a number between 1 and 1000. Hayes chose "555," the numerological translation for "promotional consideration paid for by the following." The magician then revealed a piece of paper with those exact digits scribbled down. It wasn't magic, Christy admitted, pulling back the curtain for the live studio audience, but mind control. Lord Alfred, that impressionable sap, had succumbed to his advanced hypnosis techniques.

It was Paul's first and last appearance on *TNT*. He would exit the Federation in August after a loss to Billy Jack Haynes.

While Christy programmed the mind of his Lordship, that success didn't translate to the squared circle.

His record was 0-32-1.

OPEN YOUR EYES, ZEBRA

> Event: WWF at Madison Square Garden (New York, NY)
>
> Match: Wendi Richter (Champion) vs. The Spider (Challenger)
>
> Date: November 25th, 1985
>
> Attendance: 16,000
>
> Highest Rated TV Show on this Date (tie): *Kate & Allie*; *Newhart*

"What was that … … … referee made a three count? … … It appears the referee has made a three count … … And Wendi the champ … look at that! It is Moolah! It is Moolah! Take a look, Jess!"

– Gorilla Monsoon (Fabulous One 2017).

I'm not normally a "blame the refs" guy. It's weak. It's often a case of sour grapes – a scapegoat for your favorite team's lack of talent or execution – but Lordy Lordy, do Wendi Richter and Velvet McIntyre have some legitimate gripes. In baseball, there has been chatter surrounding robo umps; computerized technology designed to create a consistent and uniformed strike zone across the Major Leagues. Its detractors remind us that the "human element" is part of the game, and I get the sentiment. I appreciate their stance. But then I think back to the mid-80's, when two high-profile women's championship matches were plagued by inexcusable referee oversights, and I'm not sure I could stomach my Phillies being Wendi Richter'd. Or Velvet McIntyre'd for that matter.

It was a risk to put your title on the line against a spider. The challenger, no surprise, resided from Parts Unknown, with a weight unknown. Did the Spider have the customary two legs, or was this arthropod sporting eight? Until she made the walk down that aisle, it was anyone's guess. You can't gameplan for six additional appendages. Consider Goro, the half-man, half-dragon. That dude was an absolute unit and he *only* had four arms. The uber-popular Richter, though, was a fighting champion. She ducked no one, arachnid or not.

Richter was the aggressor early. She was no stranger to the bright lights, capturing her first championship at MTV's *The Brawl to End It All*, so the fast start was no surprise. The Spider, however, didn't just stumble into the #1 Contender spot. She made the appropriate adjustments, and the contest settled into a back-and-forth affair. After a Richter running clothesline produced only a one count, the challenger locked Wendi in a small package. The champ's shoulder lifted off the mat after one, but veteran official Dick Kroll kept counting.

Wait, how didn't Dick see that the shoulder was up?

I'm wondering the same thing.

So how much did the Spider pay for the plastic surgery, Dave?

Hey now. That's how rumors get started.

I have no idea what Kroll saw – or didn't see to be precise – but he called for the bell. Monsoon and Ventura struggled to piece together the action. If this was Nickelodeon's *GUTS*, Mike O'Malley would've sent it to Mo ... *for the official results*, but even Howard Finkel was tongue-tied. A confused Richter again took the fight to her opponent. She yanked the mask off the Spider and BAH GAWD, it was the Fabulous Moolah! What the hell was she doing here!? SHE WASN'T THE SPIDER! She wasn't the #1 Contender! She wasn't even from Parts Unknown! The incensed champ drilled Moolah with a backbreaker while the incompetent, blind as a bat Dick Kroll looked on idly. He neither raised the victor's hand nor took any necessary steps to suppress the confusion. After a few more moments of turmoil, Howard Finkel finally, *finally* delivered the official announcement.

Whether we liked it or not, we had a new champion.

~ ~ ~

> **Event: WrestleMania 2 (Rosemont, IL)**
>
> **Match: The Fabulous Moolah (champion) vs. Velvet McIntyre (challenger)**
>
> **Date: April 7th, 1986**
>
> **Attendance: 9,000**

Velvet entered WrestleMania 2 with a plan. She knew her strengths. She wanted to push the tempo and play above the rim. McIntyre weathered some early offense by the champ and climbed to the middle rope for a splash attempt – your classic high risk, high reward move. The logic was sound. The challenger couldn't play it conservatively. Moolah had seen it all though. You don't have a near 30-year reign without banking some ring acumen. She rolled out of the way. Moolah then capitalized on the blunder by flopping on the challenger for the cover. With the wind knocked out of her, Velvet still had the wherewithal to drape her leg over the bottom rope, but the official, either due to negligence or defiance, continued the count. The Fabulous Moolah had notched yet another successful title defense.

It was a miscarriage of justice, the second in a matter of months, and a blatant disregard of the universally accepted rope break rule. I've played enough *WCW/nWo Revenge* for N-64 to know what a proper rope break is, and I expect a trained official to have that same basic understanding.

This, however, was no properly accredited official. Who was *that* guy? What third rate ref school was this scab plucked from? (I honestly don't know. I couldn't track down his identity). He wasn't even wearing a striped shirt or a bow tie. He was dressed in blue chinos and a white button down. I didn't see a ref. I saw a guy who wanted to give you a great deal on a washer/dryer set. The announce team never mentioned the mistake. I can excuse guest commentator Cathy Lee Crosby for not knowing the nuances of the rope break, but cat got your tongues, Monsoon and Okerlund? If Velvet's leg was outside the ring any further, she'd be playing footsie with the timekeeper.

Moolah benefited from shoddy officiating. There are no instant replays in wrestling. There are no do-overs. As my cutthroat mother says while playing pinochle, "A card laid is a card played." Besides, Moolah's camp probably thought the officials did a fine job, an admirable one even.

Only losers complain about the refs.

Get Well Soon, Hulk

"Last week, I asked all you Hulkamaniacs out there to show the Hulkster how you really care about him. And a lot of you did ...

But then again, a lot of you didn't. You know, maybe you didn't hear me. Maybe you didn't understand me. Or maybe you just don't realize how important this whole situation is. You know, I just came from being with the Hulkster, and he's in the – like I've never seen him before. You know, he's down, man ..."

– **Tugboat, (*Superstars*, June 9th, 1990).**

"Mom! MOM! Where are the stamps? We got any stamps!? I'm getting another guilt trip from Tugboat. Even though I'm only 6 years old, he thinks I should grasp the gravity of Hulk Hogan's situation. The stamps, ma! Where are the stamps!? Mom!"

Hulk Hogan

PO Box 911

Venice CA, 90294

Dear Hulkster,

How are you? How are you feeling? Your dear friend Tugboat (toot, toot!) ~~shamed me~~ suggested that I send you some well wishes after the vicious attack from Earthquake and Jimmy Hart on *The Brother Love Show*. It was horrible and despicable, and I haven't cried that hard since King Kong Bundy squashed Little Beaver. I hope you're doing better.

Can I ask you a question? I don't mean to overstep, Hulk, but why do you always go on Brother Love's show? It seems like nothing good ever happens there. Didn't the Big Boss Man handcuff and strangle you with a nightstick like a year and a half ago? Not like victim blaming you or anything, just something to think about.

I haven't sent much mail before, Hulkster. Aside from a few letters to the editor over at *Highlights* magazine, I've only sent a 'Get well soon' card to Matilda after she returned home to Davey Boy and Dynamite (I'll never forgive those Islanders). I hope you can read my handwriting. Anyways, I saw "Mean" Gene Okerlund wearing his Hulk Hogan Friendship Bracelet. He vowed never to take it off until you return. I hope to get a bracelet soon. I just spent two months allowance on a Hulk Rules beach towel, so I need to save up. We are all in solidarity, brother.

Oh, why again didn't President Jack Tunney exercise your rematch clause with The Ultimate Warrior? Stupid Tunney.

We need you to come back, Hulk. I need you. The Tugster needs you. We all need you.

We need Hulkamania to run wild again.

Your little Hulkamaniac,

Dave

P.S. I'm sorry this letter was so late. My mom didn't have any stamps.

Tito's Mid-Life Crisis

> **Event:** *Wrestling Challenge* (Huntington, WV)
>
> **Match:** El Matador vs. Pat Tanaka
>
> **Date:** November 3rd, 1991
>
> **On This Day:** The Indianapolis Colts dropped to 0-9 after a 10-6 loss to the Miami Dolphins.

"In order to excel to the heights that I wish to attain in the World Wrestling Federation, I know there is something I must do. I must return to my native land. I must stand before my peers. I must look into the eyes of the bull. I must come as close as possible to the menacing wreck of horns. I must know the thrill of the charge of the 2,000 lb beast. I must hear the adulation of my fans. I will become ... El Matador!"

– *Wrestling Challenge*, September 22nd, 1991 (Old School Wrestling TV 2019).

Most guys going through a mid-life crisis purchase some Ed Hardy t-shirts and a motorcycle.

Tito Santana became El Matador.

I get the need for a change or a fresh start, but start small, ease into it – maybe grow a moustache or get your ear pierced or something. Tito submersed himself in the bullfighting culture, like someone who visited Napa Valley and now won't shut up about grapes. In the fall of '91, it was all he ever talked about, bullfighting this, bullfighting that.

"There's a lot of training involved ... It takes a lot of hard work ... You must be quick on your feet ... The bull's horns are very sharp ..."

Alright, alright, WE GET IT. Sheesh. *Fighting bulls ain't easy.* Well neither is pimpin', but you don't hear the Godfather rambling on and on (Ok, that was a bad example). I don't know what triggered Santana's sudden evolution from wrestler to wrestling bullfighter, but I have a theory. I don't think the bullfighting manifested via some overnight identity crisis. Santana didn't throw his hat into the bullring on a whim. The genesis of his transformation can be traced back to 1989, when his Strike Force partner, Rick Martel, alienated him in their WrestleMania V match with the Brain Busters. Maybe Santana spent the next two years searching for validation, wondering if he was truly deserving of love? Maybe 'El Matador' wasn't a return to his roots, but rather a cry for help, a byproduct of abandonment issues.

Or maybe Tito was just really into bullfighting. I don't fucking know.

El Matador made his *Wrestling Challenge* debut on November 3rd, 1991. Santana's white trunks with the lightning bolt on the butt cheek were replaced with green pants, white boots, and a decorative jacket. An ornate pink and yellow *muleta* (cape) added to the pageantry, and the presentation was impressive. After a traditional bow and acknowledgement to the adoring crowd, the pride of Tocula then held the *muleta* off to his side. Tanaka obliged and charged wildly, missing badly on a few wild right hooks. This happened three consecutive times, and I can't believe I need to write this, but Tanaka, you are not a bull. You know that, right? The hell are you doing?

El Matador looked a step faster than Tito's past outings. Heenan and Monsoon surmised that the added quickness was a direct result of Santana's intense bullfighting training, and it's tough to argue. The two know ball. While the "why" behind the identity change is up for debate, we can't dispute the results. El Matador looked convincing in victory. *Olé!*

DAVE RUETER

"Right in the back of the neck! That's how they put the bull away. That's how he put Tanaka away."

– Gorilla Monsoon (Monsoon Classic 2021).

QUALITY OVER QUANTITY

> Event: SummerSlam 1991 (New York, NY)
>
> Match: Sgt. Slaughter, General Adnan, and Col. Mustafa vs. Hulk Hogan and the Ultimate Warrior
>
> Date: August 26th, 1991
>
> Attendance: 20,000
>
> Top Selling Video Game in the U.S: *Sonic the Hedgehog*

"The lovely Miss Elizabeth, and the 'Macho Man' Randy Savage request the honor of your presence at their wedding, where it will truly be, a match made in heaven ...

And then nuptials turn to napalm ... in a match ... made in hellllllllllll!"

— Vince McMahon (SummerSlam 1991).

I called this a *Match Made in Heck*, because I didn't need my parents on my case for cursing. The "H-word" was a big no-no at my house. I got around it by entering "7734" on a calculator and flipping that bad boy upside down. What can I say? Some mustangs aren't meant to be tamed.

On paper, this match looked like a slam dunk for Slaughter's stable. Yeah, special guest referee, Sid Justice, was an unknown variable. I'll concede that. You weren't sure if he'd call the match down the middle, or if the Hulkster's lackey, Jack Tunney, had already sunk his bureaucratic fangs into Sid. Justice aside, though, Sarge's crew had the numbers advantage. If my math's right, 60% of the contest's participants were members of the Triangle of Terror. How do you combat that? Slaughter, Adnan, and Mustafa's goals were aligned. They were a well-oiled machine.

They bent the rules – even broke them at times. How could Hogan and Warrior, in a match *literally* concocted in the underworld by Lucifer himself, conquer the diabolical trio when we weren't even sure they could coexist? Hogan's spotty past was well-documented. Every partnership ended in a messy divorce. Throw in the giant question mark, Sid, and the scales – on paper anyway – were skewed in Slaughter's favor.

But that was just on paper. Dig deeper. Who *really* faced the long odds? Whose backs were *really* against the wall because the record books suggest that the Triangle of Terror was dead on arrival. Michael Cole can shout, "The numbers game!" until he's blue in the face, but history paints a different picture. The team on the power play, the team with the man advantage *never* wins. Like ever. They've won less than the Washington Generals. I get the math – really, I do. 2 >1, 3 >2, etc, etc, but a series of coincidences eventually becomes a trend.

WrestleMania V: Demolition def. The Powers of Pain and Mr. Fuji.

Superstars **(February 25th, 1989):** Andre the Giant def. Tito Santana and Jim Powers.

Championship Wrestling **(January 11th, 1986):** King Kong Bundy def. Jeff Grippley and Paul Dose.

The list is endless.

Also, the Triangle of Terror was battling more than history. They were only facing two guys, but these were no ordinary opponents. Jeff Grippley and Paul Dose weren't walking through that door. These were Level-10 bosses, the best of the best. The Hulkster and Warrior lost like one match every five years. FanDuel had Slaughter's boys at +5000 on the moneyline and even that number looks light. You think Hogan and Warrior were worried about Col. Mustafa going off? You think they were watching film, conjuring up ways to counter Adnan's nerve holds? Slaughter could've recruited Saddam himself. He would've taken the big boot and the leg drop just like everyone else.

Sarge held his own. The former World Champ was a veteran who didn't get intimidated by the hostile crowd. The trio seized the upper hand and cut the ring in half, but their offense lacked … juice. Where were the devastating maneuvers? Who was going to deliver the knockout blow? Couldn't someone mix in a bulldog, or a reverse Russian leg sweep? Show me something, anything. I'd have even settled for a monkey flip. Adnan was a net zero. I've seen more offense in an Army/Navy game. How many times can you rake someone's eye? How often can you rake someone's back? It's unpleasant, sure, but nothing that a hot shower and some Neosporin can't fix. Adnan resorted to the rake, time and time again. It was like your first go-round with *Mortal Kombat* on SNES. Until you figured out the controls, you just mashed the X-button and hoped Raiden could protect the realm through endless jabs.

The Triangle of Terror, predictably, became another statistic. Despite the numbers advantage, it was Sgt. Slaughter who had the handicap. It was he who was spread too thin. He didn't clash with just the current and former world champions. He fought a war within his own barracks. Sarge aligned himself with teammates who lacked firepower (Seriously, where was the napalm we were promised, Vince?). Adnan and Mustafa's ceilings were low, their potential capped. Slaughter saw the writing on the wall, and soon after, he'd crawl back to the country he publicly scorned.

And we'll get to that in a later chapter.

Hogan pinned Sarge after the leg drop at 12:40.

The 1985 Manager of the Year

> **Event:** *Championship Wrestling* (Poughkeepsie, NY)
>
> **Election Results:** 1985 Manager of the Year
>
> **Date:** September 21st, 1985
>
> **On This Date:** Light Heavyweight boxer Michael Spinks upsets Larry Holmes in a 15-round decision. Holmes was one victory away from tying Rocky Marciano's 49-0 record.

I lost a student council election in 7th grade. I know why. It wasn't stolen and it wasn't my character. I was a straight shooter, and rigorous background checks by the school newspaper came up clean as a whistle. I ran a bad campaign. I didn't stand for anything, and I was light on the important issues. Moments before I delivered a speech to the student body, I crossed out one key line.

"If you vote for me, I promise to get toppings on the cafeteria pizza!"

That's all I needed to say. That was the campaign promise that would've gotten me the votes. I excluded the line because I couldn't deliver it. A pepperoni slice? In this economy? Our school was dirt poor. Pizza toppings may as well have been a dome over the football field. The school ran fundraisers every other day. We had something called "Penny Wars," which was a fancy phrase for solicitation. Kids went home and asked their parents for loose change, and we called it a "Penny War."

It didn't matter what I could or couldn't deliver, though. I just had the float the idea out there.

"You vote for the pizza topping kid?"

"Yeah, of course. He also promised a Slurpee machine in each classroom."

I don't think the candidates for '85 Manager of the Year made very compelling arguments (Partly because the award was decided with three months still to go). Their platforms lacked substance. Every manager said they were the best, yes, but *why* are you the best? Differentiate yourself, Johnny V. Sell yourself, Master Fuji. Why should I pick you? What have you accomplished? Did one of your guys capture championship gold? Talk me through that journey. In this voter's eyes, guiding your wrestler to a title is the greatest qualifier.

So, based on that criteria, Fuji and Heenan were immediately removed from consideration. Same goes for Hillbilly Jim, who somehow snuck on the ballot as a fringe candidate. Who rubberstamped his manager's license anyway? Johnny V only managed one guy, but his man, Brutus Beefcake, had won the tag titles with Valentine a month prior. Another worthy candidate, Freddie Blassie, led Sheik and Volkoff to the belts at WrestleMania I, and Captain Lou was always prevalent in the tag team scene. (For my money, though, the '85 Manager of the Year was "The Mouth of the South." Please respect my privacy).

In the ring on this night with "Mean" Gene were Heenan, Hillbilly Jim, and Albano. Bobby brought some muscle. Bundy and Studd hovered outside the ring like poll watchers; there to make sure everything remained on the up and up. Okerlund announced an overwhelming turnout – over one million votes cast and tallied. This was where the math got fuzzy.

"I'm going to explain to you what has taken place, and what I'm doing here. Through my great friends: Fred Blassie, 'Luscious' Johnny Valiant, 'The Mouth of the South' Jimmy Hart, Mr. Fuji ... by proxy vote, they have pledged me their votes. Now how many votes do I have, just for me?"

— **Bobby Heenan,** *Championship Wrestling,* **September 21st, 1985 (WWF the 80's 2020).**

I believe election integrity was just compromised. I don't think what Heenan declared was legal, and I don't know why Okerlund took him at his word. Bobby himself collected 179,321 votes. He then asked Okerlund to tally the total of his pledged ballots. Everyone waited as Gene counted ("Carry the two"), which is a *lot* of pressure without a calculator. It gave me PTSD from doing a VLOOKUP while screen-sharing on a Zoom call. I'd rather pee in front of people than enter an Excel formula. The new total for "The Brain" was 519,711, which, barring any shenanigans, would guarantee him Manager of the Year.

Enter: Shenanigans.

Hillbilly Jim and Captain Lou each accrued over 300,000 votes respectively. The man from Mudlick then gifted Albano his portion, because why respect the will of the people now? Jim's donation pushed Captain Lou's total to over 600,000 and this sham of a vote finally reached its merciful conclusion.

Heenan didn't lose graciously. He sabotaged the trophy presentation and attacked Albano. Big John Studd and Bundy then cornered Hillbilly and flattened him with a series of splashes. Historians will draw comparisons to the controversial 1977 Manager of the Year presentation. After finishing second to Arnold Skaaland, an incensed Albano swung the trophy across the Golden Boy's back. Eight years later, the tables had turned. Now, it was Lou's Manager of the Year trophy destroyed. It was Albano lying in a heap.

Karma had claimed another victim.

LUST IN HIS EYES

> Event: *The Main Event II* (Milwaukee, WI)
> Match: The Mega Powers vs. The Twin Towers
> Date: February 3rd, 1989
> Attendance: 20,000
> #1 Song on This Date: "Two Hearts" by Phil Collins

"I love Elizabeth just as much as the 'Macho Man' does ... but just in a different way."

— **Hulk Hogan**, *The Brother Love Show*, January 28th, 1989 (Wrestling with Paul 2020).

I loved *Saved by the Bell*. Even the *College Years* ones with Jeremiah Lasky, the sexual predator who moonlighted as an anthropology professor. I'm a simple man with simple tastes and someone who looks for the good in everything and everyone. I draw the line, however, at season 3, ep. 3, "The Aftermath."

In an episode prior, Kelly broke up with Zack after falling for (and playing tonsil hockey) with some college dickwad named Jeff, who was a manager at The Max and "minoring in romance languages" (puke). In "The Aftermath," Zack attempts to move on. He goes on a few blind dates and takes one suitor (Screech's cousin) to The Max, where Kelly was a server. Preppy then asked his date to dance – an odd request at a burger joint, but whatever – and plays "A12" on the jukebox. "A12," if you're not up to speed on the Bayside High drama, was Zack and Kelly's song.

And THAT'S when everyone turned heel. Suddenly, Zack was the bad guy. Kelly cheated on him and broke his heart, sure, but *Zack* had the GALL to play "A12," ("A12 is sacred") and suddenly Preppy was blackballed by the friend group. They accused Zack of rubbing "it" – whatever "it" was – in Kelly's face, as if Kelly WASN'T PLANNING ON BRINGING JEFF TO LISA'S SWEET 16th BIRTHDAY PARTY.

Sorry, I'm getting angry all over again.

Anyways, the episode is shit. Slater, Jesse, Lisa, and Screech's reactions were shit, and "A12" wasn't even a real song. It was just an instrumental or something.

This was a long-winded way to say that I don't just blame Hulk Hogan for the Mega Powers' split. Hogan's Hogan. He's as helpful as a hangover. I also blame everyone else. It's the commentators' fault, the fans' fault, the whole lot. Hulk's actions were despicable, but the defense of his actions by outside parties was even worse. Hogan was opportunistic. He knew what he was doing – butting his way into Liz and Randy's relationship – slowly tugging at the fabric of a once happy union. Capturing the championship at WrestleMania V was a bonus.

Hulk Hogan *absolutely* had lust in his eyes. Randy was right! Savage was painted as some jealous maniac, but the homewrecking seeds were planted as far back as SummerSlam '88. After defeating DiBiase and Andre the Giant in the main event, Hogan lifted Liz and hugged her for like three minutes. This wasn't some awkward embrace, like when you give your Great Aunt Mildred an ass out hug at Christmas. The Hulkster was all up in Liz' business, like it was a junior high dance and the DJ just played Next's "Too Close." Not even Will Smith was cucked so publicly. If Randy ever dared to raise an eyebrow, however, or express any sort of concern about Hogan's actions or intentions, he was gaslighted to the high heavens.

"What's Randy so worked up about? Why is Savage so jealous?"

Hulk then anointed Liz as his 'manager,' and since when did the guy who laid waste to the federation for five years suddenly need a manager? Gorilla, your thoughts?

Gimme a break.

Exactly. It was like Tom Brady saying he suddenly needed a fullback. No one looked back at the past five years of Hogan's dominance and thought to themselves, "Something is ... missing. His career lacks ... guidance. Perhaps a manager, perhaps an Oliver Humperdink-type can propel him to the next level."

Hogan didn't need Miss Elizabeth. He didn't need her to lobby the Championship Committee on his behalf. The Hulkster liked playing homewrecker. He enjoyed meddling in people's lives. It was like one of those 90s thrillers, where a live-in nanny with impure intentions gets the wife hooked on pain meds before sleeping with the husband for undisclosed reasons. Every one of Hulk's decisions followed the plot of a Shannon Tweed movie.

The Mega Powers' turbulent relationship came to a boil at *The Main Event II*. After Akeem tossed Savage outside the ring, Randy landed on Liz, knocking her out cold. Hogan ran to Miss Elizabeth's side and delivered some shoddy First Aid. He checked for a pulse a few times (good), but then also flipped and rolled her in case ... she was on fire? (In Hulk's defense, at least he tried *something*. All first responder Dave Hebner did was continue the count outside on Savage).

While Hogan channeled his inner-Mitch Buchannon, "Macho Man" battled the Twin Towers alone. It was a game effort. Randy successfully fended off the behemoths until he saw Hogan carry his woman back up the aisle like they were rehearsing *Romeo and Juliet* for their local community theater. It was the perfect out. Hulk left Savage to get his ass kicked *and* got some alone time with Randy's girlfriend. A win/win.

At wits' end, Savage attacked Hogan later that night. In the weeks that followed, both "Macho Man" and Hulk argued their case. It was that awkward period post-break-up where each party trashes the other. Break-ups are rarely amicable. Mutual friends are forced to choose sides, and outside of Jesse Ventura who called Hulk, 'Lust Hogan,' the entire world sided with the #1 contender. It was hard to fathom. Who among you are entrusting '89 Hulkster to not hit on your significant other? If your girlfriend quits her job to become Hogan's manager, sound the alarm. Savage lost the World Championship to his ex-friend at WrestleMania V. He also lost his girl. One year prior, Randy had everything. He was the champ. He was in love. "Macho Man" was happy, and the Hulkster just couldn't stand for that.

The Blockbuster Trade

Okerlund: *"The Missing Link ... your man, going against Ivan Putski. I know you have a devil of a time controlling him."*

Heenan: *"I do not have a devil of a time controlling the Missing Link."*

Okerlund: *"Sometimes you don't even get him to the ring."*

Heenan: *"Sometimes he takes the wrong turn. It could happen to anybody. Haven't you ever gone up the wrong aisle?"* (Adorable Adrian 2009).

~ ~ ~

@Wojespn

BREAKING: Bobby Heenan has acquired the rights to King Kong Bundy from Jimmy Hart in exchange for the Missing Link and Adrian Adonis

12:34 PM · 9/21/85

38,244 Retweets 619,457 Likes

@AdamSchefter

Trade: Bobby gets his man. King Kong Bundy now the newest member of the Heenan Family. Missing Link and Adonis on the move in return. @wojespn first to report

12:37 PM · 9/21/85

25,180 Retweets 482,902 Likes

It was your classic two-for-one deal. One camp was in 'win now' mode while the other accumulated assets with an eye towards the future. For Heenan, the trade was a no-brainer. When a generational talent like King Kong Bundy becomes available, you don't walk to your landline. You run.

1985 hadn't been good to Bobby. Forget the Manager of the Year vote. Heenan was fighting a war on multiple fronts. Attempting to slay Andre with his own giant (Big John Studd) while also constructing a portfolio of superstars deep and talented enough to destroy Hulkamania was a heavy cross to carry. He had also suffered some attrition. He lost strongman Ken Patera earlier that year and Paul Orndorff publicly fired him on the April 26th *Tuesday Night Titans*. Losing Link and Adonis depleted his depth further, but the Heenan Family is like the Yankees. They don't rebuild. They reload.

(It should be noted that ESPN's Bill Barnwell graded the trade favorably for Heenan's camp).

The Hart Family took a different approach. Jimmy cast a wide net, like a Spread Gun from *Contra*. He didn't want his stable's success tied only to one man. Bundy's star was bright, but he would be eyeing a huge contract extension after his bitter, nasty feud with Andre. I couldn't obtain access to Hart's financials (though I tried), but with Terry Funk and the Hart Foundation already on the payroll, Jimmy faced a difficult decision. If you re-sign Bundy, you probably don't have the cash to bring in Hoss and Jimmy Jack Funk (They joined the fray in early '86), and if you don't bring in Hoss and Jimmy Jack to appease the Funkster, does Terry walk? On a related note, and in another example of Jimmy's salary cap predicament, Hart quietly loaned out Greg "The Hammer" Valentine to Johnny V, like he was memorabilia from *WWE's Most Wanted Treasures*.

(An aside: Some managers didn't even seek wrestlers in return. The Slickster famously traded Hercules to Heenan for cash considerations. What in the name of Harry Frazee was he thinking? At least hold out for a Wrestler to Be Named Later, Slick. You could've gotten the Brooklyn Brawler in '89. It's one thing for your favorite NBA team to dump a late 2nd rounder to save a few bucks, but we're talking about the mighty Hercules here – one of the hottest commodities in wrestling. Slick got dragged in the media for his penny-pinching ways. If you search, "Slickster + Unserious Manager" on 1986 Twitter, you'll get bombarded with hits).

What was the reaction from Hart Family fans after the announcement? Little King Kongs who had begged their parents to buy them a Bundy #5 jersey or an officially licensed singlet were now forced to pivot to a Missing Link Halloween costume. I'm no cap expert, but I think Hart was playing the long game. By freeing up space in the fall of '85, Jimmy positioned himself to be a player in the '87 Bam Bam Bigelow sweepstakes (It turned out to be a moot point, however. Bigelow and his agent, Scott Boras, would sign with Oliver Humperdink).

Could Hart have negotiated a better offer elsewhere? Was there a juicier deal on the table? I played around with the Trade Simulator.

Mr. Fuji: He could have built a package around that beach bum, Don Muraco, but without George "The Animal" Steele under the Devious One's tutelage by the fall of '85, I don't think Fuji had enough meat on the bone to pry Bundy away.

Capt. Lou: Considering he was managing Andre at the time; this would've been a massive conflict of interest.

"Classie" Freddie Blassie: Two months after the Bundy trade, "The Hollywood Fashion Plate" inked Hercules Hernandez to a deal. Assuming big Herc was in the fold by Labor Day, coupling the powerhouse with Sheik and Volkoff may have been enough to persuade Hart. But alas, Hercules, like Wyclef, was gone 'till November.

Johnny V: Trading the Dream Team, then the current World Wrestling Federation Tag Team Champions, is one of those deals you only make in *NBA 2K* after a bowl. Although Mr. Fuji dumped his tag champs, Demolition, three years later in favor of Powers of Pain, so maybe it was Fuji smoking that good shit.

Miss Elizabeth: Randy Savage for Bundy. WHO SAYS NO?

Hillbilly Jim: "Aw shucks, you want my uncle or cousin?"

The Bundy for Missing Link/Adonis swap was a fair one; a rare trade that benefited both sides. Hart would manage both the Intercontinental and Tag Team Champions within two years. At WrestleMania 2, Bundy was just a few steps shy from escaping the steel cage and capturing the World Title. Heenan complained about the size of the cage door on later episodes of *Prime Time,* saying its dimensions were too small and that Bundy couldn't even fit. "The Brain" suggested that even celebrity guest timekeeper and *Silver Spoons* star, Ricky Schroder, had trouble entering and exiting the cage.

(But those allegations, at the time of this book's publication, remain unfounded).

THE MUDLICK SWINDLER

> Event: WrestleMania III (Pontiac, MI)
>
> Match: Hillbilly Jim, Haiti Kid, and Little Beaver vs. King Kong Bundy, Little Tokyo, and Lord Littlebrook
>
> Date: March 29th, 1987
>
> Attendance: 93,173
>
> #1 Song on This Date: "Lean on Me" by Club Nouveau

"And I'll tell you something. I'm mighty concerned here today, Gene. Because, you know, I'm not really worried about myself in this match here, because I know how King Kong Bundy is, and I believe I can take whatever he dishes out. But I'm worried about my little buddies here. And I'm here to tell you, and Imma tell everybody, and you two guys, I'm gonna do my doggest to make sure everything is ok with you little fellas."

– **Hillbilly Jim (WrestleMania III).**

Never again. Never again will I trust the man from Mudlick. We put our faith in Hillbilly Jim and why? Why did we bang the drum for this guy? What did Jim do to earn our trust?

"That man is only wearing overalls. He must be a good seed."

Is that the bar to clear? Buy a pair of OshKosh and earn our blind allegiance in perpetuity? Jim's credentials were lukewarm at best. He – what – spotted the Hulkster on the bench? Stood at his uncle's wedding? Yet despite the shaky résumé, we entrusted him to keep Bundy's meat hooks off Little Beaver and the Haiti Kid. Hillbilly Jim was in over his head. He wasn't equipped to handle the responsibility. Kid and Beaver didn't need a spotter. They needed a protector and a bodyguard. Bundy's reign of terror never would've happened on Virgil or Mr. Hughes' watch.

Jim came across as this 'salt of the earth' type, this "aw shucks" kinda guy with a big heart and jolly personality. Boy, did he have us all snowed. In 1984, he popped up in the front row of World Wrestling Federation events and tell me how a guy from Mudlick (population: 2,402, according to the latest census) afforded multiple cross-country road trips *and* ringside seats. Sell a few prize pigs, did ya? There was always something fishy about White-Collar Jim, but what could we do? He was Hogan's boy. Hulk vouched for him, and if you considered stepping out, that Jim feller would lull you back in with a song.

"Don't go messin' with a country boy, a country boy, a country boy ..."

Thousands instantly break out into dance

There was an old rumor that said if you play, "Don't Go Messin' with a Country Boy" backwards on vinyl, you can hear the lyrics, "*Fuck Cousin Luke and Junior, too, Junior, too, Junior, too.*"

I advise you to do your own research.

So back to WrestleMania III. Listen, Little Beaver isn't absolved from blame here. He felt the rules didn't apply to him. He came and went as he pleased, treating the contest like it was a Tornado Tag. Five of the six combatants played by the rules, while Little Beaver ran amok. King Kong Bundy had Hillbilly Jim in a front face lock. Beaver snuck in and belted him with his SHOE. Later, with Jim laboring in the corner, Little Beaver again interjected. This time, though, he got caught. Bundy got 'em. He body slammed Beaver and followed that up with a massive elbow drop. Jim, the Good Samaritan that he is, took a passive approach. He sat on the bottom turnbuckle and provided a first-hand account of Little Beaver's flattening. That's doing your 'doggest?' Hillbilly didn't look like a concerned friend. He looked like he was on his lunchbreak.

(Also, let's not excuse Bundy here. His actions were so despicable that partners Little Tokyo and the venerable Lord Littlebrook told the big man to go screw. Bundy rode the wrestling cart back solo).

~ ~ ~

> **Event:** *Prime Time* (Boston, MA)
>
> **Match:** Hillbilly Jim (with Little Beaver) vs. One Man Gang (managed by Slick)
>
> **Date:** February 11th, 1988
>
> **Attendance:** 7,004
>
> **#1 Movie on This Date:** *Good Morning, Vietnam*

"That leaves Little Beaver. Oh no … oh my word … that's terrible. Aw, Little Beaver is down, and there's nothing he can do about it! Oh my word! He splashed him right in the middle of the ring! That is awful! That is a shame! That is just a terrible thing to happen! Slick didn't stop his man there like he should've done.

Hillbilly Jim now only just able to get back into the ring."

– Lord Alfred Hayes (*Prime Time*, February 11th, 1988).

You are USELESS, Hillbilly Jim. How do you let Beaver get squashed a second time? I wouldn't trust you to pick up a loaf of bread. One Man Gang was callous. A few months prior, President Jack Tunney fined him $10,000 for assaulting an official. He was literally the only member in his gang. You think the Chicago street tough was going to show Little Beaver some leniency? You think Gang wasn't prepared to follow Bundy's blueprint if the opportunity presented itself? If Jim was worried about the

Slickster on the outside – a valid concern – then call in a favor to Luke or Junior. That's what family is for. Hadn't Hillbilly put Little Beaver through enough?

Beaver was a shit starter. He kept Gang off balance with his antics. He stole the Slickster's hat. He hit One Man Gang with his shoe. He bit him. Then he walloped him with a *broomstick*. Little Beaver was hardcore. He would've mangled Gang with a cheese grater if one was accessible. Through his confidant's tireless efforts, Hillbilly Jim won via count-out. Things, though, quickly deteriorated. Gang attacked the victor and tossed him on to the Boston Garden floor. He then turned his attention towards his tormentor. Gang clobbered Beaver with an overhand right and finished him off with a devastating 747 Splash.

Can I backtrack for a second, Dave?

You may.

Where was Hillbilly? Why didn't Jim just get back in the ring? Why didn't he save Beaver?

Oh, that sack of shit? Hillbilly Jim couldn't be bothered. Haven't you been paying attention? Jim already locked up the winner's purse. He caught a breather on the outside, sitting on all fours like he was looking for a missing contact lens. There was no sense of urgency, no race against time. Hillbilly was on the outside so long you'd think he had been extradited. When he finally resurfaced, Jim launched into his familiar routine: This incredulous, dumbfounded act where he pleaded with the ref for an explanation.

"What happened? Why is Little Beaver unconscious? I only turned my head for a minute …"

Not this time, buddy. Fool us once. He knew exactly what happened to Little Beaver. He knew the damage done. Hillbilly Jim just didn't care.

INMATE #902714

> **Event:** *Superstars* (Syracuse, NY)
> **Match:** Big Boss Man vs. Dave Roulette
> **Date:** May 30th, 1992
> **Attendance:** 4,500
> **#1 Country Song on This Date:** "Achy Breaky Heart," by Billy Ray Cyrus

McMahon: *"No one deserves a beating like this! No one deserves a beating like this!"*

Mr. Perfect: *"Unless he got beat himself like this, McMahon!"*

McMahon: *"Even then!"* (*Superstars*, May 30th, 1992).

I watched this Netflix series that followed inmates at the Sacramento County Jail. The prison is a tower, meaning that the pipes don't run horizontal, but rather up and down from the 8th floor to the bottom. The prisoners smartened up. They discovered that by emptying out the water in their cell's toilet, they could talk through the bowl to fellow inmates on different floors. The pipes acted as an amplifier, like putting your phone inside a cup because you're too hard up to buy a speaker.

They also developed an importing/exporting technique called 'fishing.' Fishing allowed them to pass contraband between floors through the toilet. Inmates created a fishing line – tying, for example, string or t-shirt pieces together to whatever goods they were moving. The inmates then cast their line and flushed their respective toilets simultaneously. The lines would catch/tangle, allowing the person to pull either up or down. The documentary showed this technique countless times, and my mind was blown. It was amazing, a masterclass in ingenuity and modern engineering. All this to say that, no, I don't know how Nailz cut promos on *Superstars* and *Wrestling Challenge* while still in prison, but I'm not surprised he figured out a way.

In May of '92, the Big Boss Man's past reared its ugly head. He painted himself as one of the good ones – a fair and just man in a position of authority that never abused his power. We had mounting evidence to the contrary. Could we even count how many times Boss Man handcuffed and beat an opponent with a nightstick? Antonio Alfonseca only has so many fingers and toes. When Nailz said he was mistreated by the Boss Man, I tend to believe him. I don't know what Nailz did, or didn't do, to land in a cell, but boy, did he hold a grudge. He was so pissed he never bothered to change into his civilian clothes. He went directly from jail to Syracuse's War Memorial arena and that's a long ass bus ride from Cobb County.

I wish Nailz had ditched the orange jumpsuit. If I was handling his PR, if I was put in charge of rehabilitating his image, it would've been my first suggestion. If you only dress like a convict, then people are going to label you a convict. No one looked at Phineas and Henry O. and thought to themselves, "Maybe they're actuaries?" Nailz, you say you were wrongly convicted, and that could be the case, but the optics tell a different story. After Dr. Richard Kimble's prison bus crashed into an oncoming train, the first thing he did at the hospital was shave his beard and change into some new threads (then scarfed down an egg sandwich). You don't need to rummage I.R.S.'s wardrobe but mix in a pair of jeans or corduroys, something a bit more 'common man.' Also, I get retribution is top of mind. The Big Boss Man was a dick. He took liberties in the clink, and I won't stand in the way of your retaliation, but maybe, ixnay on the *revenge-nay*? Let's not publicize that. Lay low for a bit. I'm trying to keep your P.O. off your ass.

The Big Boss Man made quick work of Roulette on the May 30th *Superstars*. Then he slapped him around a bit. To the best of my knowledge, the up-and-comer Roulette was a law-abiding citizen, but we'll look past the police misconduct here. Boss Man had much bigger problems on his plate. Straight from the Cobb County, GA Detention Center, here was former inmate #902714. He entered through the crowd and gave his past bully an absolute ass whipping. Nailz handcuffed Boss Man to the top rope and cracked him repeatedly with his own nightstick. One shot to the leg was delivered with such brute force that Mr. Perfect speculated that the limb was broken.

McMahon: *"No one is moving. No one is trying to help the Boss Man. Where are the other officials around?"*

Mr. Perfect: *"Things are a little bit different on the other side of the fence, huh, Boss Man?"*

No one lifted a finger. It was like when Augustus Gloop fell into the chocolate river, and his mom begged for help. Willy Wonka, in the most sarcastic tone possible, said, *"Help. Police. Murder."* Maybe it was apathy; maybe it was a business decision. Maybe no one wanted to stand in the way of Nailz' pent-up aggression. Considering how many wrestlers had been cuffed and beaten by Boss Man, perhaps it was justice. There's no 10-run rule in professional wrestling. Nailz didn't stop. He didn't call off the dogs. He then cuffed Boss Man's hands behind his back and focused on the ribs. Nailz delivered boot after boot, pausing only to spit on his prey. In the following weeks, Okerlund declared this the most vicious attack in World Wrestling Federation history and I'm not going to argue.

Boss Man was put out of commission until July. He came back promising revenge, and revenge is a dish best served … on a pole. At Survivor Series '92, he defeated Nailz in a "Nightstick on a Pole Match" after a Boss Man Slam (Not much point in the nightstick, huh?).

We didn't see much more of Nailz after that. He let the Boss Man be. Both guys left the past behind them.

What Was the Worst Survivor Series Team Ever Assembled?

"Not a whole lot of doubt, Brain, who is gonna come out on top of this one."

– Gorilla Monsoon (1991 Survivor Series).

I think we can all agree that Survivor Series is a distant 4th in the rankings of flagship WWE Pay-Per-Views. The format – glorified tag matches – has been scrapped and rebooted so many times you'd think it was the Spider-Man franchise. I never saw the incentive. There are no stakes. The superstars aren't fighting for championship gold, or even a future title shot. At the 1990 rendition, DiBiase promised to handsomely compensate the Visionaries if they defeated Hogan, Warrior, and Tito in the Match of Survival. Who gives a shit, Ted? Save your money. Besides, we already concluded that handicap matches are losing propositions. The genesis of these battles always stemmed from one or two guys having beef with someone else, so they'd drag a few others into their drama. Don't confuse someone being on the same text chain with wanting to fight beside you on Thanksgiving. In Ohio of all places.

"Hulk, Randy, we get that the Twin Towers have been making you and Liz' lives hell the past few months, and we completely sympathize with your situation ... but what does this have to do with us?" – Hillbilly Jim and Koko B. Ware, probably.

It was never articulated *how* teams were formed. Did the Championship Committee play a role? Did members pack into a Radisson suite and throw names on to a whiteboard like an NFL draft war room? Is the Committee even involved, or do wrestlers recruit like it's an afterschool club?

Superstar Needed for Team 4x4s – (must be able to work Thanksgiving holiday)

Rugged wrestler who's good with their hands wanted for Survivor Series match-up against the King's Court. These aren't TURKEYS we'll be facing: Randy Savage, Canadian Earthquake, Dino Bravo, and Greg Valentine will want to beat the STUFFING out of you. Are you up for the challenge!?!?!??

Contact Jim, Bret, or Hercules if interested

- Do NOT contact us with unsolicited services or offers

No matter who drove the formation of the teams, there has always been a healthy competitive balance. The matchups were rarely one-sided; there was a natural ebb and flow to the contests. But there have been a few stinkers, a few blowouts that channeled a 'Bama/Vanderbilt game. The only way to properly gauge a *bad* Survivor Series team is to measure the number of eliminations they recorded – or in this case, didn't record. Everything else is subjective. It was the only fair measuring stick I could use. Did you pin someone or not? Did you make someone submit or no?

After scouting the first seven Survivor Series events, I took the three squads who put up goose eggs and ranked them accordingly.

(This countdown is sponsored by Triple Action Stridex: Easy on skin, tough on acne).

#3: The Vipers (1990): Jake Roberts, Jimmy Snuka, Shawn Michaels, and Marty Jannetty

Pretty darn good, right? To quote Monsoon: "Lot of heavy artillery in there," but the Vipers ran into a buzz saw. The Visionaries (Rick Martel, the Warlord, and Power and Glory), delivered a flawless performance. Tip your cap to 'em. The Warlord pinned Jannetty after a vicious powerslam, and Roma and Hercules dropped Michaels with their awesome Power Plex finisher. The Visionaries kept The Vipers off balance with frequent tags and an array of power moves. Down 4-1, Roberts unleashed Damien and chased "The Model" back to the dressing room to lose via count out. Not the most admirable of ways to go out, but that little fucker Martel did blind Jake with his cologne after all.

#2: (1991) The Berzerker, Col. Mustafa, Hercules, and Skinner

How did this ragtag bunch come together? It was like the teacher assigned a group project, and these were the only four people left without partners. Blame whom you must for this debacle but don't dare point a finger at the Berzerker. He was a one man show. I screamed at my TV, pleading for the guy to get some help. Even Barry Sanders had a better supporting cast. Every time I looked up the big Viking was fending off yet another member of Duggan's crew. In basketball analytic terms, the Berzerker had a usage rate of 78.9, shattering the previous high mark of 41.65, set by Russell Westbrook during the '16-'17 NBA season. Mustafa, Hercules, and Skinner were barely in the ring, and when they did make a rare cameo, they ate a few clotheslines before their hasty eliminations.

It's worth mentioning that managers were banned from ringside during the '91 Survivor Series tag matches (except for Sensational Sherri, who somehow circumvented the rules). If General Adnan and Fuji were allowed to supervise, maybe they could've concocted some in-match adjustments, but I'm grasping at straws. While Mr. Fuji was devious, he wasn't a miracle worker. Before departing back up the aisle, Fuji offered the Berzerker some last-minute instructions. I can't read lips, but I think he said, "You're fucked."

#1: (1993) Bam Bam Bigelow, the Headshrinkers, and Bastion Booger

There were four guys in Doink masks, but the only clowns on the night were across the ring. Fellas, fellas. Put down the turkey legs. Stuffing your face during the pre-match promo? What were we thinking? It wasn't even Thanksgiving. '93 Survivor Series WAS ON A WEDNESDAY. Who the hell eats turkey *the day before* Thanksgiving? Thanksgiving Eves are for getting drunk at a local bar and running into people from high school that you only marginally tolerated.

"Wow, what's it been, Dave? Like ten years?"

"Yeah, man ... Crazy..."

"You still wear a retainer? I remember you had a retainer."

Team Bigelow was scheduled to face four Doinks and they did, technically, but it was actually the Bushwhackers and Men on a Mission in Doink masks. Does that make sense?

Not really, Dave, no.

Ok, let me try again.

Team Bigelow faced Team Doink, but Doink the Clown wasn't in --

Just stop, Dave.

Great, now that we have that settled. Bam Bam's team was rotten, but kudos to him for seeing this through. After Samu's defeat at the 3:02 mark, I would've arranged a car service to get me to Asbury Park by morning. I have no idea what Bastion Booger was doing or thinking. He stopped halfway through the match TO EAT A BANANA. Sir, this is the 1993

Survivor Series, not a continental breakfast. Fatu had an easy pin, but stopped TO PICK UP THE BANANA PEEL, like he was part of some Adopt-A-Highway clean-up. After slipping on said banana peel (of course), he got pinned, stranding Bigelow on Doink Island. It was elementary from there.

This Tuesday in Texas

A Little Help Here

> Event: This Tuesday in Texas (San Antonio, TX)
>
> Match: Jake "The Snake" Roberts vs. "Macho Man" Randy Savage
>
> Date: December 3rd, 1991
>
> Attendance: 8,000
>
> #1 Movie on This Date: *The Addams Family*

On the January 2nd, 1988 *Saturday Night's Main Event*, Andre the Giant attacked the Hulkster after his match with King Kong Bundy. Giant choked the life out of the champ. He systematically brought Hulkamania to his knees, and he did it while wearing a checkered sportscoat. Dave Hebner first demanded, and then begged the 8th Wonder of the World to release the hold but to no avail. Then the cavalry arrived.

- The British Bulldogs
- The Junkyard Dog
- Tito Santana
- Rick Martel
- Jake "The Snake" Roberts

It didn't matter. Send the Army, the Navy. Send every ranking officer from *Stratego*. Send the whole damn locker room. Andre couldn't be subdued. Finally, and only after "Hacksaw" belted the Giant across the back with his 2x4, did he relent.

Imagine if no one got involved. Think of the permanent damage Andre could've inflicted. The intervention from the other wrestlers was futile, but at least they *tried*. They were in the back – playing cards, or stretching, or ragging on Rene Goulet's win/loss record – and jumped into action. Now, did I expect the current tag champs, the former tag champs, *The Wrestling Classic* tournament winner, and a dude with a python to find a way to peel Andre off the Hulkster? Yes, of course, but I won't fault the effort, only their execution.

(They just pulled at Andre. Like, poke an eye or something. Kick him in the shin, tickle him, I don't know).

Years later, at This Tuesday in Texas, "Macho Man" gave the sadistic Jake Roberts his well-deserved comeuppance. Savage defeated "The Snake" with his flying elbow drop at 6:25, but the pinfall didn't quench his need for vengeance. How exactly do you quantify just and fair reparations for a cobra bite? So "Macho Man" reached for a chair, then the ring bell, but before he could deliver the fatal blow, Jake blindsided him with a DDT. "The Snake" then hit him with another. President Tunney had banned reptiles from ringside after the nightmare in Fort Wayne, but this version of Roberts didn't cower to Jack's empty threats of fines and suspensions. Jake lifted the ring apron, reached for a familiar bag, and tossed it inside.

Heenan: *"He's got it! He's got it!"*

Monsoon: *"The bag that contains the cobra!"* (This Tuesday in Texas).

Yet again caught in the middle of a high-profile crisis, referee Dave Hebner and his stern warnings fell on deaf ears. Liz sprinted down to protect her husband, pleading for "The Snake" to recoil.

And … that was the extent of the help. There was no security, no outside official, no wrestler, not even the token Mario Mancini or Salvatore Bellomo run in. Hulk Hogan had a small army rush to his aid in '88, but "Macho Man?" The guy fresh off a venomous snake bite? He was left to rot.

One sec there, Dave. Sorry to interrupt.

No worries. You're good. What do you got, reader?

Wasn't This Tuesday in Texas the pay-per-view where Jack Tunney sat at ringside for the Hogan/Undertaker rematch?

That's right.

So Tunney was obviously in the arena.

You're getting warmer …

And he just sat there and did nothing? Even *after* banning reptiles from ringside?

WHERE THE FUCK WAS TUNNEY, that spineless mollusk.

To be fair, we never *did* see the snake. Tunney Apologists – and you know who you are – always fall back on that defense.

"Show me the snake, Dave. Where's the proof? What's the hour and minute mark on the Network?"

Oh, beat it, will ya. A guy nicknamed, "The Snake," pulled out a snake bag. He had been carrying a snake to the ring since 1986. I don't think it was a Cabbage Patch doll. But it wasn't *just* the cobra, which alone is a harrowing thought. After slapping and taunting a badly injured Savage, this piece of human garbage hit Liz.

> *"This is disgraceful! This is despicable! I don't believe it! He should be suspended for life! He's not a man! He's an animal!"*
>
> **– Gorilla Monsoon.**

After hitting a woman, finally – FINALLY – one person rushed down to the ring. FINALLY someone had reached their breaking point. (Seriously, guys. Where the hell was everyone? He hit Liz!).

Was it Tunney, Dave?

'Ol Country Club Tunney? No, of course not. It was the much-maligned, formerly disgraced referee, Danny Davis, the same guy who I told to go to hell earlier in this book. I guess sometimes help does come from unexpected places. President Tunney eventually moseyed on down, after finishing his scotch and cigar. I timed his arrival with a sundial.

He barked at Roberts a few times before escorting him back up the ramp.

THE '89 ROYAL RUMBLE

BAD DECISIONS WERE MADE

> Event: Royal Rumble 1989 (Houston, TX)
>
> Match: The Royal Rumble
>
> Date: January 15th, 1989
>
> Attendance: 19,000
>
> #1 Song on This Date: "My Prerogative" by Bobby Brown
>
> Entrant #1: Ax
>
> Entrant #2: Smash

I don't feel comfortable Monday morning quarterbacking one of the most decorated teams in wrestling history, but heavy is the hand that holds the tag rope. Now, I won't speak for Ax or Smash. They're adults. They made their decision, but if *my* tag partner and I were the first two entrants in the Royal Rumble, and *he* greeted me with some haymakers, then I'd be in the market for a new teammate.

"Chill the fuck out, Barry."

(My partner is Barry Windham in this analogy. Or Barry Horowitz. Or Barry "O").

Your takes are usually spot on, Dave, but not sure I agree here. Don't you remember the tagline? It's every man for himself.

The hell it is. We got 28 other dudes in this thing. Haven't you ever been on a bar crawl? It's a marathon, not a sprint. As a self-appointed Royal

Rumble expert, I know a wrestler can't win the match in the first five minutes, but he or she can certainly lose it. If you walk into an arcade with one dollar, you're not beating *The Simpsons* if you burn a second quarter on Stage 1. I don't care how lethal Marge's vacuum cleaner is. You can apply the same philosophy here.

Collectively (you, me, Demolition, the Red Rooster, etc), we knew that Andre the Giant was a participant. Every pre-match plan and approach had to be tabled until you got the 8th Wonder of the World over the top rope. (In this instance, the python, Damien, would eliminate Andre). Demolition got a shitty draw and compounded their bad luck with horrifically poor decision making. They slugged it out. They treated the first two minutes like it was a tough man contest in some backwoods bar. The Houston crowd ate it up. It wasn't like *they* had to deal with the Giant, or Big John Studd, or the Powers of Pain. What if, for example, Jacob Blu eliminates brother Eli Blu right out of the gate? Well, to borrow a line from former New Jersey Nets great Derrick Coleman, "whoop-de-damn-do." Now what, Jacob? How are you going to lift big Mabel over the top without your brother? You think Mo's gonna help? Ax and Smash's thought-process was short-sighted at best, and embarrassingly incompetent at worst. It's like co-op mode in *Double Dragon*. Just because you can punch or kick your buddy doesn't make it advisable.

Tag teams historically struggle in Rumbles because the most successful duos adhere to the same three principles:

- Frequent tags to stay fresh
- Cut the ring in half
- Keep the opponent in their corner

None of that applies in the Royal Rumble. If it did, then I.R.S., one half of Money Inc., would be a 3-time Rumble winner.

Demolition put on a show – no argument there. But at what cost? 14 minutes after the bell rang, Ax and Smash were gone. Two non-factors, two non-threats. Andre eliminated a fatigued and injured Smash just four minutes in. Ax treaded water for a bit longer, but Cinderella wouldn't wear leather on this night.

The reigning tag team champions were eliminated 1st and 4th respectively.

WHERE DID BAD NEWS GO?

> **Event:** 1988 Survivor Series (Richfield, OH)
>
> **Match:** The Ultimate Warrior, Brutus "The Barber" Beefcake, Sam Houston, The Blue Blazer, and Jim Brunzell vs. The Honky Tonk Man, Ron Bass, Danny Davis, Greg "The Hammer" Valentine, and Bad News Brown
>
> **Date:** November 24th, 1988
>
> **Attendance:** 13,500
>
> **#1 Song on This Date:** "Bad Medicine" by Bon Jovi

Ventura: *"I'll tell you Gorilla. This guy, I don't think he can get along with anybody."*

Monsoon: *"Highly unlikely."* (1988 Survivor Series).

I played this bastardized version of Capture the Flag called 'Freedom.' If you got caught/tagged, you were sent to 'jail,' which was minded by the most slow-footed and dim-witted member of the other team.

"Guard jail, Dave," was a menial task. You'd end up talking to the prisoner (let's call them 'Nailz') for hours. We'd talk sports, Pogs, the upcoming *In Your House* pay-per-view, whatever was top of mind. Help never came. The inmate served a life sentence – or until our moms called us for dinner. It's not that the prison was this Alcatraz-like fortress (it was usually someone's front porch). It was because the poor sap always had one teammate who had already gone home. Winning the game and avenging your teammate's honor was cool and all, but those Dunkaroos back at your house weren't going to eat themselves. Nailz hoped that Randy or Kevin or Tracy or Becky were plotting some elaborate jailbreak, but the truth was, they didn't care about you. You meant nothing. They were watching *Anamaniacs* on their couch.

Among his peers, Bad News Brown was perhaps the least popular wrestler of all time. He didn't like anyone. Bad News was a prick, and I don't think I'm being overly harsh or speaking out of turn. No one is reading this (well, I hope someone is reading this), thinking to themselves, "Eh, I don't know. Bad News was a good dude. He was just misunderstood."

Brown was a no nonsense, cutthroat loner (I'd argue he was "Stone Cold" before there was "Stone Cold," right down to the black trunk and black boots, but I digress). He didn't have a manager. He didn't need one, never asked for one, and no Frenchy Martin-type ever bothered to pitch him. Opponents faced a ruthless grappler; one who would break the rules and pound you into submission, but it was the guys who *teamed* with Bad News that loathed him even more. For a year plus stretch between '88 and '89, the Harlem native torpedoed every team and alliance he begrudgingly joined. His actions were a combustible combination of messy break-ups and ghosting. His teammates never got the last word in. They couldn't say their piece because Bad News was already halfway up the aisle. What a shitty arrangement. It's like an argument with your spouse. Before they drive to your in-laws, you deserve the opportunity to resurrect a grievance from a decade ago.

During the WrestleMania IV battle royal, Brown and Bret Hart formed an impromptu alliance to dispatch the Junkyard Dog. Mission accomplished. "The Hitman" then turned his back and got kicked in the back of the head.

At the '88 Survivor Series, Brown used his patented Ghetto Blaster enzuigiri kick to eliminate Jim Brunzell, who honestly had it coming. Brunzell wore a 1988 Survivor Series t-shirt to the ring, and doesn't

Jumpin' Jim know you never wear the t-shirt of the band you're going to see? Brown then turned his sights towards Sam Houston. After softening up the young Texan, Bad News reluctantly made a tag to Valentine. Shortly after, Bad News wanted back in. He had the itch. Brown wanted to treat the match like a DIY home remodeling project. Why outsource a Sam Houston elimination, when he could do it himself?

After the tag, Bad News held up the youngster for a Valentine forearm smash. It was a textbook double team, and a nice display of chemistry between two guys who weren't familiar with each other's work. The slippery Sam Houston, though, ducked. Valentine drilled Brown with a right hand and Ol' Bad News wasn't in the forgiving spirit. He didn't give second chances. Hell, he rarely gave you a first.

Bad News walked. You think he gave a shit about Team Honky Tonk Man? I'm not even sure Bad News knew Danny Davis' name. He probably just called him, "Hey you," or something. Brown headed back up the aisle, getting eliminated via count out. Live and learn, right? You couldn't trust Bad News. He was a terrific wrestler, sure, a ferocious competitor, but completely unreliable in a team format.

~ ~ ~

> **Event: 1989 Survivor Series (Rosemont, IL)**
>
> **Match: The Dream Team (Dusty Rhodes, Brutus Beefcake, Red Rooster, and Tito Santana) vs. The Enforcers (Big Boss Man, Rick Martel, The Honky Tonk Man, and Bad New Brown)**
>
> **Date: November 23rd, 1989**
>
> **Attendance: 15,294**

Aaaaand we're back. Surely, The Enforcers could've picked someone else, *anyone* else. Boris Zhukov was available. The Brooklyn Brawler had some unfinished business with the Red Rooster. What was Akeem doing? WHERE WAS AKEEM? Bad News was particularly ornery on this night. A year after doing the heavy lifting for his team, Brown took a more passive approach, refusing to tag in multiple times. He spent the first ten minutes jawing with some fans in the front row, while his Enforcer teammates jumped out to a 4-3 lead (Martel rolled up Santana).

Brown finally entered and pounded on a helpless Red Rooster. With the ref's back turned, Bad News held the newcomer as Boss Man bounced off the rope for that familiar double-team maneuver. Surely, lightning couldn't strike twice, right? This time would be different, no?

Welp. The Red Rooster was a student of the game. He had studied last year's film. Rooster ducked and Boss Man clobbered Brown with a right hand. After last year's debacle, I would've audibled. Perhaps a boot to the ribs from an abdominal stretch would've been a higher percentage play, but who am I to second-guess The Enforcers?

Bad News took offense (naturally), as Boss Man futilely pleaded his case (of course). Martel and the Honky Tonk Man jumped in to separate the two. This was déjà vu for the former Intercontinental Champion, as Honky, for the second consecutive year, was tasked with diffusing another mutiny. There was no reasoning with Bad News, nothing the Boss Man or the former champ could've said. Brown split, again. He left his teammates high and dry, again. He was eliminated via count out once more. Bad News wasn't a part of the 1990 Survivor Series, or any other Survivor Series thereafter.

It was for the best.

THE STARS AND STRIPES CHALLENGE

> **Event: The Stars and Stripes Challenge (The U.S.S. Intrepid)**
>
> **Date: July 4th, 1993**
>
> **#1 Movie on This Date:** *Jurassic Park*

Yokozuna defeated Bret Hart at WrestleMania IX for the world title. Thanks to a Bill Buckner-esque gaffe by Mr. Fuji (more on that in another chapter), his reign ended seconds later. Yoko's loss to Hogan was a fluke; an anomaly that didn't represent the enormous talent gap between the two superstars in '93. At King of the Ring, order was restored.

But before we move to July 4th, allow me a quick note about the Hulkster's fifth title reign. Hogan didn't defend his title ONCE between WrestleMania IX and King of the Ring, and if you don't have a 1993 desk calendar at your fingertips, that was SEVENTY DAYS.

Quick question, Dave. I'm sorry to interrupt.

No worries, the floor's yours.

I thought every champion had to defend their title every 30 days?

Very astute! You're correct! Problem was, this was "On the Take" Tunney here. The guy was more crooked than a dog's hind leg. In the spring of '93, our President turned a blind eye to the championship title bylaws. The rules didn't apply to Hogan. They never applied to Hogan. Meanwhile,

Jack forced the Mountie to defend his Intercontinental Championship against Roddy Piper just two days after winning it.

Typical Tunney.

Unlike Hogan, Yokozuna was a fighting champion. He took on all comers. With Hulkamania firmly in the rearview mirror, he and Fuji craved new competition. They didn't run. They didn't hide behind Tunney's red tape. Fuji and his man wanted a new test, a new challenge.

Fuji introduced the Stars and Stripes Challenge shortly after King of the Ring. He invited any pro athlete to try and slam his champion on our nation's birthday. The fine print, though, said Americans only, so eat shit Bushwhacker Luke. The Devious One rented out the U.S.S. Intrepid for the occasion, treating the World War II vessel like a banquet hall. And if the adoration and eternal gratitude from your fellow Americans wasn't enough, the winner of the Stars and Stripes Challenge also received a brand-new Chevy Silverado.

"Honey, whose car is that out in the driveway?"

"That's ours, sweetie. I got it for body slamming a grand Sumo champion on a U.S. Naval aircraft carrier."

"I thought you were just running out for milk?"

I had some concerns about welcoming Yokozuna onto the U.S.S Intrepid. With the sinister Mr. Fuji behind the wheel, I couldn't rule out some Trojan Horse type coup. The event, however, went off without a hitch. Todd Pettingill and Randy Savage emceed the festivities. Pettingill wore a pair of jorts, but looked like a guy who never wore shorts if that makes sense. You just know he runs errands in Air Monarchs.

Former New York Giants running back, Lee Rouson, started things off. He wasn't Ottis Anderson or Rodney Hampton, but that didn't damper the crowd's spirits. Rouson was followed by another G-Men back. 2x Pro

Bowler, Joe Morris, was a step up in name recognition, but you're never going to body slam the World Champion dressed like a guy selling timeshares. No one has ever vanquished a foreign threat in khaki shorts.

Sandwiched between Flyers defenseman, Shawn Cronin, and Dolphins offensive lineman, Keith Simms, was 110 lb jockey, Julio Pezua. Was this a joke? Was everyone having a good laugh? A few weeks prior, Yokozuna DESTROYED Hulkamania, and here we were now dancing on the Hulkster's grave. Julio Pezua? A journeyman NHL defenseman? Where art thou, Ted Arcidi? Our nation turns its lonely eyes to you (woo, woo, woo).

The cagey vet, Bob Backlund, then tried his hand, along with hockey pro Peter Taglianetti. Taglianetti held a putrid 51 rating in Sega Genesis' *NHL '93*. I know EA Sports' opinion held little weight in this competition, but I would've felt better with *NHL '93* gods Chris Chelios or Phil Housley in this spot.

Scott Steiner gave a gallant effort. So would his brother, Rick. (Though Rick attempted a belly-to-belly suplex, which was a loose interpretation of the body slam challenge). NBA wingman Scott Burrell also stepped into the ring. This was a few years before Burrell was bullied mercilessly by teammate Michael Jordan.

"Burrell just kept picking MJ to play one-on-one. Scott got close to him. He got within a point, but Jordan won. Scott wanted to play again. So Jordan said, 'I'm sure you do want to play again. You want to tell your grandkids that you beat Michael Jordan. What the hell am I going to tell my grandkids? That I beat Scott Burrell?'" (Feldman 2020).

That's some good shit talking. Burrell took one look at Yokozuna and walked out. Dolphins running back, Mark Higgs, failed, and so did defensive lineman Gary Baldinger. Next was Tatanka. Instead of taking the traditional scoop route, the Native American climbed the top turnbuckle and popped the champ with a chop right between the eyes. It wasn't exactly in the spirit of a body slam challenge, but I'll allow it. Tatanka then hit the ropes and got leveled with a savate kick. So long, Tatanka.

After two more New York Giants skunked up the joint, Bill Fralic, took his cracks. Fralic was no stranger to the squared circle. You couldn't intimidate the All-Pro lineman. He was a cult hero of sorts, calling out Studd and a host of others before the WrestleMania 2 battle royal. (On the March 21st, 1986 edition of *Tuesday Night Titans*, he called Heenan's man, "John Dud"). Fralic was game, and even managed to lift Yokozuna off one leg.

Wide receiver Joey Smith was overmatched and so was Green Bay Packer, James Campen.

"Wow, what an opportunity. 4th of July, Stars and Stripes, and the WWF. I have one thing to say to you, Yokozuna. I catch 1,600 lb grizzlies with these traps in the offseason. I'm positive I can slam you." – James Campen (*Superstars*, July 3rd, 1993).

Yokozuna wasn't your run of the mill, grizzly bear. Miami Dolphins receiver Jim Jensen gave an embarrassing effort, which was disappointing for a guy who's in *Tecmo Super Bowl*. I like to think Mark Duper and his two-bar facemask would've shown more grit. Finally, it was Kona Crush's turn. Crush was a powerhouse, a physical specimen who had recently slammed Bastion Booger on *Monday Night Raw*. He had the pedigree. The big Hawaiian had Yokozuna up off the ground until that pesky lower lumbar gave out. "Macho Man" then called his own number, trying to salvage what little was left of America's pride. Yoko, however, held his ground.

Hope was lost. The finest athletes the United States could offer – or the ones who didn't have holiday plans anyway – all failed. Yokozuna had flexed his dominance. Hogan wasn't walking through that door. Neither was a seventh Giants running back. The country was out of athletes, and out of time. Fuji only booked the venue for two hours after all.

Then suddenly in the distance a helicopter flew towards the Intrepid. The murmurs in the crowd grew louder. Who was it? Who was fashionably late? Who was this last-second entrant into the Stars and Stripes Challenge?

It was …

…

…

"The Narcissist" Lex Luger?

Ugh, not this fucking guy. That's not "Mr. USA" Tony Atlas. At least bring back Crush for another go – at least he had intestinal fortitude. I despised "The Narcissist," a goon who took joy in knocking out opponents with an (illegal) bionic elbow. In fact, the day before on *Superstars – the day before* – he sent the youngster Rich Myers to another dimension with that steel plated 'bow. Then he pinned him with one knee while flexing.

So color me skeptical.

There was something off, though. Luger didn't carry his full-length mirror. He also dressed differently. He didn't sport his customary white tights. He wore a United States flag shirt, which, come to think of it, is EXACTLY what someone would wear if they wanted to falsely gain our nation's trust before humiliating us. Tricky, tricky.

You almost had me, Lex. Almost. But whatever you're selling, I'm not buying.

He then shoved Bobby Heenan aside, and I admit, that raised an eyebrow. It was at that year's Royal Rumble where "The Brain" fawned all over "The Narcissist," sexting him in front of a sellout ARCO Arena crowd.

Lex stepped into the Intrepid ring and shouted some racially charged rhetoric towards Fuji and his man. His support grew.

"You know something, Doris, that "The Narcissist" makes a lot of sense. Yokozuna *is* an 'overstuffed, sushi eating, rice chompin' wrestler.'"

Not even Jim Duggan could've said it better. I was reminded of the scene from *Con Air* when John Cusack realized he had an ally on the plane. Lex Luger was his Cameron Poe. Lex was *one of us*. He was maybe still a Narcissist, but he was an American first and foremost, and nothing unites the country more than hating someone else. He converted the U.S.S. Intrepid spectators into believers. I drank the Kool-Aid, too.

Pick his ass up, Lex! Do it for our country!

And that he did. Luger body slammed Yokozuna on America's birthday.*

*Bobby Heenan said it was a hip toss.

THE ROAST OF GEORGE WELLS

While researching this book, I binged every episode of *Prime Time* (every episode that was available on the Network anyway). *Prime Time* became my comfort food. I worked around the house and cooked dinner with Bobby and Gorilla bickering in the background. I fell asleep to it. I'd forget to turn the TV off and wake up to an S.D. Jones headbutt. It was therapeutic, good for the soul, and the old school wrestling equivalent of a weighted blanket. But *Prime Time*, for all its glory, has a blemish on its résumé, a few dark months that history won't look upon fondly. Great moments in the summer of '86 (the replay of Muraco and Fuji's stand-up act and the search for the new Japanese tag team, the Machines) were overshadowed by a relentless barrage of body shaming orchestrated by, of all people, two of America's sweethearts turned Mean Girls: Gorilla Monsoon and Lord Alfred Hayes.

June 23rd, 1986: Hoss Funk vs. George Wells

Lord Alfred: *"You're right about Wells. He's put on a lot of weight recently."*

Monsoon: *"All in the wrong places..."*

Lord Alfred: *"He's not that nice slim figure that he once was..."*

Lord Alfred: *"But he's moving slowly. He's not moving with any real cause."*

Monsoon: *"As of late, his matches have been following a pattern. Start slow, and get slower..."*

Lord Alfred: *"I think George ought to see about getting a new trainer, in all honesty..."*

Lord Alfred: *"I know he has been teaming with Tony Atlas, so maybe Atlas can help him along a bit better than that."*

Monsoon: Well Atlas wouldn't let his body look like that." (*Prime Time*, June 23rd, 1986).

What the hell? Where did that come from?

"Well Atlas wouldn't let his body look like that." Good grief. Did George Wells morph into Haystacks Calhoun and no one told me? Was George Wells even fat? A week later, the insults continued. The only saving grace here was that Monsoon flew solo.

June 30th, 1986: Hercules vs. George Wells

Monsoon: *"Wells, to me, Jesse, has been putting on some weight. I saw a couple of matches where he appeared to be a bit lethargic."*

Monsoon: *"I think George Wells best take a couple of weeks off... and regroup, Bobby."*

Damn, Gorilla, did George kick your dog or something? You made your point. I watched these matches with a tinge of sadness. Any lull in the action was filled with a comment about George's sudden bout of lethargy. If you listened to the play-by-play via transistor radio, you'd have thought that Ol' George entered the ring via a stairlift. (How known body guy, Hoss Funk, got a free pass is beyond me). I sympathized with Wells; I found myself pulling for him. I wanted him to stick it in the faces of Gorilla and Lord Alfred, like Minnesota Twins designated hitter, Jerry Johnson, after being released by manager Billy Heywood in *Little Big League*.

Besides, I didn't even think Wells was *that* big.

Even as my *Prime Time* binge marched into the fall of '86, I kept circling back to June. Late nights were littered with Google searches.

"Did Monsoon hate George Wells?"

"Gorilla Monsoon + George Wells + fat."

It consumed me. When I created an outline of this book's potential essays many moons ago, The Body Shaming of George Wells hadn't made the list. But things change. The book evolved. The overarching question I can't answer is 'why.' What was their deal? Where was the value add, and most importantly, where was Monsoon and his Lordship's sympathy? A couple months prior at WrestleMania 2, a boa constrictor almost swallowed Wells whole, like he was an antelope.

"Hey, where did George go? He was just here a minute ago."

"Oh, he's in the snake's stomach now. The ref threatened Damien with a five count if he didn't break the hold, but that wasn't a real deterrent."

Now these two guys were here taking potshots. I don't remember anyone busting Jonah's balls when he got swallowed by a whale. We can agree that WrestleMania 2 was pretty traumatic, no? Wells was foaming out of his mouth. I can excuse the guy for indulging in some late-night sweets as part of his recovery. I'm also a stress eater. I've housed an entire bag of Sun Chips just because the Philadelphia Eagles offense started a game with a three and out. On the July 7th edition of *Prime Time*, Wells was back – this time teaming with Leapin' Lanny Poffo vs. Rusty Brooks and Johnny K-9. My heart sank. *Here we go again.* For a second, I hoped Wells would change into like a swim shirt to ward off the peanut gallery, but then I snapped out of it. Ignore the haters. Love yourself, George. Do you, pal.

Monsoon, though, surprised me. Gorilla behaved and the commentary was cordial. Maybe he had seen the error of his ways.

Maybe Monsoon realized his criticism wasn't constructive. Or maybe, just maybe, Gorilla ran out of material.

The Avenger, Ron Bass

> Event: *Superstars* (Wheeling, WV)
> Match: Brutus "The Barber" Beefcake vs. Tony Burton
> Date: August 27th, 1988
> Attendance: 7,200
> Top Selling Video Game in the U.S: *Double Dragon*

"This is utterly horrible. This is despicable. President Jack Tunney needs to make a stand on this, because wrestlers should not be humiliated like this. This makes me sick."

– Jesse Ventura, while Brutus Beefcake cut the hair of Danny Davis (*Saturday Night's Main Event*, April 30th, 1988).

Brutus Beefcake wasn't a barber. He was a frat guy who hazed half the roster. What, couldn't find any live goldfish to shove down your opponent's gullet? Teabagging wasn't your speed? I suppose Brutus could've branded his adversaries, but Terry Funk already had that market cornered.

Beefcake cut his opponents' hair after knocking them out with a sleeper hold (see: illegal choke hold). Seriously, you gotta be one sick pup. That's assault, right? Keep me honest here. Scissor-thirsty wrestling fans, though, ate it up. They craved more humiliation. They wanted more locks detached from a victim's head, and their twisted demigod was more than happy to oblige. At least Sweeney Todd gave his customers a decent trim before turning their bodies into meat pies. Brutus' cuts were hatchet jobs; his shop's Yelp page littered with 1-star reviews. (On the April 10th, 1989 *Prime Time*, Heenan said, "I wouldn't even let this guy do my bushes").

Against his will, Darlene Snell shaved Jonah's head on Season 2 of *Ozark*, and social media was apocalyptic. Roddy Piper cut the Haiti Kid's hair in '86 and the live audience was livid. So why did Beefcake get a free pass? Why were his assaults celebrated? Brutus' opponents didn't sign permission slips. There was no consent. They walked into the squared circle oblivious, there only to wrestle. These upstarts wanted to test their mettle against a former tag team champion and top contender for the Intercontinental Title. Instead, they got ambushed, helpless vessels of a superstar's warped fetish. These poor saps woke up butchered and traumatized, heading straight to the nearest Fantastic Sams to right a horrific wrong. On the June 23rd, 1987 *Superstars*, Beefcake battled Chris Curtis. You can catch the action online, where the clip is titled, "Chris Curtis vs Brutus the Barber Beefcake hair vs hair match" (Jake JP 2019). With all due respect to the YouTube poster, Jake JP, I don't think Chris Curtis was privy to the hair vs. hair stipulation. I don't think Curtis brought his clippers.

Brutus' origin story began on *Superstars*, February 28th, 1987. Teaming with Greg Valentine and "Adorable" Adrian Adonis, the trio battled the Can-Am Connection and Lanny Poffo. Adonis was involved in an intense feud with Roddy Piper (more on that later) and on the precipice of their WrestleMania III hair vs. hair match. You never want to go into a cut cold, so Adrian decided to get a few practice clips in – get some reps – like how you finetune your chili before entering a cook-off.

With Rick Martel trapped in the opposing corner, and the ref distracted by a frustrated Tom Zenk, Adonis grabbed a pair of scissors from Jimmy Hart and clipped the tag team specialist's luscious locks.

WHOOPS.

It was the wrong tag team specialist. Adonis accidentally cut Bruti's salad, and HE WAS PISSED. Martel had flipped Beefcake into the corner and the Adorable One didn't recognize it until it was too late. At WrestleMania III, Brutus got his revenge. He revitalized a nearly zonked out Piper and shaved Adonis' blonde locks after Roddy's victory.

And I get it. That's fair. An eye for an eye, a strand for a strand. Adonis got what was coming to him. Brutus, though, wasn't satisfied. It created a thirst that not even some ice cold SunnyD could quench. WrestleMania III triggered a tour of perverse sadism – sleeper hold after sleeper hold, nonconsensual haircut after nonconsensual haircut – with no end in sight.

Enter "The Outlaw" Ron Bass. Not the hero we deserved, but the one that we needed. Bass, admittedly so, shouldered his own checkered past. Most superheroes do. On the August 20th, 1988 *Superstars*, "The Outlaw" made quick work of a fresh-faced Jim Evans, and post-match, wanted to send a gentle reminder that the beatings would continue until morale improves. The cowboy reached for his spurs, which he affectionately named "Bret" and "Bart," like how I'd rub my elbows, "Woodward" and "Bernstein," before hitting one of my drunk buddies in the ribcage. Evans, though, dodged a beatdown when Beefcake wedged himself into the drama. He chased off Bass, cut up Ron's bull whip, "Miss Betsy," and disfigured his cowboy hat. Texans don't like their hats messed with. Heck, Terry Funk pummeled Mel Phillips just for putting his hat on. I'm not defending Bass' actions here, but tend to your own garden, Bruti. He had a huge Intercontinental Championship title match on deck at SummerSlam – *a golden opportunity* – yet here he was, butting into "The Outlaw's" business.

After Brutus slapped Tony Burton in the sleeper hold the following week, Bass retaliated. He attacked Beefcake from behind and choked him with the remnants of "Miss Betsy." Then "Bret" and "Bart" joined the party. The King of Hardcore sliced and diced Brutus with his spurs as countless cueballs and wrestlers with uneven fades celebrated in the back (so I imagine anyway). Bret and Bart left Beefcake a bloody mess.

TV producers scrambled to put up a giant "Censored" graphic over Brutus' face to avoid harsh penalties and stiff fines from the FCC. Bass' vicious payback forced Beefcake to miss SummerSlam. An opportunity missed; an opportunity squandered. Actions have consequences. Brutus thought he was invincible. Ron Bass showed "The Barber" he was anything but.

NOT IN THE FACE

> Event: SummerSlam '92 (London, England)
>
> Match: Shawn Michaels (with Sensational Sherri) vs. Rick "The Model" Martel
>
> Date: August 29th, 1992
>
> Attendance: 80,355
>
> #1 Song on This Date: "End of the Road" by Boyz II Men

Bobby Heenan: *"She fainted again."*

Vince McMahon: *"She didn't faint."*

Bobby Heenan: *"What are you trying to say?"*

Vince McMahon: *"She's watching these two men fight over her."* (SummerSlam 1992).

I'm a three-time college intramurals dodgeball champion. Not a big deal – really – so please don't feel you have to treat me any differently. Team Do It, Team Do It Again, and Team Do It Again and Again was a dynasty, a tour de force who steamrolled every ensemble of suckers who stood in our path. But we got a little overconfident, talked a bit too much trash at the dining hall. Entering year three, a new contender had entered the chat: The university's baseball team. Both squads were on a collision course to the finals. While we had the championship pedigree, they played Division-1 baseball. These guys threw missiles.

The final was a nailbiter, tied 1-1 in the best-of-3 series. In the deciding game, both teams were down to their final player. For the baseball team, it was a starting pitcher, a guy who had been mowing us down with a barrage of two-seamers that couldn't be caught or dodged by the average human. And for us? Me, wily and hungover, thanks to my roommate splurging on some 7.3% ABV Molson XXX the night before, because, according to him, "I did the math. You get more bang for your buck."

The pitcher threw a rocket in my direction. I ducked the beanball and leapt up to return fire. Nolan Ryan, though, wasn't done. He had another one in his holster. I ate a fastball right in the nose from point blank, and I know it was my nose because I screamed out, "Ah, fuck, my nose!"

The Starting Nine celebrated while I asked my best friend if I was bleeding.

"Do you think it's broke?"

He wasn't pre-med, but I figured he'd know a broken nose if he saw one. But the ref (the Work-Study student tasked with supervising the finals) had blown the whistle. He pulled his own version of a Dusty Finish.

He pointed to the pitcher.

"No head shots. You're out."

Team Do It Again and Again limped away with our titles. You could hit someone anywhere, just not in the face.

~ ~ ~

On the July 20th, 1992 *Prime Time*, Rick Martel squared off against Bret Hart for the Intercontinental Championship. The Championship Committee had deemed Martel the #1 contender (much to the chagrin of Shawn Michaels) and here was Rick, looking good and feeling good, and moments away from his first career World Wrestling Federation singles title. Martel locked "The Hitman" in his lethal Boston Crab, the same finisher utilized by my older brother (though he re-named it the "Philly Crab" for geographical consistency). I tapped out to the Boston Crab hundreds of times, so no one could better empathize with Hart's predicament. I didn't know a counter outside of grabbing a couch leg and yelling, "Rope break!" Bret, fortunately, showed a bit more resolve. Martel sank in deeper, bending the champ's back into a U-shape. But before "The Hitman" could tap, before Martel could get his hand raised, a jaded and jealous Michaels ran down and pummeled Hart. The interference triggered an automatic disqualification.

In retaliation, Martel took on the role of homewrecker. He slid into the DMs of Michaels' manager and suitor, Sensational Sherri. While Shawn was at work, disposing of some ham and eggers on *Wrestling Challenge* and *Superstars*, Martel was liking Sherri's posts, littering her feed with fire and drool face emojis. Despite the awkwardness of Rick and Sherri *sharing a last name*, she liked the attention. She reciprocated. As far as work husbands go, you could do much worse than an international model. The confrontation came to a head at SummerSlam, but with one very important stipulation. Both wrestlers were entirely too beautiful to get hit in their perfect mugs. Strikes to the face were outlawed.

Both wrestlers abided by the unique provisions – initially anyway. The faces were kept clear, like after a six-month Accutane regimen. Michaels and Martel couldn't stop cheating, though. They couldn't help themselves. Both guys pulled the other's tights on pin attempts. Michaels tucked his feet inside the middle rope on another. Halfway through the match, and with both guys at wits end, Shawn slapped Rick across the face. Martel returned the favor. Sherri jumped on the apron to deescalate, but her intervention had no effect. Pushing led to shoving and both IC title contenders ramped up for a brawl.

So Sherri ... fainted, like one of those myotonic goats. Michaels attempted to revive her. "The Model" then shoved him out of the way.

Wait, where were London's Emergency Responders, Dave?

From the best I could gather, they were both short-staffed and preoccupied with Virgil who got choked out by Nailz moments earlier. Martel jumped in to give chest compressions, but after a few reps, he got popped with a Michaels right hand. The war was on. So was the count. The fight continued up the aisle at Wembley Stadium. Sherri miraculously awoke and saw the melee. She then fixed her hair, collected herself, and fainted again (that pesky vertigo).

Sherri was revived a second time by Martel after being doused with a bucket of water – no word on why there was a bucket of water nearby.

The match itself ended in a double count-out.

OH, HEY, IT'S SCOTT CASEY

> **Event:** 1988 Survivor Series (Richfield, OH)
>
> **Match:** André the Giant, "Ravishing" Rick Rude, Dino Bravo, Mr. Perfect, and Harley Race vs. "Hacksaw" Jim Duggan, Jake "The Snake" Roberts, Ken Patera, Tito Santana, and Scott Casey
>
> **Date:** November 24th, 1988
>
> **Attendance:** 13,500
>
> **On This Date:** The A's defeated the Dodgers in a World Series Playoff edition of *Family Feud* (hosted by WrestleMania VIII ring announcer, Ray Combs).

"That was a dumb move by Scott Casey right there."

– Jesse Ventura.

This chapter is not meant to disparage or belittle the talented youngster, but Scott Casey's head-scratching inclusion in the '88 Survivor Series must be addressed. We need to have an honest dialogue. How did Casey make the cut? How did he finagle his way onto Roberts and Duggan's team? Was this a blackmail situation? Did he have compromising photos of Damien? You're going to battle against Andre, Rude, Bravo, Perfect, and Harley Race, and you counter that heavy artillery with ... Scott Casey?

Listen, I'm not Anti-Scott Casey. The guy was a competitor. He was put together. But check the data. Comb through the numbers. As soon as the competition stiffened, Casey folded like an origami crane. He was a AAAA ballplayer, the wrestling version of a yo-yo club. If I'm putting a

Survivor Series squad together, I'm only calling Scott if Battle Kat says no. In November of '88, nice wins over the improving Steve Lombardi and the cagey Jose Estrada were overshadowed by lopsided losses to Rick Rude (2:10), King Haku (1:49), and the Red Rooster (2:43).

"You see Casey on *Wrestling Challenge* today, Chuck?"

"The up-and-comer?"

"Yep, that's the one. He didn't have it today. The Red Rooster wrestled circles around him."

My friends and I saw Linkin Park in high school. We had an extra ticket, so my buddy brought his 11-year-old brother, and I get it. It was a super nice gesture and a memory they can share for the rest of their lives, but how were the boys supposed to drink these Rolling Rock ponies in the parking lot with a 5th grader staring at us? He was our Scott Casey. Look at the other nine guys in this match. Scott was a fish out of water, and not even the most diehard Casey supporters envisioned him surviving.

Predictably, Bet MGM had Scott as the odds-on favorite (-400) to be the first wrestler eliminated. (For context, Andre was +6000). It turned out to be a sucker bet. Scott hung around; he wasn't the first man to go. That dubious honor would go to Ken Patera.

Scott Casey was the *second* man eliminated. He succumbed to a Dino Bravo sidewalk slam less than a minute later.

DID HOGAN JUST TAP?

> **Event:** Saturday Night's Main Event (Los Angeles, CA)
>
> **Match:** Hulk Hogan (Champion) vs. Hercules Hernandez (Challenger)
>
> **Date:** November 15th, 1986
>
> **Attendance:** 16,000
>
> **On This Day:** The Beastie Boys released their debut album, License to Ill

"This is robbery. This is total robbery. The man quit!"

– Jesse Ventura (*Saturday Night's Main Event*, November 15th, 1986).

Hogan, by his lofty standards, had an off night. It wasn't the dominant performance we had come to expect. What's the word? Uneven? Lackadaisical? Like when your parents told you to make your bed, and you just pulled the comforter up to the pillow. Even the Hulkster's gear was mishmashed together. Hogan wore blue knee pads – not his customary red – which was very unsettling, like seeing Michael Jordan in a pair of Filas. The title match took place in his hometown of Southern California, so maybe the champ got pulled in a few different directions. He had family to see and appearances to make. You had extended cousins hitting him up for tickets or lining up to pitch some new business venture. It'd be easy to lose focus, have a lapse in concentration. There was no rest for the weary, however, because here was another one of Heenan's henchmen (Herc being the latest addition to the Family) ready to take his cracks at the champ.

Hogan had the weight of the world on his broad shoulders. A letdown was to be expected, assumed even. After all, you can't be immortal *every night*.

The challenger was playing with house money. Despite repping a flawless physique and now under the watchful eye of one of the best managers in the business, Hercules entered the match with minimal expectations. He was a massive underdog, and even the sharpest of bettors knew that the Hulkster (-800 on the ML) was the appropriate play. This wasn't a weeknight tilt against Sivi Afi or Scott McGhee. The mighty Hercules had his hands full. Hogan was an impenetrable force on *Saturday Night's Main Event*, having already disposed of Bob Orton, Nikolai Volkoff, Bundy and Studd (while teaming with Andre), Terry Funk, Don Muraco, the Funk Brothers (while teaming with the Junkyard Dog), and Paul Orndorff in prior episodes. Hogan was a perfect 7-0 under the NBC banner by November of '86, so this result, like every other past rendition, was just a formality.

There was also the question of *how* Hercules would defeat the Hulkster. Not 'if,' which was already a legitimate concern, but 'how.' Herc liked to soften his opponents up – direct his punishment towards the lower lumbar area – before slapping on his patented backbreaker submission move. Well, not only did Hulk Hogan rarely lose; he *never* tapped. It took an Act of God to defeat the Hulkster, and even with divine intervention, that elusive miracle came via count out.

(Side note: Hogan did eventually tap to the "Hercules backbreaker," but nearly 11 years later, on the August 4th, 1997 *Monday Night Nitro*, when Lex Luger defeated him with the Torture Rack for the WCW World Championship).

The challenger stuck to the script. After Hogan missed with an elbow drop (a cardinal mistake), Hercules wrapped the Hulkster in a bear hug. He squeezed the life out of the champ, imposing his will in front of the capacity crowd. Then he went for his finisher. Feeling that enough damage had been inflicted, feeling that the champ was ripe for the picking, Hernandez lifted Hogan. The challenger locked him on his trapezius muscles as Hogan's vertebrae shuffled around like a deck of cards.

The champ appeared to shake his head, a clear sign of surrender, though veteran official Dave Hebner didn't call for the bell. Did Hogan submit or did the up and down motion of the devastating backbreaker simulate a repeated head nod is up for debate. I still can't say for certain, and I spent the entire Memorial Day Weekend dissecting the footage. The broadcast had conflicting opinions. Ventura sided with the challenger, while Vince was in Camp Hogan. They needed a third member.

"Let's bring in senior official, Mike Pereira. Mike, what did you see?"

"Well, this is a tough one, Vince. The Hulkster's head is definitely moving, but I don't see anything clear and obvious. Referee Dave Hebner is looking for a tap out gesture, a hand signal of some kind, but we don't see anything concrete with the camera angles we have. I just don't see enough evidence to overturn the call in the ring."

Well, Hercules had seen enough. In *his* mind, history had been made, so Hernandez dropped Hogan to the ground and raised his arms in victory. Hebner, though, ruled otherwise and the match continued. The Immortal One never required much wiggle room. While Hercules argued with Hebner (and then announced to the crowd in *painstakingly slow* fashion that he was about to pin Hogan for the 1-2-3), the champ recouped his strength, like Link grabbing a recovery heart in *The Legend of Zelda*. Hogan kicked out of the cover with authority. He got that familiar look in his eye. The Los Angeles crowd buzzed, as right hand after right hand from the challenger landed with no effect. The momentum shifted firmly in the corner of the Hulkster. The champ had found his second wind, and now it was Hernandez who was on the run.

Hercules had lost. He just didn't know it yet.

IF YOU AIN'T CHEATING, YOU AIN'T TRYING

THE KILLER BEES STORY

Raymond Rougeau: *"Hi, this is Jacques, and I'm Raymond, and we're the Fabulous Rougeau Brothers. Jacques, have you noticed sometimes the Killer Bees pull out their masks and cheat a little bit?"*

Jacques Rougeau: *"Well, I think everybody notices that, Raymond."* (*Superstars*, June 25th, 1988).

For eight days in 1980, Cuban American Rosie Ruiz was the recognized winner of the Boston Marathon. She finished the race in a cool 2:31:56, the fastest recorded time by a woman in marathon history. Ruiz shattered the record without breaking much of a sweat, running so quickly in fact that no spectator or participant even recalled seeing her. When asked by a reporter why she didn't appear tired post-race, Ruiz replied, "I woke up with a lot of energy." (Kidd 2007).

As the story goes, she *allegedly* jumped into the race with only a half-mile to go (Ruiz maintained her innocence).

It's my favorite sports cheating scandal because it was so brazen. Forget Deflategate. Ruiz won the 26.2-mile race by skipping the first 25.6 miles. That's like Joey Chestnut strolling in at the contest's 7-minute mark, saying he already ate 60 hot dogs. Six months earlier, Ruiz allegedly bypassed the lion's share of the New York City Marathon by taking the subway. If you're going to cheat, go big. Don't half ass it.

So how did the holier than thou Killer Bees, the biggest pair of choir boys this side of the Young Stallions, also moonlight as the biggest cheaters in wrestling history?

Because no one wanted to believe it was true.

B. Brian Blair and Jumpin' Jim Brunzell played everyone for a fool. They'd look you in the eye before robbing you blind and even when the Killer Bees cheated in plain sight, they got a pass. Their rule breaking got categorized as some next level creativity, a brilliant maneuver, if you will. The cheating was celebrated, lauded even. Fans and commentators embraced its candor. The Bees brought masks to the ring. If one was in peril, they'd put on the masks and pull the ol' switch-a-roo. One would roll out of the ring, and the other would replace him.

Wait, wait. Where was the tag, Dave?

THERE WAS NO TAG, reader! They consistently broke the rule of tag team wrestling: You can't enter the ring without being TAGGED in. The Bees played under a different set of rules than every other team in the division. It was like playing Rock-Paper-Scissors, but your opponent just kept throwing out "dynamite." And if you dared to challenge their methods, the vocal majority berated you into silence. Or they'd move the goalposts.

Ventura: *"Wait a minute, McMahon! What is this now? They both have masks on! Hey, I'm gonna tell you something. This is totally illegal in my opinion!"*

McMahon: *"I don't recall anything in the rulebook stating that wearing masks is illegal."*

Ventura: *"Who is the legal man in the ring now? Who *is* in the ring?"* (*Saturday Night's Main Event*, November 15th, 1986).

Come on, Vince. Jesse isn't anti-mask. He never chastised Mr. X or the Red Demon for their choice of anonymity. (In fact, it was Monsoon who would argue about the disadvantage masked wrestlers faced, because it limited your peripheral vision). The Bees flourished on this uneven playing field. The parallels to the 1989 classic, *The Wizard*, when Lucas smoked Jimmy Woods in *Rad Racer* using his Nintendo Power Glove, were obvious – albeit an admittedly obscure reference. As the wins piled up, they pushed the envelope even more.

In the semifinals of the March 15th, 1987 Frank Tunney Sr. Memorial Tag Team Tournament – the most prestigious of all tag team tournaments – the Bees used their tried and true rule breaking to slip past Paul Orndorff and King Kong Bundy. In the finals against Demolition, they did it again. B. Brian and Jumpin' Jim couldn't help themselves. Cheating was like a drug for them, an urge they couldn't shake. They were a terrific team without the deceit; two up-and-comers who could've catapulted up the tag ranks on their own merit. They didn't have to cheat, but I suppose Winona Ryder didn't need to shoplift either. At the '87 Survivor Series, Blair and Brunzell followed the same blueprint, masking up in a sneaky elimination of the Islanders.

"That is indeed B. Brian Blair, the illegal man!" – Gorilla Monsoon.

Gorilla said it with such glee, such unbridled enthusiasm, like a proud uncle telling his colleagues that his niece got into Boston College. The Bees flaunted their dirty tactics with an air of entitlement. Guys like the Junkyard Dog, George "The Animal" Steele, and Koko B. Ware would join the masked fray. On a few occasions, with Koko specifically, they'd *still* try and pull off the switch-a-roo, skin color be damned.

There was a double standard with the Killer Bees. Another masked team around that time, the Conquistadors, who resided from "Somewhere in Latin America" (that narrows it down), incorporated the same underhanded methods. Conquistador #1 and #2 rotated in and out of the ring like hockey defensemen and were vilified for it. The Conquistadors weren't clever. They, too, were cheaters, but when you're beloved, you can get away with murder. Any action can be justified, any alibi verified. The Bees were adored. They had an army of defenders. Jumpin' Jim and B. Brian Blair didn't cheat their opponents, you see.

They outsmarted them.

Second Intermission

"He Should Be Fined and Suspended"/ "He Didn't Do His Homework"

(We interrupt this program to discuss Ventura and Monsoon catchphrases).

The following is a running list of wrestlers and officials who:

- According to Jesse Ventura, should've been fined and/or suspended.

Or

- Per Gorilla Monsoon, did not do their homework.

The Junkyard Dog should've been fined and suspended for his actions on the November 2nd, 1985 *Saturday Night's Main Event*, when he branded Jimmy Hart with Terry Funk's iron. You can't go around branding people, JYD.

Speaking of the Dog, **King Harley Race** didn't do his homework at WrestleMania III, when he went for the headbutt (a big no-no).

Everyone was worthy of suspension on the January 3rd, 1987 *Saturday Night's Main Event*. **George "The Animal" Steele** should've been rung up for not one particular incident – but just general behavior really. (Soon after Ventura's observation, George kidnapped Miss Elizabeth which didn't help his defense). **The Junkyard Dog** later headbutted official, Danny Davis, which should've warranted an immediate suspension. **Ricky "The Dragon" Steamboat** also should've faced the wrath of Jack Tunney's office after his blatant interference in the Savage/Steele Intercontinental Championship match.

Mr. Perfect didn't do his homework at WrestleMania V, when he was woefully unprepared for the Blue Blazer's aerial attack.

Tito Santana should've had to write a big, fat check when he assaulted the Doctor of Style (and ripped his threads) at WrestleMania III.

Same with **Jim Duggan**, after he leveled the Iron Sheik with his 2x4.

The Nasty Boys didn't do their homework on the March 15th, 1993 *Monday Night Raw*, when Knobbs gave the Headshrinkers' Fatu and Samu a double noggin' knocker.

Joey Marella, not Danny Davis, deserved a suspension for his incompetent officiating during the Hogan/Andre match at WrestleMania III. Ventura made his case on *Saturday Night's Main Event*, May 2nd, 1987.

Terry Funk didn't do his homework on November 9th, 1985, during *World Wrestling Federation on NESN*, when he, too, headbutted the Junkyard Dog (see above).

Brutus Beefcake was a repeat offender. He attacked "The Hammer" Greg Valentine with a pair of hedge clippers on the March 12th, 1988 *Saturday Night's Main Event*. The incident warranted an immediate suspension.

The youngster **Jim Haley** didn't do his homework on the June 9th, 1986 edition of *Prime Time*. He punched Special Delivery Jones in the head, which was the wrong part of the anatomy to attack ol' S.D.

"Rugged" Ronnie Garvin should be hearing from Jack Tunney's office any minute now, after he delivered the Garvin Stomp to poor Frenchy Martin at WrestleMania V.

The Red Rooster didn't do his homework at the '88 Survivor Series, when he futilely rammed Koko B. Ware's head into the turnbuckle. **Steve Lombardi** missed the exact same assignment. He made the mistake against Koko on the November 8th, 1988 show at the Maple Leaf Gardens. **"The

Model" Rick Martel** must've played hooky with Rooster and Lombardi because he, too, ineffectively smashed Koko's head into the turnbuckle at WrestleMania VI.

The actions of habitual rulebreaker, **"Hacksaw" Jim Duggan**, warranted a fine and suspension at SummerSlam '89, after he *very illegally* hit Akeem with a 2x4.

On the same night, **"Superfly" Jimmy Snuka** *could have* faced a fine and suspension for his post-match extracurricular activities. After losing via count out to Ted DiBiase, Snuka took his frustrations out on the hapless Virgil. Ventura wouldn't *officially* call for a fine and suspension in this case, but he did float the idea out there.

The dog must've eaten ring vet **Tony Garea's** homework at The Big Event in 1986, when he tried to match strength with the powerhouse, Ted Arcidi.

The ring technician himself, **Bret Hart**, received failing marks on the June 16th, 1986 *Prime Time*. He slammed Siva Afi's head into the turnbuckle (no effect).

Brutus "The Barber" Beefcake should've had his wages garnished at this point. He deserved a hefty fine and suspension at WrestleMania VI, after he cut The Genius' hair.

~ ~ ~

(According to my research, none of the wrestlers listed were fined or suspended for their actions).

We now return to our regularly scheduled programming.

The Other, *Other* Streak

There are two prominent streaks in contemporary wrestling.

1) Goldberg's 173-0 masterpiece in '97 and '98.
2) Undertaker's 21 consecutive WrestleMania victories.

Kudos to Goldberg. I'm not going to diminish his extraordinary accomplishment. Whether or not there was a rounding error – counting a victory over Brad Armstrong or Sick Boy as four or five wins, like how guys round up on the number of women they've slept with – isn't for me to debate. I also don't think it matters. The former United States and WCW World Champion won a boatload of matches. He passed the eye test. Tallying up the exact number of times Goldberg steamrolled Yuji Nagata is a pointless exercise.

The Undertaker's streak, however? It always seemed watered down. For years, manager Paul Bearer hand-picked tomato cans for Taker. When Mike Tyson got out of prison, his team lined up Peter McNeeley and Buster Mathis Jr. to knock off the ring rust. Bearer cherry-picked an over-the-hill Jimmy Snuka, a past-his-prime Jake Roberts, and a King Kong Bundy on the downslope of his career. If this was '83 Snuka or '86 Bundy, ok; I'd give the devil his due. Name recognition, though, isn't the only qualifier. Context matters. Like striking out Babe Ruth is a tremendous achievement, but sitting down the 40-year-old version, the Babe who hit just .181 for the Boston Braves diminishes the feat. Sure, Taker's run got more difficult from there, but the Dead Man fattened up that record on a smorgasbord of low-hanging fruit.

Yet in the annals of squared circle lore, there's another streak that has been forgotten; another streak that over time has been scrubbed from wrestling's consciousness. Some pundits argue that this streak was even more impressive than Goldberg and Undertaker's. (It's me. I'm one of those pundits). In fact, I wrote my college thesis on the exact subject. This streak is an afterthought in comparison to the above, and its past time we changed that. You see, before Taker's WrestleMania record hit double-digits, there was Goldberg.

And before Goldberg, there was Tatanka.

From 1992 until October of '93, YOU DID NOT BEAT TATANKA. Countless tried. Everyone failed. The only more dominant entity from that era was the Dream Team (The U.S. Men's Basketball Team, not Johnny V's beauties), but even *they* lose points for rostering Christian Laettner. While Goldberg feasted on the C-List members of Raven's Flock, Tatanka ducked nobody. He took on all comers. Just have a look for yourself:

- Skinner
- The Warlord
- Rick Martel
- Kato
- Col. Mustafa
- Kato a few more times
- The Mountie
- Repo Man
- Papa Shango
- Damien Demento
- The Berzerker
- Doink
- Terry Taylor

- One of the Beverly Brothers
- Bam Bam Bigelow
- Adam Bomb
- Bastion Booger
- Mr. Hughes

People slept on Tatanka's dominance, like how most forget that "Semi-Charmed Life," "Graduate," "How's It Going to Be," and "Jumper," all came from Third Eye Blind's debut album. One of the greatest wrestlers of this generation never beat Tatanka, but it's rarely mentioned. It's never discussed. His rivalry with the Heartbreak Kid was completely one-sided. During this span, HBK defended his Intercontinental Championship against Tatanka on eight different occasions. Michaels went 0-8. In a stroke of good luck, however, Shawn lost all eight matches by either disqualification or count out, thus keeping the title. Like what are the chances? You'd think the Championship Committee would've sprinkled in a Lumberjack Match or two to keep the combatants in the ring, but I digress.

~ ~ ~

> **Event:** *Superstars* **(Worcester, MA)**
> **Match: Tatanka vs. Ludvig Borga**
> **Date: October 30th, 1993**
> **Attendance: 2,000**
> **#1 Movie on this Date:** *The Beverly Hillbillies*

On October 30th, something had to give. Tatanka put his unblemished record on the line against the Finnish powerhouse, Ludvig Borga. Borga had been outstanding since his arrival, albeit a bit ornery, which was perplexing considering the United Nations Sustainable Development Solutions Network ranks Finland 'the happiest country in the world' every year. Ludvig looked indestructible. His string of victories included a convincing triumph over Marty Jannetty at SummerSlam '93 and next up, Tatanka: The Irresistible Force against the Immovable Object.

The Native American came out firing, unleashing a flurry of chops and clotheslines. He knocked Borga down, but only temporarily, and Ludvig took control from there. He parlayed a sidewalk slam into a textbook vertical suplex. The big Finn then sapped his opponent's energy with a series of devastating chin locks. All eyes were on this contest. Even the Devious One had made his way ringside. Fuji's man and current World Champion, Yokozuna, was set to captain "The Foreign Fanatics" against "The All-Americans" at the Survivor Series next month, so Fuji was there scouting. He was old school. He wasn't an analytics guy; his decisions weren't determined by numbers and spreadsheets. Anxious to get a closer look, Fuji took one too many steps towards our fallen hero, who languished outside the ring. The ref stepped in, warning the manager to maintain an appropriate distance, and Ludvig capitalized on the distraction. With the official's back turned, while the ref admonished Master Fuji, Borga wrecked Tatanka with a chair shot. Ludvig then dragged him back into the ring – and in the ultimate sign of disrespect – pinned the unconscious Tatanka and ended his undefeated streak with one measly finger.

After the decision, Yokozuna added insult to injury. He decimated him with a Banzai Drop and the injuries sustained prevented Tatanka from representing "The All-Americans." Candidly, I don't know if Tatanka ever recovered from that night. His game slipped in later years. Was he still good? Of course, but he was now far from invincible. Did the Federation finally figure him out? Was it Father Time claiming another victim? Or were the struggles he endured later due to mounting stress, a once perfect wrestler now drowning in paperwork and red tape.

How can one remain focused after all, when you're being audited by the IRS for failure to pay a gift tax on a ceremonial headdress?

Jimmy Hart

The King of Kings?

Back in high school, I went through a Nickelback and Puddle of Mudd phase. I'll be damned, though, if I ever admitted that out loud. It was my dirty little secret. You took that to the grave, like disclosing that your favorite film of the *Jaws* franchise was *The Revenge*. I had a reputation; I had street cred to maintain. I told people my favorite bands were Pearl Jam and Radiohead and hoped they'd never find the *Silver Side Up* CD underneath my passenger seat.

Liking Jimmy Hart wasn't cool. Hart wasn't funny like Heenan. He wasn't classy like Blassie, and he didn't hang with Cyndi Lauper like Captain Lou. Hart paired his obnoxious megaphone with an assortment of goofy, colorful suits to create one irritating package. Jimmy was less Colonel Parker and more Matthew Lesko, the 'free money guy.' "The Mouth of the South" was so despised that at WrestleMania III, celebrity commentator Mary Hart publicly announced that there was no relation between the two. Yes, Jimmy looked like a hack but looks can be deceiving. Appearances can disarm you. Billy Hoyle hooped in a tie-dye hat and a long-sleeve shirt. Rams running back Eric Dickerson rushed for an NFL-record 2,105 yards in 1984, and he did it while wearing prescription goggles.

Bobby Heenan is the consensus greatest manager of all time, and I don't dispute that. "The Brain" has my vote. What's odd, though, is that no one mentions Jimmy Hart in the same breath. It's Heenan and then everyone else. Is Bobby far and away the greatest manager of all time – like is he *really* light years ahead of Hart? Or is the race not considered close due to Heenan's immense popularity? It wasn't fashionable to like Jimmy, and I think that has affected his ranking among the all-time greats. Almost

19 million people tuned into the Season 7 premiere of *The Big Bang Theory*, yet I don't know one single person who called it their favorite show. You kept that opinion to yourself. "The Brain" was amazing. He was the best. He was the greatest manager of all time, and it wouldn't be cool to suggest otherwise.

Consider this. The following is a list of champions managed by "The Mouth of the South."

World Championship

1. Hulk Hogan, 1993

Intercontinental Championship

1. Greg "The Hammer" Valentine, 1985
2. The Honky Tonk Man, 1987-1988
3. The Mountie, 1992

Tag Team Championship

1. The Hart Foundation, 1987
2. The Nasty Boys, 1991
3. Money Inc., (2x), 1992-1993

Women's Tag Team Championship

1. The Glamour Girls, 1987-1988

Not even George Santos could dream up a résumé like that.

Here is Heenan's:

World Championship

1. Andre the Giant, 1988 (co-managed by Ted DiBiase)

2. Ric Flair, (2x), 1992 (co-managed by Mr. Perfect)

Intercontinental Championship

1. "Ravishing" Rick Rude, 1989
2. Mr. Perfect, (2x), 1990-1991

Tag Team Championship

1. The Brain Busters, 1989
2. The Colossal Connection, 1989-1990

Pretty close, right? And this is *after* my admittedly generous inclusion of Ric Flair's two title reigns under the Heenan Family banner.

(Collectively, Hart and Heenan's men were responsible for four separate World Championship title wins, but neither manager was at ringside for any of them. That's like if Bill Belichick used PTO on the day of each of the Patriots' six Super Bowls).

Hi, thanks for your email. I will be out of the office on Sunday, February 1st. Please contact Josh McDaniels or Matt Patricia if you need assistance. – Bill.

The two's managerial styles were quite different. Heenan had in-ring experience. He teamed with Andre, Haku, and Arn Anderson at the '89 Survivor Series. "The Brain" fought at both WrestleMania IV and V, and he picked up a win over the cagey vet, Salvatore Bellomo, on the May 5th, 1986 *Prime Time*. Bobby could devise a schematic advantage to ground any opponent.

Hart wasn't a wrestler. He didn't know a suplex from a duplex. (Though it should be noted that he won a $50,000 cash prize battle royal on July 12th, 1986. He hid underneath the ring the entire match, but still, the check cleared all the same). Jimmy didn't teach X's and O's. The extent of his advice was reminding the ref to "Watch the hair!" What he lacked as a tactician, however, he made up for in motivation. Hart was a wrestler's manager. I didn't necessarily agree with his methods, but I can't argue with the results. Just see above. Guys bought into his system. Wrestlers wanted to fight for him. (Well, except for the Hart Foundation after Bret and "The Anvil" discovered Jimmy was giving a cut of their earnings to the Fabulous Rougeau Brothers. I mean, that was pretty messed up).

The pivotal year in both managers' careers was 1987. Heenan focused on the World Title, recruiting Andre to dispatch the Hulkster. Bobby aimed high. Every other prize was secondary. Yeah, he found the time to ink a deal with the Islanders, and later got involved in some light animal kidnapping, but I think dog theft was more a hobby than a full-time occupation. While "The Brain" channeled his efforts towards Hogan, Jimmy racked up the secondary championships. He snatched up the Intercontinental Title, the Tag Titles, and the Women's Tag Titles in the same calendar year. In the case of the Glamour Girls (Judy Martin and Leilani Kai), they were already champs. They already did the legwork. Hart just talked his way into their managerial rights.

Jimmy and "The Brain" had a difference of philosophies. In Monopoly terms, Heenan only wanted Boardwalk and Park Place, while "The Mouth of the South" was perfectly content hoarding the railroads and collecting $200/ride. Whether Hart avoided Hogan (and by proxy, the World Title), out of fear, or because of careful calculation, I can't say. Either way, Jimmy played the long game.

In 1993, eight years after joining the World Wrestling Federation, Hart aligned himself with the Hulkster. It was a decision that must've been wildly unpopular among managerial inner circles. Hogan spent a decade terrorizing Jimmy, Bobby, Fuji, Slick and every other member of the fraternity, but Hart sold out for wrestling's biggest prize. He joined up with the one superstar every manager swore to destroy. It's easy to see why Bobby stumped so hard for Yokozuna in '93, and why "The Brain" ranks above

Hart on everyone's list of top managers. Standing beside Hulk Hogan wasn't Bobby's former colleague. It was a traitor. Heenan never would've sold his soul – not for Hogan. He never would've stooped to Hart's level. Bobby was way too cool for that.

What I'd Like to Have Right Now ...

"Ravishing" Rick Rude and the Art of Trash Talking

As legend goes, Larry Bird walked into the locker room before the 1988 NBA Three-Point Contest and asked fellow participants, "Who's gonna come in second?" After South Carolina thumped Kentucky, 54-3, in 2011, Gamecocks head coach, Steve Spurrier said, "Kentucky has a heck of a punter. I know that." Shit-talking is a skill, and an innate one at that. Not everyone has it. I worked a summer as a camp counselor and reminded the kids to throw their popsicle wrappers in the trash. I told them that litterbugs suck and without missing a beat, some camper goes, "Your face sucks," and I've been reeling ever since.

I respected "Ravishing" Rick Rude's range. He was multi-faceted. He didn't belittle people through *just* his punchlines (Although, calling the fine people of Connecticut, "Fat, out of shape, Hartford heffers" certainly hammers the point home). Rude insulted his opponents through his interviews, his actions, and the clothes he was wearing. He tailored his entire presentation to the chirp. There were no wasted words, no wasted motions ... actually, strike that. There were A LOT of motions ...

Now hit the music.

The Rick Rude Dance

There's disrespect, and then there's gyrating over a fallen opponent. Find one person who hasn't done the Rick Rude dance, and I'll find you a liar. It plays in any social setting. Win a game of flip cup? Clasp your hands behind your head and swivel those hips counterclockwise. Get a big promotion at work? Well, look away if my gyrations offend you, Linda from Accounting. My brother once broke out the dance in our parents' living room and I think he got grounded for a month. I've done the Rick Rude dance so many times that if I owned a boat, she'd be named, "Cut the Music." In 2015, Kansas City Chiefs running back, Charcandrick West, did his best impression after a touchdown, and I haven't taken off my Charcandrick West jersey ever since. The NFL frowns upon 'suggestive' celebrations, but those bureaucratic prudes wouldn't know a Sexual Awakening from a Rude one.

Rick's movements were effortless and smooth, like the first time a scooper slides through a freshly opened carton of ice cream. Slow and meticulous hip rotations followed any Rude body slam or clothesline, because only "Ravishing" Rick could beat a man while reenacting a scene from *Showgirls*. He also won in bunches. There is a very short list of wrestlers who pinned the Ultimate Warrior. Randy Savage isn't on there. Andre the Giant never got the job done, and I'll have to re-check my Excel spreadsheets, but I don't think Jose Luis Rivera got in the win column either. Rude snatched the Intercontinental Championship away from Warrior at WrestleMania V (partly due to some 'light' interference from Bobby Heenan), but it counted just the same. Rick was confident going into the contest. So confident in fact, that he spraypainted the IC title on his trunks. Speaking of …

The Tights

There's disrespect, and then there's airbrushing a picture of your opponent's wife ON THE CROTCH OF YOUR TIGHTS. Holy hell. Imagine going to the local playground for pick-up, and some dude is wearing a pair of And-1 shorts *with your girl's face* over his junk. How could you possibly elevate for a mid-range jumper when your lovely, sweet Janice is staring right back at you?

After mopping the floor with the chump of the day, Rick would invite a woman from the crowd for a make-out session – standard protocol really. The arrangement was purely physical. No dinner, no small talk, just a little first base action between Rick and that night's lucky lady. After quickly disposing of the young Jake Milliman on the April 23rd, 1988 *Superstars*, Rude addressed a beautiful woman in the front row. Fans expected to bear witness to another in-ring spit swapping, like playing Seven Minutes in Heaven with the closet door open.

The mysterious woman, though, was less than enthused with Rude's advances. She rejected Rick at every turn and Heenan's man was incredulous. This was Rick fuckin' Rude here. The guy had more abs than I had '88 Topps baseball cards. What was her deal? It was just a little smooch and maybe, *maybe* some heavy petting. We then discovered that she was married to a wrestler – not Jake Milliman as "The Brain" had guessed – but Jake "The Snake" Roberts. Of all the gin joints in all the towns, Rick Rude hit on Cheryl Roberts.

"The Snake," still soaking wet from his post-match shower (he defeated Chris Curtis earlier in the night), charged down to ringside. He and Rude brawled in the aisle until officials broke up the melee. In the aftermath, Rick had two viable options:

A) Apologize to Roberts for hitting on his wife.
B) Order custom-made tights with Cheryl Roberts' face airbrushed on his crotch.

Rick Rude wearing the Cheryl Roberts tights is maybe the most fucked up thing I've ever witnessed, and I watched her husband once coerce the Ultimate Warrior into some snake-infested funhouse. The tights weren't just a one-time thing. Never doubt Rude's commitment to a bit. He did this for *months*. Rick had a closet full of Cheryl tights, an entire Cheryl Roberts collection, and they all looked *exactly* like her. The resemblance was uncanny. He had the Leonardo da Vinci of airbrushing on his payroll. He'd reveal a pair of Cheryl tights from *under* his other tights which seems impossible to pull off, until you remember that guys in the 1990's routinely wore khakis over a pair of boxers that were three sizes too big.

Your Mom

And just for good measure, Rick Rude had a few Yo Momma jokes in his arsenal.

> "If the Big Boss Man doesn't like me standing here ... calling his mother 'a stinkin' sweat hog,' he needs to come out, and talk to me about it. If the Big Boss Man doesn't like the fact that I know his mom is nothing but a slimy swamp sow, he needs to talk to me about it. And if the Big Boss Man doesn't like the fact that his mother, in my mind, is nothing but a snaggletoothed sea hag, then he needs to talk to me about it. What the Big Boss Man and his mother prove to me, is that cellulite is hereditary. What the Big Boss Man and his mother are, are the perfect example of bad genetics.
>
> **– "Ravishing" Rick Rude (*Wrestling Challenge*, September 30th, 1990).**

Jack Tunney, that bozo, whose disciplinary measures shifted with the wind, tolerated an almost year-long assault on Cheryl Roberts. Airbrushing someone's wife on your crotch was no problem; that expression of free speech fell well within the boundaries of good taste. Calling the Big Boss Man's mother, a "snaggletoothed sea hag," however, was apparently a bridge too far.

In late October, President Jack suspended Rude indefinitely.

NO MÁS

THE 1987 SLAMMY AWARDS

> **Event:** The Slammy Awards (Atlantic City, NJ)
>
> **Date:** December 16th, 1987
>
> **Hosts:** Gene Okerlund and Jesse Ventura
>
> **On This Date:** Sting (the singer, not the wrestler) performs at Wembley Arena. He ends the set with "Message in a Bottle."

"That donkey should've sat right on that ass Heenan."

— Gorilla Monsoon.

And the winner for Most Disappointing Streaming Platform is ...

Peacock, who just edged out Quibi.

Peacock did *not* have the 1987 Slammy Awards on the Network, which was incredibly frustrating. I don't ask for much. I really don't. I want to resurrect the European Title and watch an award show from over 35 years ago in HD. Is that so hard? I was able to track down the Slammys eventually, albeit through backdoor channels. I sank into the underbelly of the interwebs and purchased it from a tape trader who operated out of an Angelfire website. The show was sandwiched between episodes of *ALF* and *Head of the Class*.

I didn't *love* the '87 Slammys. Ok, I hated it. Now, that didn't stop me from watching it three consecutive times for the sake of this book, but I won't be ordering seconds. (Afterwards, I cleansed my pallet with the 1990

Royal Rumble). The Slammys are an acquired taste. Maybe it's me. Maybe I'm an old man shouting at a cloud, but I prefer my action *inside* the squared circle. I caught myself daydreaming on multiple occasions, harking back to a Bob Orton/Jerry Allen *Prime Time* match I watched weeks prior. The Slammys weren't so much an awards ceremony, but a variety show. The awards were just a backdrop for these song and dance numbers that left me questioning the entire validity of this project. It reminded me of my 7th grade talent show where every act either sang "My Heart Will Go On," or did the dance from *Space Jam*. It was June 2022. The sun was shining, the birds chirping, and I was sitting in my basement listening to Jimmy Hart sing the lyrics, "Girls in cars" over and over.

Touch grass, Dave.

You ain't kidding.

Before the first award, "Mean" Gene told us the votes were calculated and tabulated by Jack Tunney, which was like asking the fox to babysit the chickens. Tunney would rig a student council election if he had enough skin in the game. Given the news, I expected Hulk Hogan to win every Slammy, even the awards for Woman and Manager of the Year. Tunney didn't receive a hero's welcome. The live audience rightfully booed the World Wrestling Federation President, giving him a reception that'd make even Commissioner Roger Goodell blush. Tunney popped his head in, heard the boos, and hightailed it right back to the craps tables.

Songs were sung. Awards were awarded. Sika ate the envelope containing the winner of "Song of the Year," so we'll have to use our imagination there. "Hacksaw" Jim Duggan had an eventful night. He received two accolades, "Greatest Hit" and "Best Vocal Performance," finding the time to accept both awards while brawling with Harley Race all over the Caesars Hotel. Monsoon chased the two around and provided play-by-play, but mostly used the opportunity to eviscerate Bobby Heenan.

"Atomic drop right into the carrot cake! Bobby 'the Brain' Heenan, what a slime, what a piece of garbage."

The evening's final performance was a rendition of "If You Only Knew" (not to be confused with Aaliyah's "If Your Girl Only Knew," or the raunchier 7th Floor Crew version). I loathed it. Forget the number; the song and dance were whatever. The ensemble featured just about every wrestler not named 'Andre,' and my first reaction was, "Why?" Why was our World Champion hobnobbing with Heenan, Fuji, and co.? Why was Strike Force performing with the Hart Foundation? The Honky Tonk Man recently shoved Liz on *Saturday Night's Main Event*, and here was Savage now one beat away from breaking into an "Islands in the Streams" duet. Everyone was too chummy for my liking.

"Our next caller is Dave from the Delaware Valley. Hey, Dave, thanks for calling into Pro Wrestling Spotlight Radio."

"Hey, John, first time, long time, thanks for taking my call. The last caller stole my thunder, but I, too, wanted to express my complete and utter disgust for the '87 Slammys. Earlier in the night, Hulk Hogan presented Billy Graham with the 'Real American' Award for his determination and bravery. Then, minutes later, our champion is playing Rockettes with Butch Reed and the Gang, the two guys, who I need not remind you, ended Graham's career a month earlier in Syracuse. Make it make sense, John. Imma hang up and listen …"

The hypocrisy oozed from the stage, but in the face of darkness, there was one shining light. Virgil, OUR Virgil. He refused to comply. He kept a close eye on the Hulkster and his cronies, like any good bodyguard would do. Virgil didn't sing. He didn't dance. He stood stone-faced on stage with his arms crossed and I never respected anyone more. He looked like me when my wife drags me to HomeGoods. Virgil didn't win a Slammy, but he should've. He should've won all the awards.

There fortunately wouldn't be another Slammys for seven years.

The Barber Shop Window

> Event: *Wrestling Challenge* (Corpus Christi, TX)
>
> Segment: *The Barber Shop*
>
> Date: January 12th, 1992
>
> #1 Movie on This Date: *Hook*

Gorilla Monsoon: *"Right through the glass window of the Barber Shop!"*

Bobby Heenan: *"Jannetty tried to dive through the window to escape!"*

Gorilla Monsoon: *"Are you blind!?"* (*Wrestling Challenge*, January 12th, 1992).

Poor Marty Jannetty. Poor, poor Marty Jannetty. Marty's story is a tragic one, his name to this day still a euphemism for any 'less than' partner of a team or tandem. I got dumped at a roller-skating party in 5th grade which was traumatizing enough, but having my friend afterwards call me "The Marty Jannetty" of the relationship only poured salt in the wound. The Rockers' break-up is the most recognized tag team split in wrestling history, and it's not particularly close. They made the Strike Force split seem amicable, and even the Mega Powers parted ways without one chucking the other through a window.

I've never passed one barbershop without making a Rockers reference, and yeah, my act is tired and played out, but dance with the girl you brought to prom, I say. The backdrop of this break-up added to its pop culture staying power. This schism didn't occur on *The Brother Love Show* or *Piper's Pit*, two programs that were littered with monumental moments. Shawn canned Marty on the B-rate *Wrestling Challenge*, on the *fucking* Barber

Shop of all places. I'd rather get dumped at an Applebee's. If *Piper's Pit* and *The Brother Love Show* were Oprah and Jerry Springer, respectively, then *The Barber Shop* was Jenny Jones or Ricki Lake – a blip in time, a 90's afterthought like Nickelodeon's Gak or those Ecto Cooler juice boxes that are forgotten more often than remembered. Brutus Beefcake hosted *The Barber Shop* for ten months, and outside the infamous Rockers appearance and the final episode with Sid, I can't recall one other interview. Would Jannetty and Michaels' split still be relevant thirty years later if it wasn't a glass window that Shawn hurled Marty through, but rather Brother Love's podium? Would Shawn and Marty's break-up top the list of memorable moments on *Piper's Pit*, ahead of Jimmy Snuka and the coconut or the Hogan and Andre confrontation from early '87? You can't discuss *The Barber Shop* without mentioning the Rockers, like how every conversation about *Diff'rent Strokes* includes the one with Gordon Jump and the bicycle shop.

The red flags were at full staff. Michaels wore a black leather jacket for the interview, and if the nWo's surplus of fanny packs taught me anything, it's to never trust a wrestler in black leather. Both parties resuscitated old wounds, harping on past events where the offending partner wronged the other. Marty brought up their tag match from *Superstars* in November, where Michaels was preoccupied with some girls in the front row. Shawn fired back. On *Prime Time* in December, he wrestled Flair in singles action. Michaels had Ric staggering, vulnerable and hurt on the outside. Shawn sprung over the top rope for one of his classic high-risk maneuvers, but Mr. Perfect pulled his man out of the way. Michaels crashed into the guardrail, knocking himself unconscious. Jannetty then joined his partner at ringside. He complained to the ref, arguing, though, for what I'm not sure (Mr. Perfect never put his hands on Michaels). As Shawn laid there on the outside, Marty then made the inexplicably bad decision to roll his fellow Rocker back inside the ring. (Seriously, what the hell was Marty thinking? I've seen more ring awareness in a George Steele/Kamala match). Ric thanked him for the assist and pinned the unconscious Michaels for the easy 1-2-3.

The Rockers' dissension, however, can be traced back even further than the events from late '91. Shawn and Marty's estrangement was a culmination of squandered opportunities, and the dam broke after their tag title match against LOD on the December 28th, 1991 *Superstars*. A Rockers miscue decided that contest; the final crack in a relationship that couldn't be repaired. Their run was punctuated by years of frustrating losses and hollow victories. What if, though, in an alternate universe, one of those wins weren't just empty calories? Would the Rockers have survived a tumultuous 1991 if they had tasted championship gold just once? Maybe if they cleanly pinned the Nasty Boys for the titles on *Superstars* in May of that year, instead of walking away with a DQ victory. Or more infamously on October 30th, 1990, when Marty and Shawn defeated the Hart Foundation in a controversial 2 out of 3 Falls match for the championship belts. The combatants navigated the contest with a broken top rope, which led the bungling President Tunney to intervene. What if Jack simply decided to "play it as it lies," instead of playing God, and overturning Marty and Shawn's victory days later? Some of the Rockers' bad luck was self-inflicted, but some of their bad luck was just that. Frustration mounted. Pundits assumed at least one title reign by '92, in part because Marty and Shawn self-identified as "tag team specialists." This was their domain. They were the specialists here, not Haku and Andre, or Knobbs and Sags. On the nuances of tag team wrestling, Marty and Shawn were the self-assigned subject matter experts.

Not all great teams are championship teams. In sports, when stars can't get over the hump, they first blame their supporting cast. Then they blame the coach. Eventually, they point fingers at each other. By early 1992, the Rockers were broken.

Shawn tossing Marty through the window was inevitable. We shouldn't be surprised it happened. Just shocked that it didn't happen sooner.

Marty's Revenge

> **Event:** *Monday Night Raw* (Manhattan, NY)
>
> **Match:** Shawn Michaels (Intercontinental Champion) vs. Marty Jannetty (Challenger)
>
> **Date:** May 17th, 1993
>
> **Attendance:** 1,000
>
> **Highest Rated TV Show on this Date:** *Murphy Brown*

"You know as well as I do, I'm the best in the World Wrestling Federation. I will defend this title anywhere, anytime, against anybody, because I'm the man. I'm the Heartbreak Kid. When you're Shawn Michaels, you fear no man. Anywhere, any place, anytime ... Jack."

(***Monday Night Raw***, May 17th, 1993).

Why champions continued to extend open challenges on the heels of the Honky Tonk Man's SummerSlam '88 folly is beyond me. I'd be milking every one of those thirty days between mandatory title defenses. That imbecile Tunney wouldn't even see me until Day 29, and even then, I'd be scouring the rulebook for any sort of loophole.

"I can't and won't defend my title on Friday. You're infringing on my constitutional right to celebrate Arbor Day."

"Every 30 days, huh? Well, that's interesting, Jack. Tell me, how many title defenses did Hogan have between WrestleMania IX and King of the Ring? I'll wait."

I'm not scared, just pragmatic. Do you know what's worse than a fighting champion? A former champion. The art of the open challenge is a delicate one. More than anything, it's a bluff. The title holder doesn't expect anyone to *actually* answer. Like, who'd be crazy enough to accept, to jump the line of the Championship Committee's established contenders? Certainly not me, I got a family. You think I'm getting Shake, Rattled, and Rolled in front of millions? A funny coincidence about these open challenges, though: The wrestler who accepted was ALWAYS the champ's worst nightmare.

The Honky Tonk Man didn't want Warrior. Are you crazy? The first thing he hoped to see through that curtain was Lanny Poffo's sequin jacket. When Shawn Michaels said he'd take on *anybody*, that invitation came with an asterisk. Michaels would fight anyone *except* his former best friend who he chucked through glass. Open challenges have a way of drumming up your greatest fears and biggest skeletons. If I issued an open challenge, it'd be answered by a snake holding a printout of my search history.

If we don't learn from the past, we are doomed to repeat it. Almost five years after the Honky Tonk Man's blunder, Michaels, too, fell victim to his own bravado. Jannetty played with house money, firing on all cylinders as the partisan crowd serenaded him with chants of "Mar-ty, Mar-ty." On his heels and on the run, Shawn had had enough. He walked off with the title, correctly calculating that a loss via count out would spare him his championship. It was a flight mentality, a 'break glass in case of emergency' strategy dusted off by desperate champions, and a tactic perfected by Money Inc. (DiBiase and I.R.S. were seemingly part of more count out decisions than the Berzerker). I thought it was a chicken shit move myself, but I've also never defended my Intercontinental Championship in front of a hostile crowd against a hungry Marty Jannetty.

Michaels never did get that count out decision. Mr. Perfect, who had his own beef with the champion, blocked the aisle, leaving Shawn stuck between a Rocker and a hard place. Out of options and out of exits, Michaels fought through the adversity. A series of near falls highlighted a back-and-forth contest. Then Shawn got sloppy. He got distracted. He turned his focus towards Perfect on the outside, and have we learned NOTHING from Butch Reed at WrestleMania IV, people? Opposing managers and spectators are like mall kiosk vendors. It's best to mind your business and never make eye contact.

On the November 3rd, 1991 *Wrestling Challenge*, the Rockers battled Earthquake and Typhoon. In the waning moments, Jannetty got preoccupied. He chased Jimmy Hart up the aisle, leaving his partner to fend off both members of the Natural Disasters (a total combined weight of 843 lb).

Almost a year and a half later, Shawn followed suit. He, too, neglected his opponent inside the ring. The outside distraction led to a Jannetty small package, and history was made (and repeated) at the 10:57 mark.

CRAZY LIKE A FOX

THE WRESTLEMANIA IV BATTLE ROYAL

> Event: WrestleMania IV (Atlantic City, NJ)
> Match: The Battle Royal
> Date: March 27th, 1988
> Attendance: 19,199
> #1 Song on This Date: "Man in the Mirror," by Michael Jackson

"You know that guy might be smarter than everyone thinks. Maybe he's gonna wait for everyone to eliminate each other, then climb in there."

– Jesse "The Body" Ventura (WrestleMania IV, March 27th, 1988).

In 1951, a neurologist recommended that an infant named Kim Peek be placed in a mental institution. Coupled with cerebellum damage and a birth defect called, Agenesis of the Corpus Callosum, which causes a disruption between the white matter connecting the brain's two hemispheres, the doctor told Peek's parents that Kim would never gain the capacity to walk or learn independently (Christian H 2013).

Later in life, he would be labeled by neuroscientists as a "mega-savant." Peek displayed a superhuman ability to comprehend and store information. He could read books in an hour, simultaneously reading the left page with his left eye and the right page with the other. He memorized dates, numbers, and statistics, and could recall the contents of over 12,000 books. The 1988 film, *Rain Man*, was inspired by Peek's extraordinary life.

~ ~ ~

There is one head-scratching Royal Rumble strategy I never understood:

Sprinting down the aisle.

What's the rush? Why the hurry and where's the tactical advantage? You got these wrestlers hauling ass without any semblance of a plan. Jumpin' Jim Brunzell bolted to the ring at the '88 Royal Rumble like he was the McCallisters trying to catch their holiday flight to Paris. Like cot damn, Jumpin' Jim, apply a little critical thinking. Inside, the Hart Foundation, Roberts, Tito, and Harley Race were licking their chops. Slow it down a few paces.

I'd milk my Royal Rumble procession. I'd treat my jaunt down to the ring like a Sunday stroll. I'm stopping at the concession stand. I'm posing for pictures and signing autographs. I'd lease a WrestleMania III cart and travel in luxury. If I timed it right, six more wrestlers would hit the ring before my foot even touched the steel steps.

"After you, Sam Houston. Gotta gas up my ride here."

Battle royals, though, are different. You can't stall. There's no clock to milk. Officials pack you inside the ring like sardines and off you go. Before you can even collect your bearings, Nikolai Volkoff is working you over in the corner. Unless there is a wink and a nod during introductions, you can't really form alliances ahead of time. This isn't *Survivor*. How do I communicate with Sika that removing Ken Patera from the equation is the optimal play? These matches are a complete crapshoot. There are no rules and no universally accepted strategy.

But what if? What if I told you that the unlikeliest of wrestlers rigged the system? What if there was one superstar, typecast as slow-witted and barbaric, that managed to outsmart nineteen other competitors through an ingenious and elementary tactic that makes you wonder why every other wrestler doesn't implement the same approach. Everything can be gamed. There's always an angle. Ohio resident, Michael Larson, proved that when he hustled the game show, *Press Your Luck*, for $110,000. It just takes a little time and effort.

Bad News Brown didn't win the WrestleMania IV battle royal.

George Steele did.

"The Animal" was never eliminated. There's your victor. Now, I guess I should point out that Steele never stepped foot into the ring, but I didn't want to burden you with these minor details. George set up shop outside and let 19 other ham and eggers blindly follow battle royal protocol. It was innovative and creative and I'm onboard with declaring turnbuckle stuffing the original smart food. Steele wasn't stupid – far from it. He just let people underestimate him. Hell, the guy notched a win over Hulk Hogan in '84 and that doesn't happen by accident.

No one paid George any mind. Officials occasionally barked out these hollow threats, but "The Animal" just went about his business. Two minutes into the match, he yanked Jim Neidhart out of the ring by his goatee and refs deemed it a valid elimination, the ultimate low-risk, high-reward strategy. Monsoon, Ventura, and Mr. Baseball (Bob Uecker, not Tom Selleck) were on the call, and even they were perplexed by Steele's involvement.

"I'm not sure he ever got in there."

– Monsoon.

A moment later, without a shred of evidence or video footage:

"The Animal is already out of there as well."

– Also Monsoon.

To hell he was. The announce team couldn't grasp Steele's next-level thinking. It was like that West Canaan practice where Coach Bud Kilmer watched Mox run the Oop-dee-oop and then wondered aloud if his quarterback even knew the difference between a sneeze and a wet fart. People fear what they don't understand. In Atlantic City, George Steele changed the game. He may not have 'won' in the traditional sense, but he damn sure didn't lose.

Officials declared Bad News Brown the 'winner' of the 20-man battle royal.

Eighteen wrestlers in total were eliminated.

The Destruction of "Superstar" Billy Graham

> Event: *Superstars* (Syracuse, NY)
> Match: "Superstar" Billy Graham vs. "The Natural" Butch Reed
> Date: November 14th, 1987
> Attendance: 6,000
> #1 Movie on This Date: *Fatal Attraction*

"Bologna. This is disgusting. Let the man in the ring and be a man and start the match properly."

– Bruno Sammartino (*Superstars*, November 14th, 1987).

The medical term for suppressing traumatic memories is 'Dissociative Amnesia.' I self-diagnosed, because I didn't recall this episode of *Superstars*, only the aftermath. I remember Billy Graham with his cane. I can picture him managing "The Rock" Don Muraco, but I had forgotten how we got there, and this chapter served as a painful reminder.

Billy Graham was one of the best to ever do it. He had all the tools. A colorful, boisterous personality complemented massive 22" arms, but "Superstar" didn't *only* spend his time in the gym. The dude was also a karate master. Think of the time management skills required to lift all those weights *and* earn a black belt. I can't even get my kid to change into his pajamas and brush his teeth in under an hour. In 1977, he defeated Sammartino for the World Championship, ending Bruno's second title reign at a ridiculous 1,237 days. The moniker fit. Graham was unquestionably a Superstar, and not many superstars leave on their own terms. "Rowdy" Roddy Piper and John Elway were anomalies. Elway hung them up after winning Super Bowl XXXIII, and "Hot Rod" put a bow on his illustrious career with a victory over Adrian Adonis (I don't believe Piper wrestled again after WM III, but I'll confirm). Those two are the exceptions. Most superior athletes hang on too long, clinging to past success that is far too dated to repeat. In 2017, I bet my friends that I could make a 35-yard-field goal. I played soccer all my life. How hard could it be? I had soccer patches stitched onto a duffle bag and everything.

I left the kick … short (though it was good from 34, I promise), and have been wrestling with my own pending mortality ever since. The end isn't always pretty. People lose their fastballs. In 1988 alone, Hall of Famer Steve Carlton had a 16.76 ERA for the Twins, and Ken Patera stumbled through a 31-match losing streak. In the case of Billy Graham, this was a forced retirement. Slick's henchmen delivered his walking papers. "Superstar" might've had something left in the tank, but he – and we – would never find out.

The World Wrestling Federation documented Graham's recovery from hip surgery in the spring of '87. On the May 30th *Superstars*, Craig DeGeorge pulled back the curtain in a Special Report. They showed footage of the operation, providing a detailed and *extremely* graphic look at Graham's innards. I didn't personally need to see how the sausage was made, but DeGeorge thought otherwise. Billy's comeback was inspirational, a testament to his hard work and perseverance, and despite the attrition, "Superstar" still maintained that incredible physique.

"The Natural" Butch Reed was also put together. The only thing bigger than his muscles was his ego, so when the beloved Billy Graham and his incredible story reentered the spotlight, Reed scoffed. The title of biggest and strongest belonged to him. In the 1980s, you settled a dispute through dance, but if there was no music, you pivoted to the next best thing. On the August 1st *Superstars*, Reed and Graham had themselves a good ol' fashioned pose down.

Who won? Well, I'm the wrong person to ask. I don't know a good pose from a bad one. I couldn't gauge proper form or mechanics. My only exposure to the bodybuilding world is a jar of unused whey protein powder buried in the back of my cupboard. Jesse Ventura thought Butch's body of work was sound, but the Glens Falls, NY crowd preferred Billy's presentation. I've seen two pose downs in my day (Ultimate Warrior and Rick Rude at Royal Rumble '89 being the other), and both ended in violence. Men are fragile beings. We don't like being told that someone has bigger appendages than us, so Reed jumped "Superstar" after the event.

Defeating Graham that November took a backseat to a more sinister plan. Butch blindsided the Hall of Famer before Billy entered the ring. Reed choked "Superstar" with his tie-dye shirt and then shifted his focus towards that surgically repaired hip. It was despicable, vile behavior that Sammartino rightly called out ("*Bologna.*"). This wasn't a match. It was a hitjob. The resilient Graham rallied, but interference from the One Man Gang derailed his comeback. Gang hit him with three 747 Splashes before Don Muraco charged in to make the save, clearing the ring of Slick and his goons. First Responders hurried to the aid of Graham, working with urgency to get "Superstar" on a stretcher and out of harm's way.

I thought there was an unwritten rule about stretchers, like how you can't bunt to break up a no hitter. Beating an opponent so badly that he required a stretcher was tolerated – the examples are endless – but you never continued the attack once the injured wrestler was *on* the stretcher. Butch Reed and Gang showed no such decorum. Muraco did all he could, but twice Slick's men pummeled Graham when medical personnel attempted to carry him out. The second time, Gang pancaked "Superstar" with another 747 Splash, like a kid jumping on a pile of leaves while his dad was stuffing them into lawn bags.

The timing of the attack was calculated. This assault occurred right before the inaugural Survivor Series, where Graham was set to team with Hulk Hogan, Paul Orndorff, Ken Patera, and Bam Bam Bigelow. An episode of *Prime Time* later replayed the horrific events, and moments after the clip ended with Graham screaming in agony, Monsoon (callously) added:

"Perhaps the World's Champion better look for another member of his team."

(*Prime Time*, November 19th, 1987).

Damn. While the rest of the world mourned Graham's career, Gorilla encouraged the Hulkster to hit the waiver wire. Billy Graham did not compete in the 1987 Thanksgiving extravaganza (DNP: Hip). He never wrestled again.

CANADA'S GREATEST ATHLETE?

> Name: "Iron" Mike Sharpe
> Height: 6'4"
> Weight: 283 lb
> From: Hamilton, ON
> Career Record: None of your business

"He has had a bad forearm for nine years. You might say his recuperating powers stink."

– Gorilla Monsoon (*Prime Time Wrestling*, July 28th, 1986).

At one point in my life, I claimed to be the greatest *No Mercy* player on the planet. I expected others to bow down just because I won in Championship Mode with Essa Rios. (My friend later bodied me with Steven Richards, so I pivoted to the 'World's Greatest Ping-Pong Player'). So, I can relate to Mike Sharpe's candor. I get where he's coming from.

With respect to Gene Kiniski, the crown has always topped the head of one "Iron" Mike Sharpe. In a nation of 40 million people, the grizzled vet dubbed himself "Canada's Greatest Athlete" and who were we to question that level of self-confidence. Bret Hart was the "Excellence of Execution," sure, and "The best there is, the best there was, and the best there ever will be," but we're talking *athlete* here. There's a difference, albeit a subtle one, like when Vanilla Ice explained to MTV that the bass line of

"Ice, Ice Baby" wasn't *quite* the same as Queen and David Bowie's "Under Pressure."

In an era of hot takes, we're gonna buck the trend. We're going against the grain. We are going to settle this debate not through raised voices and opinions masked in half-truths, but with thorough research and undeniable facts.

So, who really is Canada's Greatest Athlete?

Wayne Gretzky

Brantford, ON's native son holds, ahem, a handful of NHL records.

Case For

- NHL Leader in Career Goals (894)
- NHL Leader in Career Goals, Including the Playoffs (1,016)
- Single-season leader in Goals Scored (92)
- NHL Leader in Career Assists (1,962)
- NHL Leader in Career Assists, Including the Playoffs (2,222)
- Single-season leader in Assists (163)
- NHL Leader in Career Points (2,856)
- NHL Leader in Career Points, Including the Playoffs (3,238)
- Single-season leader in Points (215)
- Career Hart Trophies (9)

Case Against

- Never defeated (David) Sammartino at the Broome County Arena in Binghamton, NY on September 9th, 1987.

Steve Nash

The pride of British Columbia, Steve Nash evolved into one of the best pure point guards of the modern era.

Case For

- The 2005 and 2006 NBA MVP
- 8-time NBA All-Star
- 3-time First-Team All-NBA
- 5-time NBA Regular Season Assist Leader
- #4 on the All-Time Assists Leaderboard (10,335)
- Member of the NBA's 75th Anniversary Team

Case Against

- Never reached the Quarterfinals of the 1988 King of the Ring Tournament

Gordie Howe

Born in Floral, Saskatchewan, Mr. Hockey's influence on the sport is undeniable.

Case For

- 23-time NHL All-Star
- Played 26 NHL seasons
- Second in Career NHL Goals (801)
- Second in NHL Career Goals, Including the Playoffs (869)
- Most Consecutive 20-goal seasons (22)
- Oldest player to ever play in the NHL (52)
- Career Hart Trophies (6)

- Has a bridge named in his honor (The Gordie Howe International Bridge)

Case Against

- Zero victories over the young upstart, Lanny Poffo.

Ben Johnson

The Scarborough, ON sprinter was the fastest man on the planet in 1987 and 1988.

Case For

- Won 100m gold at the 1987 World Championships
- Won 100m gold at the 1988 Olympic Games

Case Against

- Later stripped of his medals for doping

But you know who didn't get caught for cheating? Do you know who once discreetly pulled a foreign object from his leather forearm sleeve, belted Brady Boone for the 1-2-3, *and* got away with it? The pride of Hamilton, Ontario, that's who. Sharpe was a bigger bully than Busick. Just ask the youngster Steve Gray, who had his toupee ripped off by "Iron" Mike. Sharpe then held the hairpiece over his head like a spoil of war (Gray later sued the toupee manufacturer, as documented on the August 27th, 1984 episode of *Tuesday Night Titans*). Mike may have lost a match or two along the way, but no one's perfect. What beloved protagonist is? Gretzky, Howe, Nash, Johnson, they were all terrific, some of the best at what they did, but only "Iron" Mike Sharpe notched victories over the likes of S.D. "Special Delivery" Jones. He battled the up-and-comer Sivi Afi to countless 15-minute time limit draws, and he reached those great heights while injured.

He competed with a pesky forearm injury that dogged him throughout his entire career (Sharpe and Cowboy Bob Orton must've gone to the same lousy, low-rent orthopedic physician). Mike never got healthy. He always wrestled hurt. Imagine what he could have achieved with two healthy wings.

Occam's razor suggests that the simplest answer is often the correct one. I buy that. The numbers are right here in front of us. Wayne, Gordie, both strong candidates, both guys were considered, but the moniker belongs to only one. There will be no title change on this day. History will NOT be made.

Your winner ... and STILL ... Canada's Greatest Athlete ... "Iron" Mike Sharpe.

THE KEN PATERA STORY

"You're not going to walk right up the ladder to the World Wrestling Federation top. If I gotta get every member of my family and make sure you're mentally, physically, and financially busted, I'll do it. All you ever concerned yourself with was pressing weights, pressing weights, and all you're good for now is pressing license plates.

Well, I'll tell you something pal. You never brought me a championship. You never brought me nothing."

– **Bobby Heenan** (*Superstars*, **May 2nd, 1987**).

In the spring of '87, Olympic strongman, Ken Patera, returned to the ring after a two-year prison sentence. I wanted details on the arrest, but the internet, like Luscious Johnny V, is a fountain of misinformation. Who's pushing an agenda? What sites can you trust? Who's looking at you with a straight face, telling you that Dustin Diamond and the Beastie Boys' Mike D. are indeed brothers? Trying to sift through fact and fiction was a hopeless endeavor, a futile exercise that left me no closer to the truth than when I started. After weeks, no, months of research, I found only one trustworthy resource; just one lone news outlet who wouldn't spin the story. If I wanted to know the truth about Ken Patera's past, I had to focus on the present. An old Christmas present that is.

I dusted off my copy of Coliseum Video's *The Ken Patera Story*.

(Ok, ok, I re-watched it on the Network. Just go with it).

Investigative journalist "Mean" Gene Okerlund gave us the lowdown. Late one snowy night, Patera was hungry – no crime in that. He went to a fast-food chain, but the place was closed. So instead of just trying another restaurant, he and an unnamed co-conspirator allegedly threw a rock through the establishment's window. Break glass in case of emergency is usually set aside for fires, so these guys must've really been hungry. The cops were called to their motel and a fight ensued.

"In these days of rapists, kidnappers, and murderers plea bargaining for a fraction of their sentences, or even getting off scot-free, Patera was sentenced to two years in prison. There were many that felt a first-time offender, a man who represented his country in international competition, should not have received such a harsh sentence."

– "Mean" Gene Okerlund (*The Ken Patera Story*, **1987**).

The root cause of the arrest is why I think Coliseum Video got it right – and where every other outlet who reported the story missed the mark. *The Ken Patera Story* theorized that the Olympian's behavior can't be isolated to one, singular incident. His actions weren't merely an outlier. Ken Patera was being carefully groomed. That night's events were the culmination of gradual manipulation, a calculated transformation from American hero to monster masterminded by none other than "The Weasel" Bobby Heenan. Bobby was to blame, you see. Bobby made Ken Patera this way. The strongman got recruited to the dark side under the guise of empty promises, and when things got heavy, when things got real, "The Brain" left Patera holding the bag.

But, Dave, surely Heenan called up Patera while he was in prison, right?

No phone calls.

Ok, well, Bobby at least sent him a letter or two, no?

No letters.

Well, maybe Heenan prefers a more direct approach. He probably visited Patera in-person?

No visits.

Ken left prison with a higher purpose. His freedom wasn't enough. The redemption of Ken Patera required the total elimination of bloodsucking vultures like Bobby Heenan.

But first, a debate.

On May 2nd, Okerlund emceed an animated discussion between Heenan and Patera. Bobby left his civility at the door, calling the powerhouse an "ex con" at every turn. Ken, to his credit, accepted responsibility. He paid his debt to society. He had every right to move on, but his manager's lack of accountability really gnawed at him. Why couldn't Heenan see that his influence played a role in the incident?

"I'm a businessman. I'm not a babysitter. And what you do outside the ring, you big, big ex con punk, is your business. Not my business."

Not exactly the apology Patera hoped for. Heenan continued with a tirade so heinous, so despicable, that I can't even put it into words.

Can you try, Dave? You can't leave us hanging now. What did Heenan say?

Seriously, I can't put it into words. His entire rebuttal was bleeped out, and a message flashed across the bottom that read, *"The producers have been forced to censor Mr. Heenan's remarks due to their heinous nature."*

Like I said, it was heinous.

The debate went off the rails. Bobby attacked Patera with his belt, whipping his former family member into the corner. The onslaught, though, wouldn't last. Patera was a U.S. representative at the '72 Games, a former Intercontinental Champion. He turned the tables, wrapping Heenan's own belt around his neck and tossing him across the ring.

I don't know if Ken Patera's story got a satisfying conclusion. He sought an apology, or at the bare minimum, an acknowledgement from the stubborn Heenan that he could've handled things differently. Ken got neither. Patera's retaliation on debate night left "The Brain" in a neck brace for months. It wasn't the public admission of guilt that Patera sought, but it would have to do.

THE U.S. EXPRESS AND THEIR TERRIBLE, HORRIBLE, NO GOOD, VERY BAD DAY(S)

> **Event:** World Wrestling Federation at the Philadelphia Spectrum (Philadelphia, PA)
>
> **Match:** The U.S. Express (Champions) with Capt. Lou Albano vs. The Dream Team (Challengers) with "Luscious" Johnny V
>
> **Date:** August 24th, 1985
>
> **#1 Song on This Date:** "The Power of Love," by Huey Lewis and the News

I told my wife I want to be cremated. I have my reasons, none bigger than the potential of a zombie apocalypse. The last thing I want to do is rise from underground and terrorize the living. Figure I won't be much of a threat to mankind if I'm a lump of ashes in one of Paul Bearer's urns. In pro wrestling, though, even ashes have been weaponized. At This Tuesday in Texas, Hogan blinded the Undertaker with the remnants of someone's remains, which is as low as it gets. Hulk literally threw Taker's grief back in his face, but a win's a win, I suppose. It was cheap, but I picked Oddjob in *Golden Eye*, so I can't really throw stones.

Wrestlers capitalizing off a foreign object isn't a novel concept. Countless titles have changed hands as a result. The British Bulldogs lost the tag belts thanks to Jimmy Hart's megaphone. The Nasty Boys won the titles with the help of Jimmy's motorcycle helmet. Strike Force was undone by Fuji's cane and the Ultimate Warrior took a scepter to the head at Royal Rumble '91. The list goes on and on. Perhaps no team, though, suffered worse foreign object luck than the U.S. Express. Mike Rotunda and Barry Windham got clipped not once, but two separate times in 1985 thanks to manager interference. As if overcoming cagey duos like Sheik and Volkoff or the Dream Team wasn't difficult enough, the U.S. Express' title defenses were sabotaged by outside factors beyond their control. It's like leading a race in *Mario Kart*. You're making sharp turns. You're dictating the pace, but then hear the ominous sound of a blue shell heading your way. In a controlled environment, in a match where managers were banished to the dressing room and the contest was decided solely based on wrestling ability and tag team cohesiveness, I'd take the U.S. Express over the field. Freddie Blassie and "Luscious" Johnny V couldn't dethrone the U.S. Express by taking a passive approach, so they did what any effective manager would do. They got their hands dirty.

At WrestleMania I, Sheik and Volkoff were under siege, reeling from a fiery Barry Windham onslaught. The MSG crowd roared in approval, but there are no timeouts in wrestling; nothing Blassie's men could do to stem the tide. Rotunda drop kicked the former World Champion outside the ring, as the official struggled to maintain any semblance of order. Mike wasn't the legal man, and the ref correctly reprimanded him. That was Freddie's opening. With the official's back turned, Blassie handed his cane to Sheik. The Iron Sheik cracked Windham and Volkoff flopped on him for the cover.

Okerlund: *"In a very controversial match..."*

Blassie: *"What do you mean controversial? He pinned him right in the center of the ring, didn't he?"*

Okerlund: *"Where's that cane of yours?"*

Blassie: *"What cane? I didn't have no cane."* (WrestleMania I, 1985).

I admired the U.S. Express' resolve. Despite the miscarriage of justice (h/t Gorilla), the duo rebounded and recaptured the belts on the July 13th, 1985 edition of *Championship Wrestling*. (You may have missed it. The impressive win was overshadowed by Live Aid, which took place the same day and had an estimated viewership of 1.9 billion).

Now it was Johnny V's turn to screw over the American heroes. Blassie created the blueprint; all "Luscious" had to do was follow it. Windham hit Greg Valentine with a running bulldog, but Beefcake broke up the count. This brought Rotunda into the fray. (I've always advocated for two officials in tag team title matches, and this contest only strengthened my case). While the official admonished Rotunda (again), Johnny V handed his cigar to Beefcake. Brutus treated Windham's eyeball like an ashtray, blinding the champion in horrific fashion. Valentine then measured him with a big elbow and stole the win.

The U.S. Express never recovered. You start to think that the universe is against you. Getting screwed once is a coincidence. Twice is fate. Defeating the Dream Team and Johnny V two separate times in six-man action (once with Hillbilly Jim, another with Captain Lou Albano) provided little consolation, and the team disbanded shortly thereafter. Rotunda would later try to recreate the magic. He recruited Danny Spivey to form the American Express, a cheap knockoff of the U.S. version, the *Superhuman Samurai Syber-Squad* to Rotunda and Windham's *Power Rangers*. It didn't work, and by February of '87, the American Express was finished too.

The Recruit

> Event: *Championship Wrestling* (Poughkeepsie, NY)
>
> Match: "Macho Man" Randy Savage vs. Aldo Marino
>
> Date: July 6th, 1985
>
> #1 Movie on This Date: *Back to the Future*

(*Editor's note: This chapter discusses the managerial recruitment of "Macho Man" Randy Savage, not the 2003 spy thriller starring Al Pacino and Colin Farrell*).

Vince: *"The 'Macho Man,' Randy Savage, who is quite a competitor. Making his World Wrestling Federation Debut … a colorful robe there … A well-built young man, Bruno."*

Bruno: *"Yes he is, I'll tell you. He has made quite a reputation for himself. I hear a lot of great things about him. Not too pleasant as far as his style. He's a very good wrestler, but a very mean individual. But he certainly has been a winner and is well known all over the world."* (WWE 2014).

I, too, know what it feels like to be wanted. A few very, *very* small colleges recruited me to play tennis. (Think Michael Chang with Andre Agassi's hairline). I had a lot to offer, and not just a middling forehand and a weak second serve. These schools recognized that. And while I appreciated coaches telling me what *I* could bring to their program, I was more interested in hearing about what these schools could *give me*. I've seen *Blue Chips*. Neon Boudeaux got a car. Butch McRae's mom got a house, and Western University boosters bought Ricky Roe's dad a tractor. No one offered me shit. I'm not greedy. I didn't need a tractor. I didn't even need a lawnmower, but I also didn't see the harm in these schools greasing the wheels with an envelope full of cash or *Sunday Night Heat* tickets.

The recruitment of "Macho Man" Randy Savage was a bit more competitive. In an era where every wrestler with a bad attitude had representation, here was an honest to God free agent — and a 5-star one to boot. Savage was the total package: speed, athleticism, an in-ring IQ off the charts. World Wrestling Federation managers salivated over his potential. Who wouldn't welcome Savage into their stable? The guy had everything. Randy could've been a cat person, and even Matilda would've looked the other way. His debut brought out all the blue bloods: Mr. Fuji, Blassie, Heenan, Jimmy Hart, and Johnny V, the best of the best, managers with résumés a mile long. They congregated outside the ring to get a closer look, appearing friendly and amicable, just a bunch of colleagues talking shop. They exchanged pleasantries, but I questioned their sincerity. Managing was a cutthroat business. Everyone was looking for an edge. Deep down you knew these fountains of misinformation were dying to bad mouth the other if given the chance.

"Randy, baby! It's me, Jimmy Hart, baby, the Mouth of the South! I know he's devious, baby, I know, I know Mr. Fuji's credentials, but what about his man, Don Muraco! Why wasn't he at WrestleMania!? He was sitting on the sidelines, baby! Lemme tell you, Macho Man, lemme tell you, that would never be you in the Hart Family, baby! Baby, your star would shoot straight to the top — straight to the top! Put on your swim trunks, Macho Man because you'll be swimming in gold, baby! Swimming! Jimmy Hart promises you that!"

You think Blassie or Heenan wouldn't have trashed the other guys in a sales pitch? Over a business lunch with Randy, Johnny V would've called every one of his fellow managers, 'Grandma'. They knew what was at stake. These guys drooled over Savage's work, and, boy, was he impressive. Every move from the "Macho Man" was a thirst trap. Each running clothesline or flying elbow drop elicited comment after comment from Savage's horny Reply Guys.

"Good morning beautiful."

"The pink tights and yellow boots suit you!"

"You always turn a good day into a great one, my love!"

The managers joined Savage inside the ring following the match. They watched in awe, as Randy further flexed his dominance. He tossed Marino outside the ring for shits and giggles, and then flattened him with a double axe handle from the top rope. Blassie grinned from ear to ear, clapping in delight. I've never seen someone so proud. These managers were the top talent evaluators in the game, and they had seen wrestlers bigger than Randy Savage, but perhaps not better. The following week on *Championship Wrestling*, Savage appeared as a guest on *Piper's Pit*. He didn't hide his intentions. He called out the champion, Hulk Hogan, and no amount of pandering could have ingratiated someone more.

When the managers flooded the ring, Bruno commented, "Here comes Blassie. He'll be the first one to open his big wallet to see if he can get this guy" (WWE 2014). It was an astute observation. Superstars like Randy Savage didn't grow on trees. You built your stable or family around guys like him. "Macho Man" wasn't a complementary piece. He was the foundation. Managers knew they'd just witnessed the next big name in wrestling.

Or, like Randy Savage would don on future tank tops, "Hulk Who?"

Uncle Elmer's Wedding

> **Event:** *Saturday Night's Main Event* (East Rutherford, NJ)
> **Match (Made in Heaven):** Uncle Elmer and Joyce's Nuptials
> **Date:** October 5th, 1985
> **Guest Count:** 8,000 (It was a big wedding)
> **#1 Song on This Date:** "Money for Nothing," by Dire Straits

Jesse Ventura: *"It looks like two carp in the Mississippi River going after the same piece of corn."*

Vince McMahon: *"Alright, Elmer planting one on Joyce! There's a little hug from Hillbilly Jim as well. 'Mean' Gene playing them out of there. This was – this was fabulous. This was something very, very special, Jesse."*

Ventura: *"Where's the slop bucket? I'm getting sick."* (*Saturday Night's Main Event*, October 5th, 1985).

Dearly beloved, we are gathered here today in the presence of family, Hulk, Andre, and Captain Lou to celebrate the joining of this man and woman in the unity of marriage …

That's right. Dust off your gaudiest cummerbund. We got a wedding to attend.

On the second ever episode of *Saturday Night's Main Event*, that lovable ol' galoot, Uncle Elmer, got hitched. This momentous occasion holds a special place in my heart. Years ago, a buddy edited Uncle Elmer's Wikipedia page with the tidbit, "Dave was the ring bearer for Elmer's wedding," and I wore that badge proudly. For 48 hours (per the internet anyway), I was part of television and World Wrestling Federation lore before the Powers That Be over at Wiki undid my boy's handywork. This night wasn't your run-of-the-mill Saturday programming. Televised weddings were a rarity; this being the first one on broadcast TV since Tiny Tim tied the knot with Miss Vicki on *The Tonight Show* in 1969. (Tiny Tim would gift Uncle Elmer a ukulele, and later appear on Jerry Lawler's *King's Court* during the July 17th, 1993 *Raw*).

Weddings sandwiched between wrestling matches present some challenges. Andre attended, but later teamed with Tony Atlas against King Kong Bundy and Big John Studd. He watched the ceremony in a pair of red trunks and boots, a formal ensemble on par with a Canadian tuxedo.

And Elmer?

Minutes before he exchanged vows, Uncle Elmer wrestled! He squared off with ring veteran, Jerry Valiant, which gave me crippling anxiety. I hyperventilated into a paper bag during ring introductions.

"I can't believe Elmer risked injury right before his wedding," I said to my dog, who was equally horrified. He barked twice in agreement, then went back to licking his penis.

I get wanting to collect one more winner's purse to help subsidize the cost of the reception, but geez, aren't we burning the candle at both ends here? Who wrestles the day of their wedding? Who takes that kind of risk? Uncle Jesse went skydiving the morning of his nuptials and I hated that, too. Also, Valiant was no slouch. Jerry was a former world tag team champion! He was more than capable of chopping the big pig farmer down to size. One patented sleeper hold, and Valiant would've changed his moniker from "Gentleman" to the "Wedding Crasher." Elmer would dispatch Jerry quickly (a record-breaking six second victory), but still, it was an unnecessary risk.

Now, it wouldn't be a wrestling wedding without a bit of controversy. In November of '99, Stephanie McMahon and Test's wedding was derailed, because – surprise – Steph had already married Triple H at a drive-thru chapel in Vegas. Elmer and Joyce's nuptials were smooth sailing in comparison, but not without an appearance from residential shit starter, Roddy Piper. I've never attended a wedding where the officiant asked if anyone objected, but I guess it's a thing, or was a thing anyway. "Hot Rod" had some opinions.

"There is no room here for romance and wrestling. I object. There is no room here for a pig farmer in the ring marrying anybody during a wrestling match. I say that, 'You stink, you stink, and the whole damn wedding stinks.'"

Despite the objection, the couple said their 'I do's.' They had a low-frills reception, a country hoedown type deal (Totally Elmer and Joyce if you knew them). Perhaps the MVP on this night, though, was the Poet Laureate, Lanny Poffo. He recited an original piece at the reception *seconds after* losing a tag team title match. He watched a victory slip away as his partner Tony Garea submitted to Greg Valentine's figure four. Then, drenched in sweat and still in his gear, he sprinted to the wedding hall and regaled the guests with a poem. And he did it all with a smile on his face. Poffo was a pro's pro, and a friend's friend. With the wounds fresh, I would've forgiven Lanny if he snuck in a potshot about Garea's weak will – or weak legs in this case – but Poffo was a better man than me.

All in all, it was a beautiful night, and a wonderful ceremony. We were all witnesses.

(Uncle Elmer and Joyce tied the knot at the 6:18 mark).

The Legion of Doom and Rocco

"You know, this is the best thing that ever happened. I really like this. I think this is the best thing to ever happen to the Legion of Doom. Rocco! Let me bring Rocco to the ring. So that you will never forget your past."

– Paul Ellering (*Superstars*, June 27th, 1992).

It was a strange pairing. The biggest and baddest tag team of all time parading around with a puppet. Hawk and Animal were violent individuals, so I'm not gonna make any cracks about Rocco ... but seriously, fellas, what was with the puppet? You don't hear Vin Diesel introducing Jeff Dunham as his co-star for *Fast and Furious 11*. The Beverly Brothers calling LOD, "The Legion of Sissies," was the exception, not the norm. Opponents feared Hawk and Animal, and for good reason. If I'm wandering around Chicago, lost, and needing directions, I'm certainly not asking the two guys wearing spiked shoulder pads. Unless you were a linebacker in Sega Genesis' *Mutant League Football*, I didn't see the need for the spikes, but I also wasn't going to tell Hawk and Animal how to accessorize. In the arcade game, *WWF WrestleFest*, the Legion of Doom are your reigning tag team champs in Saturday Night's Main Event Mode, because even Technos, the game's creator, respected LOD's greatness.

Upon their arrival in the summer of 1990, Hawk and Animal notched win after win, systematically turning the tag team division into dust. Their rivalry with Demolition was demonstrably one-sided, like how Aaron Rodgers had a "rivalry" with the Bears. They steamrolled Fuji's Orient Express over and over, and discarded Power and Glory in under a minute at WrestleMania VII. On the June 27th, 1992 *Superstars*, manager Paul Ellering took the boys back to their old stomping grounds. LOD had captured the tag titles at SummerSlam '91 (defeating the Nasty Boys) but got clipped by Money Inc. in February the following year. I understood Ellering's thought process. A quick trip home, a little chicken soup for the soul. After the championship loss, Hawk and Animal needed to hit the reset button. They had to rediscover their love of the game, like when Hans' brother, Jan, gave Bombay a timely reminder in *D2: The Mighty Ducks*.

Turns out, LOD's old home had been demolished. Whoops. The reason why was never provided, but I'm guessing real estate tycoon Paul Christy purchased the land for some luxury apartments. Hawk and Animal rummaged through a demolition site, wandering through piles of debris, and the homecoming looked increasingly like a fool's errand. But then Ellering spotted something. Buried under the rubble was a ventriloquist dummy who was the childhood friend of Young Hawk and Young Animal. A friend who practically raised the two; a friend who taught them right from wrong. A puppet, like your Hulk Hogan or Ultimate Warrior Wrestling Buddy, or that gorilla named Davy, who took his orders from a talking walnut so it wouldn't be your bad thing. The puppet, named Rocco, meant the *world* to Hawk and Animal. He was the guy Legion of Doom "toasted to all those nights." Rocco was their everything, their best friend and confidant. (Pay no mind, though, that LOD left this guy to rot in their abandoned home).

"Thanks for being a pillar of support all these years, Rocco, but we recently discovered girls and made the wrestling team."

Hawk tosses Rocco in the dumpster – *Toy Story 5: Rocco's Revenge*.

Ellering and LOD promised to clean Rocco up, rescuing him from a near certain death. If you look closely at the motorcycles from their Wembley Stadium entrance later that summer, you'll even notice a "Who

Saved Who?" bumper sticker. Now, I didn't care for spruced up Rocco. He didn't have a trusting face. There was something off. You think Rocco wasn't talking shit about you as soon as you left the room? You know if you got one drink in him, Rocco was running down the entire tag team division.

Bushwhackers: Too dumb.

Beverly Brothers: Too soft.

Natural Disasters: Too slow.

Nasty Boys: Smell like shit.

High Energy: What's Frankie's deal anyway?

Paul stuck to his word. Rocco accompanied LOD down to ringside, supervising the proceedings while dressed like one of the Outsiders (S.E. Hinton's version, not Hall and Nash). He didn't offer much from a tactical standpoint, but it's probably tough to focus with Ellering's hand up your ass. I didn't see Rocco's value add, and candidly, I don't think grown up Hawk and Animal did either. The Legion of Doom lost like one tag match in a year and a half. Life after Rocco was prosperous; LOD was thriving. When Ellering resurrected Rocco, he figured the dummy would be a good reminder of Hawk and Animal's roots, a symbol of their humble beginnings.

Eh, The Legion of Doom was doing just fine on their own.

Rocco's final appearance was on that SummerSlam '92 motorcycle. Nobody ever saw him again, and no one really seemed to care.

The Hart Foundation

Fighting for Pride, and Only Pride

> Event: SummerSlam 1989 (East Rutherford, NJ)
>
> Match: The Hart Foundation vs. The Brain Busters (Champions)
>
> Date: August 28th, 1989
>
> Attendance: 20,000
>
> On This Day: You may have missed SummerSlam because you were playing the recently released Sega Genesis (August 14th).

On the December 1st, 1984 edition of *Championship Wrestling*, Big John Studd and Ken Patera wrestled Andre the Giant and a mystery partner, who turned out to be …

Pausing for dramatic effect …

Still pausing …

…

…

…

S.D. Jones.

Womp womp. Patera backdropped Special Delivery over the top rope, and that was that. S.D. laid outside the ring for a half hour, leaving Ken and Studd to cut Andre's hair. I don't think Jones was the partner the crowd expected or wanted to see walk through that curtain. For wrestling fans, being let down is an occupational hazard. It's included in the job description and almost 40 years later, ol' S.D. remains an inside joke amongst my friends.

"Dave, I'm bringing a surprise guest tonight."

"Anyone but S.D. please."

The Hart Foundation can relate to disappointment. The closest I got to the WWE was seeing Maven at a mall meet-and-greet, but battling the tag champs on a major pay-per-view in the wrestling equivalent of a spring training game had to be deflating. From '88 through '93, the tag titles were defended every year at SummerSlam *except* 1989. According to "The Body," our boots on the ground, the non-title stipulation stemmed from a simple timing issue.

"I believe it was because they weren't the champions when the match was signed. This match was signed ahead of time before the Brain Busters won the titles, so there was no title to put on the line."- Ventura (SummerSlam, August 28th, 1989).

I suppose that's iron-clad? I guess match contracts have as much flexibility as a blood oath. On the July 29th *Saturday Night's Main Event*, Tully and Arn defeated Demolition for the belts in a two-out-of-three-falls contest. After the title change, pundits devoted a lot of airtime to the SummerSlam non-title stipulation. Roddy Piper and Monsoon discussed the Brain Busters' potential strategy on the August 7th *Prime Time*. "Hot Rod" hypothesized that Heenan would instruct Arn and Tully to not show anything – run a vanilla-style offense, perhaps even wrestle the contest at half-speed to avoid any potential injury. Gorilla countered. A passive approach against the dangerous Hart Foundation would lead to a sure-fire loss, and an inevitable title shot for Bret and Jim down the road. The Brain Busters couldn't duck everyone, though. Death, taxes, and champions are required to defend their title every 30 days. Yeah, Heenan's men could hide behind the cloak of a well-timed contract signing for one night, but

Demolition and their rematch clause, the Powers of Pain, the Bushwhackers, and the Fabulous Rougeaus were all lurking in the shadows. That's a lot of heavy artillery.

On the following week's *Prime Time*, Gorilla pressed Heenan on the stipulation.

Monsoon: *"Why isn't it a title match?"*

Heenan: *"Because I don't feel the Hart Foundation deserves a title match. How do you like that?"* (*Prime Time*, August 14th, 1989).

Just so we're clear, a manager does *not* have that authority. Neither did WCW's Bret Hart when he dubbed El Dandy as the #1 contender to his United States Championship. In the final *Prime Time* before SummerSlam, it was Piper's turn to antagonize Heenan. He called Bobby a 'chicken,' an insult that cut deeper than when my prom date's little brother said I looked "like the guy from Smashing Pumpkins." (The fuck?). "The Brain" didn't take the bait. He again alluded to the timing of the contract. Then, with Intercontinental Champion Rick Rude by Heenan's side, the mild-mannered Monsoon came crashing in with a mic drop.

"I got a better answer. He doesn't want to lose two championships on the same night." (*Prime Time*, August 21st. 1989).

Ok, Gorilla. I see you.

"This is a tremendous challenge for the Hart Foundation. In a way, they are in a no-win situation. If they win, they don't win the titles. It would put them in line for a title shot, but if they lose, they may not see a title shot for the next year." – Jesse Ventura.

Nostradamus wore boas. Ventura's words proved to be prophetic. The Hart Foundation loss dropped them from that #1 contender spot. They walked into East Rutherford with everything to lose, and seemingly nothing to gain. Fighting for pride only takes you so far.

Bret and Jim would regain the tag titles – eventually. 364 days later.

The Boston Bunkhouse Battle Royal

> Event: World Wrestling Federation at the Boston Garden (Boston, MA)
>
> Match: The Bunkhouse Battle Royal
>
> Date: January 3rd, 1987
>
> Attendance: 13,067
>
> #1 Song on This Date: "Walk Like an Egyptian," by The Bangles

"The ring has been specially reinforced for this matchup."

— Gorilla Monsoon (WWE 2023).

Thank you, Gorilla.

Bunkhouse Battle Royals differed slightly than your prototypical throw 'em out contest, and it wasn't just the $50,000 prize at stake. Prior to the special attraction, we were told that wrestlers can wear whatever they want. Well, you don't need to tell me twice. I'd be working over Jimmy Jack Funk in mesh shorts and a hoodie. Attire aside, the match was standard battle royal fare. It was like a department potluck. Companies can dress it up as 'different' and 'fun,' but it's just another way to have employees eat lunch at their desk. I'm not sure where the 'Bunkhouse' piece fit in, though I suppose a "Dress Down Battle Royal" didn't have the same ring. These matches were in their infancy in January of '87, but wrestlers evolved. They'd later push the envelope. At the February 20th, 1988 Bunkhouse

Battle Royal in Pittsburgh, Ken Patera brought a chainsaw to the ring and I can appreciate the resourcefulness. (Officials took the chainsaw from Ken once the bell rang, but still. It was worth a shot).

- I try not to judge people on appearances, but Tama wore a WrestleMania 2 t-shirt, which was an immediate red flag. He had no chance.
- Sika wore an undershirt.
- It was strange not seeing King Kong Bundy in his customary black singlet. He looked like the lead singer from Smash Mouth in his bowling shirt. Still, The Walking Condominium had to be considered a favorite, button down and all.
- Reserve left guard, Don Muraco, wore a generic #64 jersey. Don't, however, let the basic threads fool you. Earlier in the night, Monsoon surmised that no one in 1986 put more wrestlers in the hospital than the "Magnificent One."
- Dick Slater wore his own "Rebel" t-shirt, like a middle seat plane passenger just dying to tell you about the importance of states' rights.
- Hillbilly Jim wore overalls. Creative.
- "The Anvil" wore sweatpants. No judgment here.
- Lord Alfred Hayes called Mike Rotunda "one of the dark horses here." Eh, I'm fading Rotunda and his Florida Gators tee. Same with Haku (a Chicago Bears shirt). Come on, fellas. At least pander to the locals and dig up a Ray Bourque or Andre Tippett jersey.
- Greg "The Hammer" Valentine wore tights and a white tank top, like an old man mowing his lawn at 7 A.M.
- Mr. Fuji gave off those 'CEO on Casual Friday' vibes. He wore jeans and a blazer.

- Blackjack Mulligan was like Superman. He only owned one outfit: blue jeans, a red shirt, and boots.
- I couldn't make out Pete Doherty's t-shirt, but you just knew the Duke of Dorchester was a union guy.
- "Ace" Bob Orton self-promoted. He wore a blue tee with "Cowboy Bob Orton" in white letters. The shirt was cool as hell, and I *need* one.
- Corporal Kirchner wore army fatigues. Were you expecting something else?
- Scott McGhee sprinted right over from spin class in his turquoise tights and a white hoodie.
- Lanny Poffo understood the assignment. He dressed like a knight, with the helmet and full suit of armor. Monsoon, a vocal critic of masks due to their hindrance of a wrestler's peripheral vision, did though question if Lanny could see out of his face plate.

~ ~ ~

The final three were Mulligan, Bundy, and Doherty, with the latter two forming an alliance. They put the boots to Blackjack in the corner. The Duke then obliged when Bundy instructed him to climb to the top turnbuckle. But once Pete reached the middle rope, Bundy dumped him on to the floor.

Fuckin' Bundy.

Monsoon: *"Aw, look at that, he suckered him from behind."*

Hayes: *"Bundy got rid of Doherty. That was really a treacherous act."* (WWE 2023).

If you can't trust King Kong Bundy to split a $50,000 prize, then who can you trust? Doherty didn't take the double-cross lying down. He reentered the ring, chair in hand. He popped Heenan's man square in the back to no effect, but the distraction allowed Mulligan to wallop Bundy with his cowboy boot.

Your Winner: Blackjack Mulligan.

Third Intermission

Don't Try This at Home

(We interrupt this program to discuss tag team finishers).

When I was 11 or so, my friends and I tried to give each other powerbombs. The powerbomb was *thee* finisher of the 1990s. Anybody who was anybody used the powerbomb. Diesel did it, Sid used it, Vader had one in his arsenal, and, of course, Razor Ramon had his own variation. Trying to readjust your fellow 5th grader's lumbar was a rite of passage, like buying a CD from Columbia House or first discovering Cinemax's late-night programming.

Delivering a powerbomb, though, was impossible. I was a cruiserweight. I weighed like 52 lbs. I could barely lift a ream of paper over my head, let alone my buddy Jason. Powerbombs were briefly replaced by piledrivers (clearly a much safer endeavor), but no one was too keen on putting their head between the legs of a gaseous classmate. Matches mostly consisted of punches and kicks, with the occasional incidental eye gouge or ball tap. No one ever took a pin. No one put anyone over, and it made booking the 5th grade territory a complete nightmare. Matches only ended in submission, and that's because this kid Eddie learned all these pressure points from his military uncle.

While writing this book, I probably watched over 500 tag matches. I wouldn't categorize myself as a tag team specialist per se – I'm no Ricky Morton – but I now fancy myself an expert. It's commonplace now, but not every duo back then had a defined finisher. Like, I watched the Bolsheviks lose a lot – like A LOT – though I did catch a handful of wins. They didn't have a finisher. They didn't put their opponents away with, just spitballin' here, their patented "Hammer and Sickle." Volkoff and

Zhukov won with like a clothesline or a well-placed knee lift or something. I made a note of teams who had a specific finisher, something they went back to the well with time and time again. I then created another column with the header, "Could my friends and I have done this?"

So without further ado, here is a list of tag finishers ranked from, "Yeah, we could've pulled that off," to "Oh, hell no."

10) The Battering Ram (The Bushwhackers): Absolutely! It's fun for all ages. When I got my high school diploma, I did the Bushwhacker dance right off the stage to a minimal pop. Guess there weren't too many Luke and Butch fans in attendance.

9) No Name (The Natural Disasters): It was their singles finishers in no preset order. Typhoon had the big splash, and Earthquake, the seated senton. You didn't grow up in the 90s unless you hit your friend with an impromptu splash while they're lying on the floor playing *ToeJam & Earl*.

8) Hart Attack (Hart Foundation): I'm not entirely comfortable with this finisher landing outside the top-7, but the rest of the list comes with a "Don't Try This at Home" disclaimer.

7) Demolition Decapitation (Demolition): The only way this move ends is with a broken nose or someone grabbing their larynx ala Ricky Steamboat. Not recommended.

6) *La Bombe de Rougeau* (The Fabulous Rougeau Brothers): Like a Hart Attack, but one brother (usually Jacques) would leap from the top rope crotch-first. Watch out for the ceiling fan in your mom's living room.

5) A tie: The Rocker-Plex (The Rockers) and The Power-Plex (Power and Glory): I can't endorse any move that begins with a suplex. The one plus here, though, is that kids *only* wore jean or cargo shorts, so the *suplexer* has plenty of pockets to dig into for leverage. Still – don't try this at home.

4) The Spike Piledriver (The Brain Busters): The rest of the list is interchangeable. The (spike) piledriver is universally banned but looks incredible. Tito Santana got hit with one at WrestleMania V, and two years later thought he was a bullfighter.

3) The Steiner DDT (The Steiner Brothers): Just your run of the mill DDT from the top rope. What could go wrong? I can't even put the star atop my Christmas tree without stumbling off the step ladder.

2) Doomsday Device (The Legion of Doom): Just don't.

1) The Shaker Heights Spike (The Beverly Brothers): Abort, abort. The Shaker Heights Spike begins with a backdrop and ends with the other brother ramming the guy's head into the mat on the flight down. On the February 6th, 1993 *Superstars* (the same episode where Yokozuna put "Hacksaw" out of commission), Blake and Beau almost decapitated the youngster, Pete Christie.

Just stick to the battering ram, kids.

(We now return to our regularly scheduled programming).

Papa Shango and the Yellow Bile

> **Event:** *Superstars* (Syracuse, NY)
> **Match:** The Ultimate Warrior vs. Brian Knobbs
> **Date:** May 16th, 1992
> **Attendance:** 4,500
> **#1 Movie on This Date:** *Lethal Weapon 3*

"I'm out of here, McMahon. I don't want nothing to do with this guy."

– Mr. Perfect (*Superstars*, May 30th, 1992).

You and me both, Perfect. Papa Shango scared the bejesus out of me and not even R.L. Stine could've dreamt up someone so sinister. Shango was a Voodoo practitioner, a mystic who mastered the dark art of black magic. He tortured his opponents, and not just in the physical sense. Papa attacked their psyche, preying on their greatest fears through spells and curses. Then he finished them off with a devastating … shoulder breaker. Foes weren't battling a mere mortal. They didn't have to *only* conquer a 6'6" 330 lb powerhouse. They had to overcome the supernatural, and how do you game plan for an opponent that invokes the spirits?

His whole presentation made you uneasy. Shango wore a bone necklace and carried a human (?) skull to the ring. (I have a complicated relationship with human skulls ever since I first saw the music video for Nine Inch Nails' "Closer"). On that May 30th *Superstars*, he slipped into a hypnotic trance, the first step in summoning his powers. What followed was mass hysteria. The lights turned off inside Syracuse's War Memorial, as blood curdling screams from the crowd filled the darkness. When the lights came to, opponent Brian Brieger's feet were on fire. That's not a metaphor. The youngster was being burned alive, feet first. You'd think that arson would warrant an immediate suspension, but maybe Tunney figured that any disciplinary action would be an infringement on Shango's right to religious freedom.

On the June 6th *Superstars*, even the amicable, usually off-limits "Mean" Gene Okerlund fell victim to Papa's sadism. After interviewing the mystic, an identifiable brown goo poured down the wrists and hands of "Mean" Gene. His knees buckled, paralyzed with fear as Shango looked on and admired his handiwork.

No one was off limits. That's what differentiated Shango from everyone else. 1988 Andre the Giant was vicious, but he only had malice for Hogan (and later Jim Duggan). I didn't live in constant fear of the 8th Wonder of the World digging his meat hooks into my trapezius muscle. With Papa Shango, though, everyone was a target. If he'd put a curse on Okerlund, then who else? You? Me? Sean Mooney? I didn't want to suffer a similar fate, so when Howard Finkel or someone told me that exciting World Wrestling Federation action was coming to *my* area, I kept my mouth shut. I didn't go begging my parents to take me to the Philadelphia Spectrum. Let some other kid get hexed. I had to look out for the guy in the mirror.

On May 9th, Shango cursed the Ultimate Warrior, but the former champ seemed unfazed. He said as much as he prepared for his upcoming match against one half of the Nasty Boys. McMahon echoed similar sentiments on commentary, but Voodoo spells are like edibles. They'll hit you, eventually. On May 16th, the Ultimate Warrior got the full brunt of Shango's spell; it just took a minute. While fending off Jimmy Hart's men,

Warrior lost his wristband. This brought Shango to ringside. You see, possessing an article of clothing belonging to your subject expedites the process. It's like going to the DMV. It really helps to have all the necessary paperwork.

Warrior took care of Knobbs and while he celebrated, Papa reappeared. Shango slipped into that familiar trance, the skull in his hand swaying from side to side as his body convulsed. Suddenly, Warrior collapsed off the apron. He clutched his stomach, writhing in pain. McMahon, an amateur gastroenterologist, made an initial diagnosis.

"Certainly hope it's not appendicitis or something."

Mr. Perfect knew better.

"No, he put a curse on him, McMahon! Look at him! He took the wristband! I don't know too much about Voodoo, but I'm gonna tell you right now, McMahon. The curse has been placed on the Ultimate Warrior."

(*Superstars*, May 16th, 1992).

As medical personnel attended to him in the back, the Warrior projectile vomited yellow bile. McMahon suggested that everyone gets sick from time to time, but I'm no dummy. This was too much of a coincidence. Warrior didn't eat some bad oysters. Papa Shango had summoned the spirits, and not even the Power of the Warrior had immunity from that.

Jim Neidhart: The Final Boss Before Hogan

> **Event:** Saturday Night's Main Event (Des Moines, IA)
> **Match:** "Macho Man" Randy Savage vs. Jim "The Anvil" Neidhart
> **Date:** May 27th, 1989
> **#1 Movie on This Date:** Indiana Jones and the Last Crusade

"You want Hulk Hogan's belt? You gotta get through me."

– Jim Neidhart (*Saturday Night's Main Event*, May 27th, 1989).

Ok then. The Savage/Anvil match wasn't your run-of-the-mill singles contest. Its circumstances were one of the more peculiar things I witnessed in my *Saturday Night's Main Event* rewind, and I, hand to God, watched Jimmy Hart race the Junkyard Dog down a water slide. This match had shockingly high stakes. The "Macho Man," the former World Champion, a former Intercontinental title holder, couldn't simply avenge his WrestleMania V loss to Hulk Hogan. No, no, no. If he wanted redemption, if he wanted the Hulkster back in the squared circle, he first had to beat ... Jim Neidhart?

Savage was World Champion for an entire year. He beat Andre. He beat Akeem. He beat Conquistador #1 (or was it #2?). What else did the guy have to prove? King Kong Bundy got a title shot at WrestleMania 2, and all he had to do was break a few of the Hulkster's ribs. Yet the "Macho Man" was held to a different standard. I'm not a big supporter of the automatic rematch clause, but sheesh, if there ever was a time to validate it. Despite the Championship Committee yanking Savage's chain, the conditions attached to this match were universally agreed upon. Savage was the #1 contender, technically, but if, and only if, he satisfied the requirements in the fine print.

"Beat 'The Anvil' or else."

It seemed arbitrary, and the question, "Why Neidhart?" was never answered. Why did Randy have to beat a tag team specialist to secure his spot atop the list of contenders? Did Hogan dispatch Raymond Rougeau before WrestleMania V on a Coliseum Video exclusive I've never seen? I just ask for consistency. If I were Savage, I'd have screamed bloody murder. "This isn't fair to Flair," etc, etc. I would've taken my gripe to the Nextdoor app. All my neighbors would've heard about this bullshit. Savage, to his credit though, didn't balk. He's a better man than me. Randy took the detour in stride. Perhaps he realized that you can't fight city hall, or maybe he knew that "The Anvil" was a fish out of water without Bret.

"We're gonna climb that first step of the mountain. Get past Jim Neidhart, and then on to Hulk Hogan."

Ventura didn't get it either. He theorized that Hogan feared Savage; that Neidhart was an obstacle planted by the champion. "The Anvil" wasn't a legitimate World Title contender. He was just a warm body, another impediment to Savage's quest for a rematch. Neidhart could've just as easily been Luke or Butch, or Marty or Shawn, or any member of the scrappy Young Stallions.

Vince McMahon, of course, wouldn't engage. He refused to entertain Ventura's conspiracy theory.

"I don't know about that, Jesse."

(Before you poo poo Ventura's hypothesis, let me remind you that Hogan threw the same speedbump at Goldberg. On the 1998 *Nitro* where Hollywood lost the WCW World Title to Goldberg, he first made the challenger get past fellow nWo member Scott Hall).

Well, Savage won. His newly obtained manager, "Sensational" Sherri, paid immediate dividends. A Sherri distraction led to a "Macho Man" flying elbow drop, and no one kicked out of that* **.

*Except Hogan.

**Ok, the Warrior, too, and more on that later.

The 1990 Survivor Series and Great Expectations

(Part I)

> **Event: Survivor Series 1990 (Hartford, CT)**
> **Date: November 22nd, 1990**
> **Attendance: 16,000**
> **#1 Movie on This Date:** *Child's Play 2*

"The kids are going nuts. They love 'em."

– Roddy Piper (Survivor Series, November 22nd, 1990).

It would be disingenuous to say that the 1990 Survivor Series ruined my Thanksgiving. I didn't watch the pay-per-view live, and I wouldn't see it until months later after a video store rental. (I had to first work off a debt to my parents after losing a rented copy of NES' *Ninja Gaiden*).

BUT I'm retroactively pissed, so yes, that year's Survivor Series *did* ruin my Thanksgiving. I've been part of some doozies, too. When I was in second grade, dinner was sabotaged after an undisclosed relative asked my sister's college boyfriend how often he masturbated. (I didn't know what 'masturbate' meant, but it sure sent the night into a tailspin). Someone broke into my car on another. They stole my entire steering column, and I had to tip my cap at their incredible efficiency. All that remained were three loose wires that looked like the strands of hair atop Homer Simpson's head. Still, I rank Thanksgiving '90 right up there with the worst of 'em because

I can't separate the holiday from the wrestling extravaganza. The big Survivor Series reveal was so deflating that I'm throwing that year's Turkey Day right into the trash. Does my mom's wonderful green bean casserole deserve to be lumped in with that Survivor Series flop? No, probably not, but them's the brakes. Don't blame me. Blame the Gobbledy Gooker.

In the weeks leading up, a mysterious giant egg began appearing on World Wrestling Federation programming. I was intrigued, I admit. Unless you stumbled across an ostrich or two, you never saw a big ass egg. Speculation about its contents grew. Aside from who, or what, was inside, I had some additional questions, mostly logistical. How did the egg travel from arena to arena, and why was everyone so convinced it was gonna hatch at Survivor Series? Alas.

Okerlund asked some young fans about the egg, and they offered their haphazard theories. Balloons, money, etc – all valid guesses. One, though, suggested the Ultimate Warrior was inside. Now, I don't make a habit of trashing the opinion of a *literal* youngster, but what the hell would our World Champion be doing inside an egg? How's he supposed to defend his title? Other guesses from the kids "Mean" Gene polled had more backing from the scientific community. A snake (sure), a lizard (possible), a dinosaur (guess we can't rule it out), and a turkey (winner, winner).

The unveiling of the Gobbledy Gooker before the night's main event generated a collective "What the fuck," and a square dance with Okerlund in the center of the ring did nothing to suppress the negativity. People had talked themselves into an actual wrestler hiding out in that egg (or at least a balloon or two). The Hartford crowd didn't want a turkey. They never asked for a turkey, and their booing echoed those sentiments. We should've seen this dud coming. Ric Flair from WCW, a returning King Kong Bundy, what were we thinking? Who spread those rumors? What evidence, outside our own lofty, unrealistic expectations, gave us any inclination that an actual human being was living inside an egg for a month? Ric Flair was a limousine riding, jet flying son of a gun. He *literally* told us how he traveled from city to city, and it wasn't via eggshell.

It wasn't just that the Gobbledy Gooker was lame. It also overstayed its welcome. After a hoedown, the turkey started running the ring ropes – killing time – like how every host of a Zoom call starts with, "How's the weather where you are?" Was the Gooker showing off? Were fans supposed to be impressed? We had just watched Sgt. Slaughter steamroll through Nikolai Volkoff and the Bushwhackers with a series of elbow drops and clotheslines, so excuse us for not fawning over the Gooker because he did a summersault.

Next time, leave the surprises to Ted DiBiase.

THE 1990 SURVIVOR SERIES AND GREAT EXPECTATIONS

(PART II)

> Event: Survivor Series 1990 (Hartford, CT)
>
> Match: The Dream Team (Dusty Rhodes, Koko B. Ware, and the Hart Foundation) vs. The Million Dollar Team (Ted DiBiase, the Honky Tonk Man, Greg Valentine, and a Mystery Partner)
>
> Date: November 22nd, 1990
>
> Attendance: 16,000

Now this is how you do it. This is how you execute a surprise reveal. The ol' "Mystery Partner" bit always delivers. (Well, almost always. We'll set aside DX introducing Savio Vega at 1998's No Way Out: In Your House). You had Hogan at Bash at the Beach '96. Owen introducing Yokozuna at WrestleMania XI. It's always a big name. Like, if you're DiBiase, you're not keeping everyone on pins and needles if your fourth is Buddy Rose.

My friend and I took this premise and applied it to a bachelor/bachelorette/birthday party coming to an area near you. The best man/maid of honor plans a bar crawl, and each new location has a mystery pal there waiting. Think of the anticipation, the buzz surrounding each stop. Will it be a buddy from high school? A college friend who flew in from the west coast? It's the ultimate hot tag situation. Starting to wear down three bars in? No worries. You just gotta get to O'Leary's, because the groom's college roommate, Ned, has a row of shots lined up and is more fired up than Rick Martel after a Tom Zenk tag.

The Million Dollar Team's fourth member was, of course, the debuting Undertaker, who was led to the ring by a baby-faced, red-faced Brother Love. The 'mystery partner' tactic was already a cunning move by DiBiase – keep your opponents on their heels – but its success was magnified by Taker's anonymity. No one knew who he was. You can't prep for a ghost. Hell, even the Vegas books were scratching their head. The Undertaker wasn't even on the board for Ted's partner. Books listed Saba Simba as the clubhouse favorite at +250.

In the weeks leading up to the event, the Dream Team said all the right things. "It doesn't matter who 'The Million Dollar Man' gets, we'll be ready, etc, etc," but of course it matters. It's all that matters. DiBiase played his hand to perfection, and his in-game tactics proved equally crisp. The captain didn't trot out one half of Rhythm and Blues to begin the match. He went right to Taker, this lethal, seemingly impervious to pain mercenary. It was like a new age baseball skip calling for his closer in a high-leverage situation, regardless of the inning. The Undertaker delivered. He dispatched the Bird Man moments in with an inverted piledriver that only Gorilla Monsoon knew the name of.

Monsoon: *"He just got nailed with a Tombstone."*

Piper: *"What is it?"*

Monsoon: *"I think it's a Tombstone, and it's over."*

Good guess, Gorilla. And here I thought only Mike Tenay knew every wrestling hold in existence.

The Undertaker would be eliminated via count out, but not before recording a second elimination. He would go on to have a moderately successful career from there.

"Three years to be a champion. It's a long time."

Hogan: *"When I think about climbing into the ring with Andre the Giant, I'm nervous. If this was under normal conditions, if it was the old Andre, that, you know, was kind –"*

Andre: *"Old Andre?"*

Hogan: *"The old Andre, man. The old Andre that was different."*

Andre: *"I'm still the same."*

Hogan: *"Yeah, well everyone can see you've changed, otherwise you wouldn't have went ahead … you never would … have gotten back into wrestling with Bobby Heenan."*

Andre: *"He's the only one who backed me up. None of you guys showed up that day."*

– The WrestleMania III Press Conference (WWE 2020).

In the season 3 premiere of *Boy Meets World*, Cory tries to muster up the courage to ask out (the way out of his league) Topanga. Cory's best friend, Shawn, who pulled more strange at John Adams High than the entire student body combined, capitalizes on Cory's procrastination and asks out Topanga instead. The controversial move leads to a discussion about Bro Code and what's within the pale. Who, or what, is considered off-limits? What boundaries cannot be crossed?

~ ~ ~

In January '87, Hulk Hogan's best friend demanded a world title shot.

The sudden break-up of Hulk and Andre created a bitter, highly publicized feud. This rivalry wasn't a slow burn. There weren't warning signs that we somehow missed. When Andre poured champagne on Hulk after his championship win over the Iron Sheik in January 1984, that celebration came from the heart. There was no ulterior motive, no hints of jealousy. It stemmed from genuine love. Be your best friend's hype man. Celebrate their successes. Andre was thrilled for the Hulkster and neither hindsight nor revisionist history will make me believe otherwise, but a late '86 suspension hearing clouded in mystery triggered a chain of events that culminated in the most anticipated wrestling match of all time. The abrupt end to their friendship naturally led to finger pointing, but truth was, no one was absolved from blame. Everyone was complicit. Everyone played a role.

First, some historical context. In the spring of 1986, Jack Tunney, that doofus, suspended Andre for missing a few matches. The President always played his suspension card without much rhyme or reason.

Miss a few dates? Suspension.

Dabble in chemical warfare? Here's a world title shot.

(What? What else would you call Killer Kahn's green mist?).

Bobby Heenan had pressed Tunney for a strict punishment. It behooved his Family to have the Giant out of the picture. Later that summer, though, a new masked team from Japan debuted in the World Wrestling Federation. The Machines, composed of Giant Machine and Super Machine, were led by Lou Albano, and set their sights on Studd and Bundy. While the men under the masks were unknown, Giant Machine – admittedly – looked a bit like Andre. Heenan was convinced of it, but others weren't sold. On an episode of *TNT*, Monsoon and Heenan debated his identity.

Monsoon: *"You know, Gene, I've been to Japan, oh, I don't know, dozens of times over the years."*

Okerlund: *"Beautiful country ..."*

Monsoon: *"And those are two of the biggest Japanese guys I've ever seen."*

Heenan: **"**Monsoon ... please! Don't try to – don't try and pull a number on these people. They're not bright anyway. But don't try and make it look any worse than it is. That is Andre the Giant. You know it, you know I know it, and these poor humanoids know it." (*Tuesday Night Titans*, July 23rd, 1986).

Tunney confirmed that suspended wrestlers could not compete under masks or pseudonyms. If Heenan was correct, if Bobby could prove the Giant Machine's identity, then Andre would be banned for life – like a real lifetime ban, not the Danny Davis version. But a hunch isn't proof. Conjecture doesn't earn you a conviction. "The Brain" may have been right, but a lack of evidence torpedoed his case, and the Machines would quietly depart from the Federation in November with their privacy still intact.

Then came the hearing. On the November 29th episode of *Superstars*, esteemed international journalist, Gary Davie, delivered some breaking news from London. President Jack Tunney had overturned Andre's suspension.

Hmm.

On December 6th, Ventura pressed Tunney for more details. The President was tight-lipped, only offering that the hearing was "most unusual" and "bizarre." Very helpful, Jack. I've gotten more dirt from the WCW Hotline. The following week, Jesse tracked down Heenan. "The Brain" talked up the Giant's size and athleticism, saying that Andre had every right to be back in pro wrestling. He elected not to divulge anything further.

Curious indeed.

The circumstances surrounding Andre's abrupt reinstatement triggered more questions than answers. There was little time to unearth the truth, however, because the aftermath of this hearing rolled right into awards season. In January of '87, President Tunney got himself on a trophy kick and handed out more hardware than a Little League coach. On *Piper's Pit*, he presented Hulk Hogan with a massive award for his three-year reign as champion, as if his own cartoon, universal accolades, and over 1,000 days of winner's purses weren't enough. The Hulkster was honored, gushing all over himself with a self-congratulatory speech. The Oscars would've played music to expedite the champ's exit stage right, but Andre thankfully appeared to break up the love fest. He shook the champ's hand with a grip tighter than maybe you'd expect from two longtime friends. The Giant prefaced that embrace with the ominous line:

"Three years to be a champion. It's a long time."

Tunney was back on *Piper's Pit* the following week. Now, it was the Giant's turn to receive his flowers. President Jack had another award, though, this one considerably smaller. For 15 years, Andre ran the table. He hadn't lost a match since 1972 (!), yet all that got him was this sorry ass trophy from Tunney. I've seen people awarded brand new Kias for way lesser feats. Despite the dog shit participation award, the Giant was all smiles. He was gracious. He waved to and acknowledged the East Rutherford, NJ crowd. He prepared to say a few words – they were to be modest and brief I'm sure – but before he could utter that first syllable, the champion arrived. Hulk grabbed the mic. The champ hijacked the Giant's acceptance speech, placing the spotlight right back on himself. Andre didn't cause a scene, but he curiously didn't stick around either.

On the January 31st edition of *Piper's Pit*, "Hot Rod" introduced guest, Jesse Ventura. "The Body" acknowledged the optics. He commented on the disparity of each respective trophy, and much to my chagrin, made the argument that size matters.

"Look at them. Here's Hogan's trophy. It looks about one foot bigger, don't it? Andre's looks a foot smaller. Now you take a look at the records, man. Andre the Giant, fifteen years he has never been beaten. Fifteen years. Hulk Hogan has been champion for three years and believe me, he has ducked some people."

(*Superstars*, January 31st, 1987).

(Jesse also speculated that Hogan's trophy was made of real gold, and the Giant's was fake. Despite my extensive research, however, I cannot confirm the authenticity of each respective award).

Roddy and Jesse agreed to bring both men on *Piper's Pit* the following week. Let's clear the air. Neither Hogan nor Andre had publicly disparaged the other. Up to this point, the perceived tension between the two – if you can even call it that – was dramatized by the Federation's talking heads, a bunch of Skip Baylesses and Shannon Sharpes speculating and theorizing. Was it odd that the underhanded Heenan appeared at Andre's hearing? Of course – no argument here, but don't a victim's loved ones often show up at a parole hearing? The giant had battered his Family for years. Bobby had a vested interest in the proceedings. Was the disparity between trophy sizes strange, if not insulting to Andre? Absolutely, but counterpoint: Tunney was a complete idiot. Don't confuse the President's alleged malice with blissful ignorance.

When the two men met on *Piper's Pit*, we assumed a laugh and a handshake. Our two heroes would assure "Hot Rod" and Ventura that this trophy nonsense was much ado about nothing. Andre was back. Hogan was the champ, and the good times would roll. 1987 would be just like 1986, which was just like '85, which took its lead from '84. All was right in the world, you see.

Except Andre wasn't alone. Where there's smoke, there's a weasel. The Giant had aligned himself with – of all people – Bobby fucking Heenan. Only the most morally bankrupt wrestlers joined his Family: Studd, Bundy, blonde-haired Patera – these guys were assholes and bullies, pieces of garbage who were the antithesis of the Hulkster's three commandments. And now Andre? *Our* Andre? The Giant had joined *him?* Hogan pleaded for answers, desperately trying to wrap his head around this new partnership.

During his three years as champion, Hogan never offered Andre a title shot. Not once. This was the crux of Heenan's argument. Now Hulk defenders (Monsoon and McMahon being the most vocal) later claimed that the Giant never asked for one. Well, that's a convenient excuse. I shouldn't have to ask my son to eat his vegetables either. Hogan *was* a fighting champion. He *did* defend his title all over the world … if those challengers weren't 7'4" and over 500 lb that is. Andre's résumé spoke for itself. He clearly deserved the opportunity, and now he demanded it.

When the Giant finally addressed the champion, he didn't rehash past wrongs. How much do I hate thee? Andre didn't count the ways. He was cold and callous, speaking to the Hulkster as if they were strangers on the street. It was just business. Could Andre have gone about this better? I think so. Should it have been a non-issue, though? Should the Championship Committee have declared him the #1 contender at any point in '84, '85, or '86? Absolutely, it was a glaring oversight.

At some point during his suspension, Heenan got to Andre. He planted the seeds of disrespect.

*Why is Hulk champion, and not you? Where is *your* opportunity?*

The Giant had gotten complacent, too comfortable in his position as Hogan's wingman. Heenan's sales pitch was both a wakeup call and a kick in the pants. Did Andre want more? Did he want the World Championship, a title that would vindicate his awesome talent, or was he content with the status quo? Consider one year prior. While Hogan headlined WrestleMania 2 in Los Angeles, the Giant was ushered like cattle to Rosemont for a battle royal. A man undefeated for 15 years left to toil with NFL players far below his stature. Being best friends with the champion has its perks, but it also has its limits. You don't reach the top by being a sidekick.

Andre didn't join the dark side. He just finally stepped out from Hulk's shadow.

AND THEN THE RAINS CAME

> Event: Wrestling at the Hiram Bithorn Stadium (San Juan, Puerto Rico)
>
> Match: The Killer Bees vs. Barry "O" and "Iron" Mike Sharpe
>
> Date: October 19th, 1985
>
> Attendance: 1,200
>
> #1 Song on This Date: "Take on Me," by a-ha

"Look at the sheets of rain coming down here in San Juan, Puerto Rico, as the sky has literally opened up, but this tag match ... still going on! Jumpin' Jim Brunzell, B. Brian Blair taking on "Iron" Mike Sharpe and Barry "O". Should be a beauty.

Although, the footing has to be very treacherous out there right now. So the wrestlers could break a leg very easily.

— **Gorilla Monsoon (Love 2013).**

In 1985, the World Wrestling Federation held an outdoor event at a baseball stadium in San Juan. The first time I watched this match, I thought it was doctored footage. No way this could be real. Why were the Killer Bees wrestling Barry "O" and Mike Sharpe in a Splash Zone? Rain pelted the four competitors, flooding the ring with a relentless barrage of precipitation. This wasn't just a drizzle. This was a Category 4 hurricane.

The tag contest was the fifth match on the card and the first three finished without a hitch.

- Tony Atlas def. Steve Lombardi
- Ricky Steamboat def. Moondog Spot

- Wendi Richter (with Cyndi Lauper) def. The Spider (with the Fabulous Moolah)

The trouble began in match #4. The skies opened when champion Hulk Hogan squared off against longtime rival, Big John Studd. Studd lost via count out, when he pulled a Craig David and chose to walk away from the troubles in his life. Fans shared the same sentiment. The brave few who remained (and there were only a few) used umbrellas and chairs to shield themselves from the onslaught. It didn't work. Gorilla did play-by-play underneath a plastic tarp. He also doubled as the ring announcer. Ventura, according to Monsoon, was "conspicuous by his absence," but I think Jesse looked at the weather report and bailed.

I don't know why there wasn't a rain delay. I don't know why officials didn't throw a covering over the ring and wait out the storm. In Little League, coaches huddled us into the snack bar, and we'd feast on soft pretzels and slush puppies. The inaction didn't make sense, but I also watched Ronnie Garvin and Greg Valentine try to pin the other countless times in their Royal Rumble *submission match*, and that didn't make sense either. You couldn't conjure up worse wrestling conditions. The guys moved in slow motion. They took careful, deliberate steps like a blindfolded Sandra Bullock in *Bird Box*. I don't blame them. Monsoon has been known to exaggerate *slightly* ("They're literally hanging from the rafters"), but when he said the ring was covered in one to two inches of rain, I believed him.

The combatants worked an opponent's arm, isolating a body part. Options were limited. The downpour grounded Jumpin' Jim, neutralizing his biggest strength, the dropkick. It was like watching Mega Man trying to navigate the Ice Man stage. If Dr. Wily's sinister creations didn't get ya, the slipping and sliding would. B. Brian Blair never found his footing and the ref fell on his ass. Barry "O," in particular, struggled with the conditions. He slid on two separate occasions. I don't think he had the proper boots, like when I shovel snow from my driveway in New Balances. The Bees won with an inside cradle. Sharpe made a half-assed attempt to break-up the pin, but I don't think his heart was in it. Sure, the winner's purse would've been nice, but a long, hot shower and some dry clothes sounded a whole lot better.

The World Wrestling Federation wouldn't return to the island for another twenty years.

The Jumping Bomb Angels

The Innovators of Offense

> Event: 1987 Survivor Series (Richfield, OH)
>
> Match: The Fabulous Moolah, the Jumping Bomb Angels, Rockin' Robin, and Velvet McIntyre vs. Dawn Marie, Donna Christanello, the Glamour Girls, and Sensational Sherri
>
> Date: November 26th, 1987
>
> Attendance: 21,300
>
> #1 Song on This Date: *"Mony, Mony,"* by Billy Idol

Ventura: *"What I'd like to talk about for a minute, too, Gorilla, is the women's match. Unbelievable. You know, I'll tell ya. I've seen a lot of good tag teams, and the Glamour Girls – I'm gonna go on record – they're in trouble, because the Jumping Bomb Angels are something else."*

Monsoon: *"They're championship material."*

Ventura: *"I've never seen lady wrestlers with the kind of moves they got. They're like watching a Dynamite Kid, or watching a "Macho Man" Randy Savage, or a Ricky Steamboat with those aerial moves. It was just fantastic. I enjoyed it."*

(Survivor Series, November 26th, 1987).

My baseball career ended at the age of 13. I remember the exact moment I knew I was cooked. I dug into the batter's box and stared down the big 7th grader on the mound. He threw a slow, sweeping hook, a pitch I had only seen in textbooks and on television. It defied physics, logic. It broke all accepted scientific truths and Galileo himself would've been baffled by its trajectory.

The kid had thrown a curveball. I had never seen one before – not while standing at the plate anyway. My knees buckled, like a baby calf first learning to walk.

What the hell was that sorcery? Was that legal?

I understand your plight, Pedro Cerrano. My bat, too, was afraid of curveballs. The pitcher then double downed. I flailed at his next Uncle Charlie with T-Rex arms and slumped back to the dugout. I missed the pitch by about six feet. The game evolved, but I didn't. It was Darwinism at its core, and I knew my place on the food chain.

The Jumping Bomb Angels were trendsetters. Before Noriyo Tateno and Itsuki Yamazaki's arrival, the women's division ran a largely conservative offense, the wrestling equivalent of 'Marty Ball,' where one grappler attempted to wear down the other through hair pulling and snap mares. (During the '87 Survivor Series, Ventura suggested that shaving your head would eliminate the hair pull from your opponent's arsenal, and it wasn't a bad thought honestly). There was nothing inherently wrong with the wrestlers' approach. It was just old school, like the rotary phone in the kitchen of my parents' house. It was clunky and slow, but you could still call in a pizza order with it.

It's difficult to deviate from an oft-traveled path. The Fabulous Moolah thrived with this offensive approach for like half a century, so if it ain't broke? It made sense that her challengers tried to emulate. The Jumping Bomb Angels, however, had no interest in conformity. In *Twisted Metal* terms, Tateno and Yamazaki were Mr. Grimms in a world full of Sweet Tooths. They flew around the ring, orchestrating a high-risk, high-octane style that would've been cutting edge in the 1990s, but was downright revolutionary in '87. For their Survivor Series opponents, it must've been like the first time hearing the Beatles.

Bomb Angels opponent Judy Martin got leveled with a double underhook suplex, and I'm not even sure there was a name for that move back then. It was like if you got catfished back in 2005.

"I was talking to this girl on MySpace for like nine months. We both were into Good Charlotte. But it turned out she was a 55-year-old man."

"Ah, you were internet bamboozled, eh?"

After eliminations on both sides, only the Bomb Angels and the Glamour Girls remained. Jimmy Hart's team couldn't match speed with Tateno and Yamazaki, but they weren't some geeks off the street. Judy Martin and Leilani Kai were worthy champions, a vicious blend of strength and smarts who had steamrolled the tag division since taking the belts off Velvet McIntyre and Desiree Petersen in 1985. Martin, especially, had a prolific move set. She delivered one of the first known powerbombs in the World Wrestling Federation; a move that wouldn't be executed by another superstar until WrestleMania VII, when Tenryu decimated Demolition's Smash.

Sometimes, though, it's just not your night. The Glamour Girls ran into a buzzsaw. Twice, the Bomb Angels bridged out of a pin attempt. They executed a flawless arm drag from the top rope. They multi-tasked, eliminating Martin with a flying clothesline while simultaneously taking out an intervening Jimmy Hart with a dropkick. Tateno and Yamazaki escaped the match unscathed, leaving the Richfield Coliseum as the sole survivors. Ventura's analysis was astute. The Angels' performance earned them a title shot with the Glamour Girls at the '88 Rumble, and they capitalized there too. Spare me your hairpulling. Tateno and Yamazaki captured the tag belts with a textbook double missile dropkick.

THE UNLIKELY CONTENDER

PART TWO (WRESTLEMANIA VIII EDITION)

> **Event:** *Superstars* (Amarillo, TX)
>
> **Date:** February 15th, 1992
>
> **#1 Song on This Date:** "I'm Too Sexy," by Right Said Fred

Well, I'll be damned.

"Due to the accusations made by Sid Justice alleging favoritism, as well as his recent actions in the ring, it is the decision of this office that at WrestleMania, there be not one, but two main events. The World Wrestling Federation Champion, Ric Flair, will defend his title against the new now #1 ranked contender, 'Macho Man' Randy Savage. While in the other main event, Hulk Hogan will be meeting Sid Justice."

– "Mean" Gene Okerlund (*Superstars*, February 15th, 1992).

We were shown footage of the WrestleMania VIII press conference on the February 1st *Superstars*. President Jack Tunney – taking a break from the putting green – named crony and benefactor(?) Hulk Hogan as the #1 contender to Ric Flair's World Heavyweight Championship.

The main event was set.

I was at peace with the decision. Listen, I didn't vote for Tunney. I didn't stump for Tunney, but even a broken clock is right twice a day. We could dissect the résumés of the top contenders until we're blue in the face, but the Hulkster was a worthy challenger. According to a *Little Mermaid* notebook I found while cleaning out my parents' garage, here is how I had the contenders ranked in February of '92 (Imagine this is written in a green crayon):

1. **Sid Justice:** Finished second in the Royal Rumble
2. **Hulk Hogan:** Finished third in the Royal Rumble and lost the championship under questionable circumstances at the '91 Survivor Series
3. **Koko B. Ware:** What? I loved Koko. Let me be
4. **The Undertaker:** Also lost the World Title under dubious circumstances at This Tuesday in Texas
5. **Randy Savage:** Finished 4th in the Rumble
6. **Virgil:** Vaulted up the rankings after his big DQ win over I.R.S. on the February 3rd *Prime Time*
7. **Roddy Piper:** Reigning Intercontinental Champion and thus not recognized as a true contender for the World Title

Hogan had the biggest gripe of all. I get Sid was frustrated – and I'm not here to invalidate his feelings – but Justice's pissing and moaning cost the Hulkster his title shot. Sid made some "allegations alleging favoritism," and Jack caved. It only took a little negative press for Tunney to backtrack. Stand by your decision, man. The whole thing would've blown over. The news cycle in the World Wrestling Federation was constantly influx. Sure, the backlash of the press conference would've lingered for a day or two, but another crooked ref scandal or cobra attack was always lurking around the corner. Tunney was a moron, yes, but I couldn't dwell on his incompetence, not with the World Bodybuilding Federation Championships fast approaching. Priorities, people. Now, there was some animosity between Hulk and Sid, and it's well-documented. Hogan yanked Justice out of the Rumble. Then there was the February 8th *Saturday Night's Main Event*, where Justice abandoned Hulk in their tag match with Taker and Flair. Sid later trashed the set of Brutus' *Barber Shop* (It was the *Shop*'s final segment. Brutus didn't want to deal with the insurance claims). So, I get it. The two had beef. Like a break-up, though, the best way to get back at your ex is to flourish in their absence. I can't think of a better "Fuck you, Sid, I'm *thriving*" response from Hulk then capturing the gold at WrestleMania.

(Quick aside: What a coup for Wippleman, who added Sid to his client list. The lone wrestler in his stable in the summer of '91 was Big Bully Busick, so talk about an upgrade. Shoot your shot, Harvey).

On the flip side, what a stroke of good fortune for the "Macho Man." He leapfrogged the #1 and #2 contenders thanks to a Tunney overcorrection. Savage's case for a title opportunity wasn't particularly strong, and he practically admitted as such when asked by Sean Mooney about the president's decision.

"Well, I didn't like it. Bottom line, I wish it was the 'Macho Man' Randy Savage. That's me. I like me, yeah, but since I couldn't get it, I just want to let you know that there's a piece of me that realizes that Hulk Hogan probably should've got the nod anyway. Just being honest."

That's a heckuva admission. Savage was like one of those college basketball teams on the bubble pleading their case for the NCAA Tournament, but already resigned to hosting an N.I.T. game. Should the "Macho Man" have gotten the nod against Flair? Of course not, but guys have been outkicking their coverage for centuries. J.T.'s friend, Rich, was both short and an idiot, yet somehow landed Dana Foster, who was like the hottest girl in Port Washington, WI. While viable contenders, Hogan and Sid, worked out their petty bullshit, the "Macho Man," with an assist from Tunney, seized the moment and the World Heavyweight Championship.

THE MIRACLE IN TOPEKA

> Event: Saturday Night's Main Event (Topeka, KS)
> Match: Hulk Hogan (Champion) vs. The Genius (Challenger)
> Date: November 25th, 1989
> #1 Song on This Date: "Blame it on the Rain," by Milli Vanilli

"A major upset! Brains win over brawn! What an upset, McMahon! Eat your words! Eat your words! The Genius took him!"

– Jesse Ventura (*Saturday Night's Main Event*, November 25th, 1989).

The Genius – the Genius! – shocked the world when he defeated the immortal Hulk Hogan. With the ref distracted, Mr. Perfect belted the Hulkster with the World Title outside the ring and the champion couldn't beat the official's ten count.

Titles don't change hands via count out, but that doesn't diminish the Genius' accomplishment. His win wasn't just impressive. It was improbable. If you throw out two battle royals, Hulk Hogan's record on *Saturday Night's Main Event* was 24-1. His loss to Andre aired on *The Main Event*, not *Saturday Night's Main Event*, and if *Family Matters'* Carl and Harriette Winslow won't acknowledge that they had a daughter named Judy, then I'm not gonna penalize the Hulkster for a controversial defeat on a Friday.

The upset was a perfect storm. Hogan was now a movie star, fresh off his role in *No Holds Barred* and on the heels of a violent feud with his co-star Zeus, a monster of a man who had strength for days but limited mobility. Zeus and the Genius were polar opposites. The latter utilized an unorthodox style. He relied on speed and smarts and sprinkled in some textbook cartwheels. The Genius rattled opponents through irritating and flamboyant antics, baiting them into mistakes. It was like how Don Flamenco would *beg* you to throw a punch, then unleash an uppercut.

"Meh, meh, meh."

Oh, fuck off, Don Flamenco. (Also, why did Little Mac get tired so easily against him? Did he go on a bender the night before? It was infuriating).

The Genius dug deep into his bag of tricks. First, it was gamesmanship. He offered his left hand to Hulkster in a pre-match shake. Then he paused to limber up, stretching each leg over the top turnbuckle. He fought dirty; he fought intelligently. Eye gouges and rakes of the back were coupled with Moneyball concepts. He took a page from Alexandra York's playbook, crunching numbers on his scroll in search of even the slightest schematic advantage. Applying mathematical concepts mid-match may seem like nonsense, but if Billy Beane replaced Jason Giambi and Johnny Damon's production on a shoestring budget, then what's the harm in adopting those same principles?

The champ didn't take the challenger seriously. In betting terms, the outstanding question wasn't whether Hogan would win, but would he cover the inflated spread. The champion got caught looking ahead. Even Hulk's pre-match promo reeked of arrogance, apathy even.

"Besides, if he's so darn smart, how come he doesn't know, that mathematically, he can't win, brother?"

He finished off Okerlund's interview with a poem.

"Roses are red. Violets are blue. The Hulkster's a wrestler. Genius, what are you?"

It was like the high school jock laughing off a challenge from the captain of the Mathletes. Aside from Randy Savage, Hogan seemingly only wrestled giants. Literal ones (Andre) and figurative behemoths like Studd, Bundy, Big Boss Man, Akeem, Kamala, and Zeus. He wrestled the 320 lb Sika on a 1987 *Saturday Night's Main Event*, and that was only like the 8th biggest guy he locked horns with.

Hogan (naturally) took the loss poorly. He was like Jim Duggan in that regard (or my son when he loses in Candyland). The champ chased the Genius back to the dressing room because heaven forbid the youngster get a second to bask in the biggest victory of his career. Though even an abbreviated celebration couldn't damper the Genius' moment. He had done the unthinkable. The plucky, eccentric brainiac knocked off the World Champion. The Genius was the "1" in Hulk Hogan's "24 and 1."

"I Want My Country Back"

"When I reflect back, what I wanted to become – the World Wrestling Federation Champion – I didn't care who I associated with: the scum of the earth, the slime, the sleaze, it didn't matter who I chummed with. I wanted to become the World Wrestling Federation Champion at all costs. I didn't care about my family anymore. I didn't care about my friends anymore. I didn't care about my country. I turned my back on my country. I wanted to become the World Wrestling Federation Champion. I was blinded by ambition."

– Sgt. Slaughter (*Superstars*, September 28th, 1991).

No, no, no. We're not doing this, Benedict Slaughter. You made your bed so tough shit. Don't try crawling back to us now. I've seen this movie a million times. No, literally, I saw this movie in the theater. Sgt. Slaughter's early 90s career arc mirrored Jennifer Love Hewitt's jock boyfriend in *Can't Hardly Wait*. Mike Dexter has this amazing life and amazing girl but thinks the grass will be greener in college, so he dumps Love Hewitt (what a moron). He then realizes that he dumped Jennifer Love Hewitt (idiot) and grovels back with his tail between his legs.

Sgt. Slaughter morphed from an American hero into an Iraqi sympathizer, won the World Title, then lost the World Title, and by late summer of '91, all he had to his name was the lamest stable in the history of wrestling. (You're off the hook, Truth Commission). Before WrestleMania VII, we watched Sarge burn a Hulk Rules t-shirt, and those colors don't run. Yet Slaughter did. Following the aftermath of the Triangle of Terror's humiliation at SummerSlam, the former world champ ran off and slipped into seclusion. He left Adnan and Mustafa behind while he dropped off the grid like J.D. Salinger. Not only was Slaughter a shitty American; he was a shitty friend. So, yeah, I do question the sincerity of Slaughter's apology tour. Did he *really* miss the U.S. of A? Did he *really* want his country back? Or did he contemplate a bleak future with General Adnan and Col. Mustafa, the wrestling equivalents of a cheese and mustard sandwich? I've been in my basement. I know a snake when I see one. While commentators speculated on his whereabouts, the overwhelming opinion on Slaughter was good riddance. We saw snippets from American soldiers, who were elated that Slaughter got his SummerSlam comeuppance. On the September 7th *Wrestling Challenge*, Col. Mustafa – still there, still fighting – battled journeyman Bill Pierce. The broadcast spliced in an interview with Slaughter's (former?) allies, and Mustafa and the General suggested that Slaughter "retire like Schwarzkopf."

He returned from hiding about a month later, and *lookie* here. Look who suddenly rediscovered his patriotism. (You'll have to take my word for it, but I'm sarcastically clapping right now). People are conveniently the most contrite when they've hit rock bottom. The former world champion stood proudly outside national landmarks, recounting past sins while romanticizing the country he spurned. Puh-lease. Handbags on Canal Street are more authentic.

"It's a great honor for me, Sgt. Slaughter, to be standing at the base of the Lincoln Memorial. As you know, Abraham Lincoln was a forgiving man. He served this country during its darkest hours when brother fought against brother. Now I've come here because this is my darkest hour. When I let my country down, it was like I turned my back on all my brothers. Now, I have no country. I don't ever expect to be forgiven for that, but just as Abraham Lincoln took a nation divided and made it whole again, I, too, Sgt. Slaughter, need to be made whole again. But in order to do that, I need my brothers. I need my country. I want my country back!"

– Sgt. Slaughter (*Superstars*, October 13th, 1991).

Did this MF'er just compare himself to Lincoln? Slaughter's road to redemption also included stops at the Arlington National Cemetery, the Statue of Liberty, the statue of Paul Revere, and the Marine Corps War Memorial. The message was the same – I'm paraphrasing here:

"Please take me back, Lady Liberty. I can't possibly team with Adnan and Mustafa anymore."

The pandering continued into November of '91. Slaughter visited an elementary school, calling on the kids to *ten-hut* like Arnold Schwarzenegger in *Kindergarten Cop*. Our disgraced traitor then led them in the reciting of the Pledge of Allegiance. After Sarge kissed the flag and dubiously proclaimed that he got his country back, the little ankle biters showered him with hugs.

But actions speak louder than words. On the November 24th *Wrestling Challenge,* Slaughter saved the red-blooded American, "Hacksaw" Jim Duggan, from an impending attack by the Nasty Boys and just like that, a year plus crusade trashing the red, white, and blue was pardoned. While those in attendance celebrated the return of the Prodigal Son, Heenan saw through the charade. After Duggan and Slaughter shook hands, Bobby quipped, "Another marriage made in hell."

I blame the fans. They were so quick to take him back, so eager to look beyond Sarge's past transgressions. They were overly forgiving. The guy *basically* committed treason, and people have been canceled for a lot less. That's like excusing Jeffrey Dahmer's behavior, because he held open the elevator for you once. Well, I'm not that gullible. I don't forget quickly, and I don't forgive easily.

Corporal Kirchner would have never.

Unsanctioned

Give me Dave, give me Julie.

Music plays, audience applauds

In this round, points are doubled. Top five answers on the board. We asked 100 people ... Name something that is unsanctioned.

Buzz

Julie.

"Um, the game at sunrise between the Mighty Ducks and the Eden Hall Academy Varsity Team."

Survey says ...

Ding

The #2 answer on the board. Dave, still room for you. The #1 answer is still out there. Name something that is unsanctioned.

"I'm gonna say the Million Dollar Championship, Steve."

~ ~ ~

The Million Dollar Belt was an unsanctioned title. Not that you needed me to tell ya that. Commentators reminded us every thirty seconds, like when flight attendants instruct passengers to stay seated with their seat belts fastened while taxiing. The Million Dollar Title was a beautiful belt. It was an expensive belt. It just wasn't a recognized one.

DiBiase unveiled his new championship on *The Brother Love Show*. "The Million Dollar Man" had spent 1988 pursuing the World Title. He tried to buy it. Then win it. Then he gave up. Ted then attempted to save face, a 'You're not breaking up with me. I'm breaking up with you' type deal.

> *"You see, the World Wrestling Federation Championship belt is not worthy to go around the waist of an athlete of my caliber. It is not worthy of the 'Million Dollar Man.' Before me right here is a championship belt worth a million dollars."*
>
> **– (Superstars, March 4th, 1989).**

He purchased a belt instead, kinda like Kevin Durant signing with Golden State in 2016. It was a cheap way out. Ted didn't earn the title. He didn't beat anyone for it. He just commissioned one at a jeweler. It was like losing your virginity at a brothel. It counts, sure, but you bypassed all the hard work. ie: Laboring over the cover art of a Valentine's Day mix CD you made your girlfriend. A championship is a championship, though, and if Wikipedia recognizes it, so must we.

There wasn't a governing body over the Million Dollar Championship. The rules of the title, and of its defense, were loosely defined and rarely enforced. There wasn't a 30-day defense rule. There was no #1 contender. You couldn't "win" the belt from Ted because it was never up for grabs. So, on the January 20th, 1990 *Superstars*, Jake "The Snake" Roberts just stole it. He stuffed it inside the bag with Damien. Possession is 9/10th of the law, so while Wiki doesn't recognize Jake's reign, I do. Besides, everyone's cool with Mideon's European Championship tenure, and all he did was find the belt inside Shane's bag.

Two weeks later, "The Million Dollar Man" hatched a plan. He outsourced the repossession of the belt to Slick, and step one involved a sneak attack during Ted's match with Roberts. The Slickster and Boss Man pummeled "The Snake" with a nightstick and handcuffed him to the top rope. The help-for-hire correctional officer then walked the fifty feet to the set of *The Brother Love Show* (very convenient), with Roberts' bag in hand.

It was the perfect coup, right? Kudos to DiBiase and Slick. Services rendered; title belt secured. But things quickly turned sideways when the Big Boss Man planted his flag on some shaky moral ground. He was fine taking the Million Dollar belt back from Roberts because Jake had stolen it. He took issue, however, when he discovered Slick got paid for it.

What a hill to die on. Get off your high horse, dude. The Slickster isn't a businessman. He's a business, man. You think Slickster Inc. was some non-profit? Slick tried to ease the tension. He tried to pass it off as a charitable donation, a small token of DiBiase's appreciation, but the Big Boss Man wasn't buying it. After retrieving the Million Dollar Belt from the bag (and maneuvering around Damien), Boss Man put the title *back inside* and returned it to Roberts.

The Million Dollar Title was on the line at WrestleMania VI. I understand the egos at play and the thirst for competition – and I KNOW I'm oversimplifying things – but why not just steal it again? Work smarter, not harder, ya know? If DiBiase lost via a small package, what's stopping Virgil from just taking the belt anyway? Tunney didn't give a shit. Warren G wasn't there to regulate things. Just take it and catch a cab to Toronto Airport.

Well, regardless, Ted won by count out.

"Million Dollar Man gets the belt, because as you know, Gorilla, this is a non-sanctioned belt so you can win it by a count out. You can win it by a disqualification. You can win it by a pinfall or submission."

– Jesse Ventura (WrestleMania VI).

The obvious explanation here is that Ventura is fucking with us, but let's play it out. Let's assume "The Body" *is* the foremost expert on unsanctioned title bylaws. If the Million Dollar Title changed hands via count out, then was Jake "The Snake" Roberts the defending champ? If so, get your shit together, Wikipedia, and *acknowledge him.*

AND ...

If the championship can change hands via count out, then why wasn't Virgil awarded the Million Dollar Belt at WrestleMania VII?

Was that because it was a non-title match, Dave?

Stop interrogating me – I don't know. I advocated just stealing the damn thing.

Inconsistencies aside, the Million Dollar belt had a short shelf life. Ted DiBiase abandoned it in February of '92 after he and I.R.S. captured the – sanctioned – World Tag Team Championships.

The Insincerity of Bob Backlund

> **Event:** *Superstars* (North Charleston, SC)
> **Match:** Bob Backlund vs. Anthony Howard
> **Date:** April 10th, 1993
> **On This Date:** Jason Alexander hosts *Saturday Night Live*. Musical Guest: Peter Gabriel

The warning signs were right in front of us. We should've seen this coming. When Bob Backlund snapped on the July 30th, 1994 episode of *Superstars*, locking Bret Hart in the Crossface Chickenwing after a close defeat, it wasn't this spur of the moment, rash decision. Bob always had a dark side. It was like former Arizona Cardinals head coach, Dennis Green, telling reporters after a blown lead to the Chicago Bears on *Monday Night Football*, "They are who we thought they were!"

Consider a detective or mystery show. The formula is the same. The episode's investigation in the first twenty minutes focuses on some unsavory type, someone with a bad attitude and a rap sheet longer than a CVS receipt. They have a checkered past, yeah, but they also have an airtight alibi. They were volunteering at the soup kitchen as part of their court-ordered community service or had multiple witnesses corroborating his or her whereabouts at the dog track last Wednesday afternoon. Either or. In the show's waning moments, we discover the guilty party was actually the nice guy, the one who had gladly answered Stabler and Benson's questions, or happily offered Jessica Fletcher help with the investigation. Turns out they were being *too nice* for a reason: They had just murdered the ski lodge innkeeper where Angela Lansbury was vacationing and wanted to throw investigators off their scent.

1993 Bob Backlund was too nice, too accommodating, and too generous of his time. Obviously, something was off. How did we ever fall for his act? He returned to the World Wrestling Federation after a nine-year absence, and, from an in-ring standpoint, hadn't missed a beat. He spent most of '93 showing off his extensive amateur wrestling background, pinning a long line of ham and eggers with some variation of a victory roll, twisting opponents into a pretzel for the 1-2-3. Then, and this is where the red flags should've been raised, he'd offer them some words of encouragement post-match.

"Hang in there."

"Keep your head up."

"Keep trying."

Fuck. That. Save that sanctimonious bullshit for your local pickleball league. Bob Backlund didn't care if challengers like Al Burke or Tony DiMoro improved or got better. It was all a show. His words rang hollow and dripped with insincerity. How did we not see it? In 1991, the Mountie and Jimmy Hart doused "The Hitman" with water, before electrocuting him with a shock stick. It was fucked up – it was also attempted murder – but at least you know where you stood with the Mountie.

And call me a poor sport, but if I got pinned with some like modified bridge, I'll be damned if I'm sitting through some Backlund speech. I'd have given Bob a forearm shiver after his post-match monologue. Or, at the bare minimum, done the wanking motion behind his back like when I got reprimanded by a teacher in junior high. But the shallow "Keep working hard" platitudes weren't the worst of it.

On that April 10th *Superstars*, Bob laid it on thick. He knew the cameras were rolling. After pinning Howard, Backlund morphed into preacher role and delivered his usual post-match sermon. Then Backlund wrapped his arm around Howard and ACCOMPANIED HIM BACK TO THE DRESSING ROOM! Give me a break. You already got the winner's purse, Bob. Is that not enough? You need Anthony Howard's dignity, too?

'93 Bob Backlund was a fraud, a caricature of good sportsmanship. The small nuggets of wisdom he passed on to opponents were nothing more than the shallow messages inside a fortune cookie.

'Keep trying?'

'Keep working?'

Young Anthony Howard didn't need a pep talk. He didn't need an escort back up the aisle. He needed a counter for Backlund's pinning combination, but I guess that never came up in conversation, did it, Bob?

HOGAN/WARRIOR

CHOOSE YOUR FIGHTER

> Event: Prime Time Wrestling
>
> Special Attraction: The Hulk Hogan/Ultimate Warrior WrestleMania VI Contract Signing
>
> Date: March 25th, 1990
>
> On This Date: Vinnie romances a blind girl on a brand-new episode of Doogie Howser, M.D.

"As you, Hulk Hogan ... travel to WrestleMania by conventional means, the normals you travel with experience malfunctions. As you realize that all that is left is total destruction, do you, Hulk Hogan, show self-pity? Do you, Hulk Hogan, try and reason why? Do you, Hulk Hogan, try and comfort the normals that have even more fear than you? Or do you, Hulk Hogan, kick the doors out? Kick the cockpit door down? Take the two pilots that have already made the sacrifice so that you can face this challenge.

Dispose of them, Hulk Hogan. Assume the controls, Hulk Hogan. Shove that control into a nosedive, Hulk Hogan. Push yourself to total self-destruction. As you realize, Hulk Hogan, that you are about to enter a world close to Parts Unknown ... smell it, Warriors ... Do you, Hulk Hogan, look for a place to hide? Or do you, Hulk Hogan, face that challenge?

– The Ultimate Warrior (*Superstars*, March 10th, 1990).

Despite what A&E's *WWE Biography* has you believe, I don't consider Hogan/Warrior a rivalry. They only wrestled once. Ok, twice, but the less said about Halloween Havoc '98 the better. Hogan/Warrior isn't a Team Shawn or Team Bret type deal (I'm Team Bret), where you're morally obligated to pick a side and quietly judge anyone who chooses the opposite. Between the WrestleMania VI main eventers, you may have had a lean towards one, but not demonstrably so. I loved both wrestlers and I think most young fans felt the same.

(Though the Warrior did refer to us as "normals" or "mere mortals" 90% of the time, but I'm weirdly ok with the former champ calling me 'basic').

I had a Hulk Hogan teddy bear. I also had an Ultimate Warrior Wrestling Buddy, who was ripe for full nelsons. It was an embarrassment of riches for us 90s kids, like living near both an Olive Garden and a Red Lobster. Whether its breadsticks or cheddar bay biscuits, you're gonna eat good. I wanted my favorite singles champions to co-exist in perfect harmony. I never pitted the two against each other, and it never even crossed my mind. It was Hogan and Warrior vs. everyone else. As a kid, I hated WrestleMania VI.

I didn't want Hogan and Warrior to wrestle at all.

WrestleMania main events always stemmed from personal conflict. Professional jealousy eroded Hogan and Andre's friendship. Hulk had lust in his eyes, etc, etc. The Hulkster and the Ultimate Warrior, though? Their relationship was a blank canvas. Hulk Hogan and the Warrior's paths rarely crossed before their Toronto encounter. They weren't enemies. They weren't friends, and Hulk didn't even seem fazed that the Warrior suggested he throw two dead pilots off a plane. (Metaphorically speaking of course). Heck, I'm not entirely sure they had even met until the 1990 Royal Rumble, where they shared a brief, yet electric moment. (Now, that moment *was* special – no argument here. There was a stare down, followed by a running of the ropes. The champs knocked each other out with dueling clotheslines, and the Hulkster would later throw out Warrior from behind).

Hogan's underhandedness didn't trigger any animosity, though. The Intercontinental Champion understood he was fair game. He shook off the elimination and sprinted back up the aisle like *Jackass'* Party Boy. The Ultimate Warrior didn't seek retribution. He didn't demand an explanation. He just went back to the day-to-day: Hitting the gym and whipping up on Dino Bravo.

(Quick aside: Hogan wrestled Bravo on the March 10th *Superstars*. Earthquake was at ringside in a hideous brown singlet and looked far too much like Friar Ferguson for my liking).

The title vs title match didn't originate from conflict, but rather mutual respect. They both were pillars in the community and both at the top of their game. Each superstar needed to see it for themselves, like when I chomp down on a scalding Bagel Bite right after someone says, "Be careful, they're really hot." I'm not fluent in Warrior promos, but I *think* that's what he was hinting at during the WrestleMania VI contract signing.

The Ultimate Warrior: *"Hulk ... Hogan. What lies before us in the Heavyweight Championship of the World, and the Intercontinental Championship of the World, are nothing but normal representations of why there are followers, and why there are leaders such as us. But you, Hulk Hogan, know as well as I do, that they are only receptors for the powers that we have.*

LOOK INTO MY EYES, HULK HOGAN. You see nothingness. You see no reasons for questions. You see no answers. For there is no reasoning in the thinking of the Ultimate Warrior. At WrestleMania VI, Hulk Hogan, I will take the powers of those that question, and I will take the powers of those who have no fear. As I take two and become one."

Hulk Hogan (unimpressed): *"Sign." (Prime Time,* March 25th, 1990).

(It was admittedly a bit strange to see a guy who hailed from Parts Unknown with a lawyer, but I suppose everyone needs legal representation from time to time).

What followed was a classic in Toronto. The Warrior weathered a "Hulk Up," and managed to avoid a big Hogan leg drop. He then countered with a big splash to become the undisputed champion. The Canadian crowd roared; though, I think it was because of the moment, not necessarily the result. I don't remember being ecstatic for the Warrior, or even bummed for the Hulkster.

I was just relieved it was over.

Talk Show Host

> **Event:** *Championship Wrestling* (Poughkeepsie, NY)
>
> **Talk Show:** *The Flower Shop*
>
> **Date:** August 16th, 1986
>
> **#1 Song on This Date:** "Papa Don't Preach," by Madonna

"I would like to say that you have been doing a tremendous job in my absence, and I would like to thank you for taking it over, but I'm here to take my show back. And the first thing that has to go are these damn flowers."

— **Roddy Piper, *Championship Wrestling*, August 16th, 1986 (All Out of Bubblegum 2015).**

Roddy Piper and Adrian Adonis' beef culminated in a Hair vs. Hair Match at WrestleMania III. As someone who is bald, I'm offended that there's apparently no worse wrestling fate than losing a hair vs. hair match. We're not lepers. A bald life isn't *that* bad. Adonis woke up from his nap at the Silverdome, got a look at himself in the mirror, and WAS HORRIFIED. Brutus Beefcake didn't even give him a buzzcut. He just trimmed a little off the top and sides. No matter, though. Adonis was incensed. It was a humiliating conclusion that diminished his spectacular 1986.

Months prior, the Adorable One was thriving. It wasn't just the win against Uncle Elmer at WrestleMania 2, or the count out victory over Piper on the January 3rd, 1987 *Saturday Night's Main Event*. Adonis flourished as a TV personality. The biggest names in the World Wrestling Federation lined up to appear on his talk show, *The Flower Shop*: Hogan, Heenan,

Orndorff, Muraco, Kwang, the list goes on. (Ok, not Kwang. Just wanted to make sure you were still reading). Adrian had built a brand. He had an entourage. He already had Jimmy Hart in his corner, and now he had Bob Orton. Hell, he even had prize-winning petunias. But fast-forward to March 29th, 1987, and here was "The Mouth of the South" shielding Adonis' hatchet job haircut with his sportscoat.

The Flower Shop replaced *Piper's Pit* when "Hot Rod" went on sabbatical. In Roddy's mind, the switch was temporary. Adonis was substitute teaching, like how Rod Belding took over that one Bayside history class (This was before that dick bailed on the Senior Class Trip in favor of that stewardess, Inga). When Piper reappeared, on the August 16th, 1986 *Flower Shop*, he expected a Return to Normalcy. Adonis would hand him the keys, and Roddy would reclaim his throne atop the wrestling talk show circuit. But things were different. It was like going away to sleepover camp for the summer and everyone had changed. After returning home, you learned one friend got his ear pierced, another is bragging about getting to second base, and a third is now super into System of a Down.

Perhaps no bigger shock to Piper's system was Bob Orton's new allegiance.

Adonis: *"Oh, hi, Acey."*

Piper: *"'Acey?' Did I get that right? They call you 'Acey' now?"* (All Out of Bubblegum 2015).

Cowboy Bob had been Roddy's right-hand man for years. Orton was a friend, a protector, a selfless bodyguard who put Piper's safety above his own, even while Ace struggled with his own debilitating arm injury.

Acey? They call you 'Acey' now?

It had to sting. Orton said it was just money; that Piper paid peanuts compared to what Adrian compensated him (I could not confirm Orton's salary differential at the time of this publication). While Roddy longed for the past, his friends had moved towards the future. Adonis often said that his show was so modern and cutting edge, that *The Flower Shop* was from 1995.

People change. Or, as 'Acey' said in reference to Piper's Pit on the September 27th *Superstars*, "That's old hat, daddy." The World Wrestling Federation wasn't big enough for two talk shows, and it makes you wonder how Phil Donahue and Sally Jesse Raphael ever coexisted. In the months that followed, the contention grew more heated, more personal. Sets were destroyed. Adonis and Piper lobbed jabs back and forth. Roddy, no stranger to shit talking, said that Adonis "looked like he needed a home pregnancy test" and dressed "like the curtains at a Days Inn."

Adrian left the Pontiac Silverdome disgraced and humiliated. Roddy had won. He had vanquished his talk show rival, but to quote running back Ricky Watters, 'For who? For what?' Was it all worth it? For all the back and forth over who had the superior show, neither program remained on the air after WrestleMania III. Piper retired. Adonis left quickly after, and *The Brother Love Show* would soon dominate the ratings.

Master Fuji's Betrayal

> Event: WrestleMania V (Atlantic City, NJ)
>
> Match: The Powers of Pain and Mr. Fuji (Challengers) vs. Demolition (Champions)
>
> Date: April 2nd, 1989
>
> Attendance: 18,946
>
> #1 Movie on This Date: *Rain Man*

Am I taking crazy pills? Help me understand. What am I missing? In the name of Encyclopedia Brown, what key piece of evidence am I not uncovering? When I first outlined this book, I scribbled down about forty chapter ideas; topics that I felt had to be included. Fuji's 1988 swerve was near the top. Yet this chapter is one of the *last* ones I'm writing. I've held off for so long, kicking the can down the road for two years not out of fear or apprehension, but because I expected to find a plausible explanation that I had somehow forgotten. It was only a matter of time. I'd stumble across an interview with Fuji on a *Wrestling Challenge* or something and everything would click.

"Ah! That's right! That's why the Devious One turned his back on Ax and Smash. Ax slept with Fuji's wife!"

I'd discover a key detail, a logical rationale, and scrap the entire chapter. I'd then promote the essay on Killer Khan's vast experience in Mongolian Stretcher Matches to the main roster, and we'd be back up and running. But I never found a good reason. I never heard an explanation from Fuji worth a damn. My instincts in '88 were just as sharp as they are today.

Why the hell did Mr. Fuji spurn his tag team champions in favor of the Powers of Pain?

I didn't get it then, and I don't get it now. At WrestleMania IV, he led Ax and Smash to the World Tag Team Titles, and then by Survivor Series of that year, the Devious One I guess had gotten tired of all that … winning? He aligned himself with the Powers of Pain for reasons that not even he could articulate, and willingly walked away from the current tag team champions – champions mind you, that both were dominant and adored him.

Ax and Smash *loved* Fuji. Where most managers hyped up their wrestlers, Demolition flipped the script. They always talked up the Devious One in their interviews, calling him this mastermind, this shrewd puppeteer pulling all the strings. Nobody saw the betrayal coming. How could you? There was no team dissension. There wasn't even tension. The explanation Fuji gave was always some version of this:

"At WrestleMania number four, I, Master Fuji, got you the belts. But let me tell you. After you got the belts, you had no discipline to Master Fuji. You had no want to listen to Master Fuji. So I got the Powers of Pain, bigger and stronger than you. And also, they listen to the Master Fuji. And I'll tell you, it's destined to win the World Tag Team belts and once again, Master Fuji will have belts around waist."

(*Prime Time*, March 6th, 1989).

YOU ALREADY HAD THE BELTS, MASTER FUJI! You managed the champs! They didn't listen to you? That's your gripe? Well, whatever Ax and Smash were doing, it certainly was working. Fuji did all this legwork and jumped through all these hoops – the ruses, the deception, etc – all to recapture the titles that he threw away. That's like if Hulk Hogan sold the belt to DiBiase in early '88, and the next day declared, "I'm going to win back the championship for all my little Hulksters!" This claim that Ax and Smash weren't disciplined was bullocks; nothing more than a false narrative created by Fuji to justify a terrible mistake. The move was a colossal downgrade. Fuji traded in the champs for the … not champs. At least the Vikings got 20 touchdowns from Herschel Walker after they got fleeced by the Cowboys. I get wanting a change, and the appeal of the Warlord and the Barbarian was obvious (they were a couple of powerhouses), but Master Fuji bungled this double-cross from the start.

Why con Demolition in a meaningless Survivor Series match? The execution was fine, and I suppose it was effective (The Powers of Pain were the sole survivors after all). It was the timing that was awful. Fuji should've saved this scam for a title match, right? Have some back alley talk with Warlord and the Barbarian. Instruct them to demand a title shot. Fuji then accepts on Demolition's behalf, because his men are 'fighting champions' and 'fear no team' and ta-da! Fuji is now managing the Powers of Pain, the new World Tag Team Champions.

Master Fuji made a rookie mistake, an uncharacteristic misstep from a wily veteran like the Devious One. Yeah, his scheme earned his new duo a title opportunity at WrestleMania V, but they faced a pissed off and scorned Demolition. Fuji managed to use Ax and Smash's thirst for revenge to finagle a 3-on-2 handicap stipulation into the contract, but we already discussed how those lopsided numbers are fool's gold. Fuji or not, Demolition was too damn good. Ax pinned his former manager after a Demolition Decapitation at 8:20.

(Though to be fair, Fuji wasn't the legal man).

A year later, Fuji traded in the Powers of Pain for pennies on the dollar. He sold the contracts of the Warlord and the Barbarian to the Slickster and Heenan, respectively.

The Repo Man and That One Wrestling Challenge

> **Event:** *Wrestling Challenge* (Toledo, OH)
>
> **Match:** The British Bulldog vs. The Repo Man
>
> **Date:** May 3rd, 1992
>
> **Attendance:** 6,500
>
> **On This Day:** Heavy D & the Boyz with Tupac and Flavor Flav perform on *In Living Color*

Heenan: *Now, Monsoon, are they gonna take him to a hospital now? Or just some neighborhood, run-of-the-mill vet?"*

Gorilla: *"Will you stop?"*

– *Wrestling Challenge*, May 3rd, 1992 (Monsoon Classic 2022).

In 1835, the United Kingdom passed the Cruelty to Animals Act. Along with imposing harsher penalties for the mistreatment of cattle, the bill attempted to eradicate the use of animals for blood sport. Prior to its passing, animals were freely manipulated and abused for horrific gambling ventures like bear-baiting (A tied up bear would fight multiple dogs in a pit-like structure), or badger-baiting (A cornered badger pitted against a dog in an artificial den).

While the bill covered a lot of ground, there was some ambiguity. Article III of the legislation referenced baiting or fighting involving, "Bull,

Bear, Badger, Dog, or Other Animal." 'Other animal' being the key phrasing here (The Statutes Project 2023). The Act didn't explicitly reference rat-baiting, and the 'sport' saw a surge in popularity after 1835. *Ratting* took place in another pit-like structure. A hundred or so rats were released while a dog (often a terrier of some sorts) sought to kill as many as possible in a preset time. (The "pit" is where the 'Pitbull' name is derived from). The scoring, the rules – it was all pretty official – as official as a sport whose objective was rat murder could be anyway. There was a referee and a timekeeper, and the records, even two centuries later, remain well-preserved. (For context, a bull and terrier named Jacko killed 60 rats in two minutes and 42 seconds. I know very little about rat-baiting, but I think that's elite).

Rats didn't garner much sympathy from humans. In a twisted way, *ratting* was almost a form of public service given the rodents rampant population in congested cities like London. Game organizers operated worry-free. There weren't concerns about fines or penalties. They, for all intents and purposes, were above the law.

~ ~ ~

Towards the end of 1991, anarchy reigned over the World Wrestling Federation, and I have a theory. In late '90, Jack Tunney threw the book at Rick Rude for his comments concerning the Big Boss Man's mother. The penalty didn't fit the crime. It was unnecessarily harsh, a clear example of Tunney overstepping his bounds. I think our bonehead president realized it, too. So he overcorrected. He swung the pendulum the other way. In '91, he adopted a Laissez-faire approach. Tunney got soft on crime. No action was deemed too crass. Superstars realized that Tunney wielded as much horsepower as a Chevy Spark, so without fear of repercussions, they pushed the envelope. Winning was nice and all, but attempted murder? That really got their juices flowing. All vehicles of death were considered. Weaponry?

Sorcery? Electrocution? Poison? No rock was left unturned, no option too drastic. A quick recap:

Jake Roberts' venomous cobra bit Randy Savage. The Mountie drenched Bret Hart in water, and then prodded him with his shock stick. He would later acquire a larger, industrial-sized shock stick, because temporary paralysis I guess wasn't brutal enough. This one looked like one of those Clubs that locked over the steering wheel to prevent car theft, and it contained higher voltage than Robbie Rage and Kenny Kaos. (Sgt. Slaughter took the brunt of that electrical charge on the May 9th *Superstars*).

Not to be outdone, the Berzerker of course tried to execute the Undertaker with a sword, and Papa Shango lit someone on fire.

There was so much violence around this time that you forget that THE REPO MAN TRIED TO HANG THE BRITISH BULLDOG.

(Be honest. Did you remember that? I won't judge you).

I had forgotten. I admit it. I was running through *Superstars* episodes from '92 when McMahon kicked it back to a highlight from a recent *Wrestling Challenge*.

"Oh, this is nice," I thought. "1992 *Wrestling Challenges* aren't on Peacock. Maybe it will be a High Energy match or – wait … wait, oh God, oh God, what the fuck is this? What are you doing with that rope, sir? Repo Man, put down the tow rope. PUT DOWN THE TOW ROPE."

I've seen the Repo Man use his rope to choke opponents, and to be clear, I wasn't comfortable with that either. Now he was *hanging* someone. It wasn't quite the Big Boss Man at WrestleMania XV, but still. This was fucked up. I didn't think the Repo Man walked, so the Undertaker could run, but here we were – a real life hanging, on – of all places – Sunday morning's *Wrestling Challenge*.

"Dave, it's time for church. Your dad is in the car."

"One sec, mom. Repo Man is trying to murder Davey Boy Smith."

The Bulldog was on his own. Winston was conspicuous by his absence. So, too, was Matilda for that matter. Commentary, though, didn't grasp the gravity of the situation, and Monsoon took the murder attempt in stride.

"Uh oh, lights are going out here for the British Bulldog. We're gonna need some assistance down here very shortly."

'Very shortly?' Geez, Gorilla. I've seen you more animated over Mike Sharpe grabbing a handful of Scott McGhee's tights. Help eventually came and they were able to usher the Repo Man away from ringside. As for the Bulldog? He recovered. Fortunately, his injuries were superficial – a bad case of rope burn mostly. Davey Boy would bounce back and get his revenge.

The Repo Man didn't face disciplinary action. Few did around that time. He would also tone down his behavior in later years. Repo's biggest controversy in '93 involved the repossession of the Macho Man's hat. A shitty move for sure, just not quite aggravated assault.

THE BODY SLAM CHALLENGE

PAY KING TONGA HIS MONEY

> Event: *Championship Wrestling* (Poughkeepsie, NY)
>
> Match: Big John Studd vs. Rick Hunter and Jim Powers (Handicap match)
>
> Date: June 14th, 1986
>
> Top Selling Video Game in the U.S: *Super Mario Bros.*

"Tonga, you're not getting a dime from me. Like McMahon said and you heard Sammartino and everybody else, they do not know if it was official. I'm gonna tell you right now. That was not official. Nobody is getting a dime from me and Studd."

– Bobby Heenan (*Prime Time Wrestling*, June 16th, 1986).

*****DISCLAIMER:** I'm not an arbitrator by trade, but I take my new role seriously. I promise to remain objective. I'll reject outside influences and past prejudices and rely solely on the evidence presented by Peacock and YouTube. Thank you. ***

Upon his arrival to the World Wrestling Federation, Big John Studd and then manager, "Classy" Freddie Blassie, created the Body Slam Challenge. $10K would be awarded to any grappler who could scoop up the big man and slam him down. The task proved too daunting, and the prize later increased to $15,000.

(In February of '83, Gorilla came close while wearing a black and gold #17 jersey. When I re-watched this showdown, I thought to myself, "Damn, look at Monsoon reppin' Dock Ellis," the Pittsburgh Pirates pitcher who famously no-hit the San Diego Padres in 1970 while on LSD. Alas, it was a #17 "Ayer" jersey).

Studd's record wasn't exactly pristine. Andre had body slammed Big John previously, but I guess those instances were unsanctioned, like when Rocky Balboa forfeited the championship to fight Drago in Russia. With all these asterisks and past slams stricken from the record, the contest remained intact until WrestleMania I, when Studd squared off once again with his bitter rival from the French Alps.

Let's tackle logistics first. How do you safely transport $15,000 from town to town? Do you carry around one of those massive Publishers Clearing House checks or just stuff cash inside a duffle bag? For Studd and new manager, Bobby Heenan, it was the latter. (When the Doctor of Style sold Hercules' contract to "The Brain," Slick put the proceeds in a paper bag. To each their own). Andre made quick work of Studd at WrestleMania, slamming him down on the canvas to the delight of the New York crowd. Never taking anything for himself, (see: *The Main Event*, February 1988), the loveable giant began tossing his winnings to the fans at ringside. Before Andre could disperse the cash, however, Heenan rushed in and reclaimed the bag. In the weeks that followed, the Brain and Studd matter-of-factly said the slam never happened, like when George Costanza showed up for work after quitting. It got chalked up to a misunderstanding.

"You know, he tried to slam me. He claims he slammed me. I just tripped and fell down, and he says he slammed me. And he goes and has the guts to steal my money and wants to buy himself a few friends. Well, I got a big message for you, Andrea, I'm not finished with you. You're gonna pay for trying to make a fool out of Studd." – *Championship Wrestling*, April 6th, 1985 (All Out of Bubblegum 2017).

"I tripped and fell down."

How do you refute that? How do you dispute an alternative reality where Heenan and Studd just shrugged off the defeat – mounting video evidence be damned. It's like debating Kyrie Irving over the earth's shape. I don't think a few NASA satellite photos are going to change his mind at this point. So, the Body Slam Challenge marched on. It seemed unlikely that another future winner would ever receive the full payout at this point, but *qué será, será*, whatever will be, will be. Personally, I'd have settled for $1,500 and that sweet duffle bag Heenan carried to WrestleMania. Imagine rolling into your local Planet Fitness with that kinda swag.

(It makes sense that Heenan was reluctant to part with the money, considering that Bobby put a $50,000 bounty on Paul Orndorff following his public firing. There's only so much cash to go around).

The $15,000 Body Slam Challenge didn't follow the same rules as the Hardcore or 24/7 title. Big John Studd wasn't always on the clock. The guy could sleep and run his errands stress-free. You couldn't stalk the giant at the grocery store and slam him in the frozen food aisle with referee Dick Kroll in tow. What a burden that would've been for Studd – constantly having to look over your shoulder. You'd never know if the youngster, Siva Afi, or a Moondog or two were lurking around with bad intentions. If you signed on the dotted line, if the contract contained the necessary language and was greenlighted by each party's respective attorney, etc, etc, then the Body Slam Challenge was a go.

Jim Powers and Rick Hunter had followed such protocols on this June edition of *Championship Wrestling*. King Tonga then also appeared, wanting a crack at the $15,000. No, no, no. It didn't work like that. This was the Body Slam Challenge, not open mic night. Studd reiterated the ground rules.

"*Two a night. These two are first,*" pointing to Powers and Hunter.

Jim and Rick were overmatched. They didn't soften up the big man, which is Body Slam Challenge 101-type stuff. They only saw dollar signs. After each failed attempt, both men clutched at their lower back, like they were involved in a fender bender and had an injury lawyer on speed dial.

After the romp, King Tonga darted back into the ring. He caught Big John off guard with two vicious chops and lifted the giant with ease. In fact, he slammed Studd so effortlessly, you wonder if we would've seen Tonga vs Yokozuna at SummerSlam '93 if the King was aboard the *U.S.S. Intrepid*. Studd rolled out of the ring, favoring his back, as Tonga performed a celebratory dance.

"Where's my money? Fifteen thousand dollars!" – King Tonga.

This isn't a popular opinion, I know, but, Tonga, you weren't a sanctioned and acknowledged Body Slam Challenge participant. Rules are rules. I'm sorry, but I must side with Studd and Heenan. Only Powers and young Rick Hunter had a potential claim to the cash prize. Your slam, while impressive, was as valid as Jimmy Hart counting the pinfall in the tag team title match at WrestleMania IX.

And, while we're on the subject …

Managerial Malpractice

> Event: WrestleMania IX (Caesars Palace, Las Vegas, NV)
>
> Match: Hulk Hogan (Challenger) vs. Yokozuna (Champion)
>
> Date: April 4th, 1993
>
> Attendance: 16,891
>
> #1 Song on This Date: "Informer," by Snow

I take no joy in writing this. Seconds after Yokozuna captured the World Championship from Bret Hart at WrestleMania IX (thanks to Mr. Fuji hurling salt in the Hitman's eyes), Hogan sprinted down to protest the non-call. The Hulkster had been in the refs' ears all night, practically begging to get T'd up like Hickory High Coach Norman Dale. Earlier in the day, Hulk almost laid out *reinstated* referee Danny Davis before Jimmy Hart did his dirty work for him. Now here was Hogan again, lobbying for yet another call from the official.

Fuji grabbed the mic and challenged the Hulkster. It was a curious response by the Devious One. My initial reaction probably would've been, "Are you lost or something, Hulk? Aren't you just a tag team specialist now?" But Fuji doubled down, displaying some of the worst negotiating instincts since Russia sold Alaska to William Seward and the U.S. for a paltry $7.2 million. What's the adage? The first one to speak in a negotiation loses. Hogan didn't acknowledge the initial challenge, so Fuji raised the stakes. He put Yokozuna's World Championship on the line.

Well, that got Hulk's attention. A minute later, we had a new champion.

This was the dumbest thing I've ever witnessed, and I labored through the final season of *Dexter*. What are we doing here, Fuji? Why are we handing out world title shots all willy-nilly? The World Wrestling Federation Rule Book clearly states you have 30 days to defend the title. 30 DAYS, Devious One. Not 30 seconds.

It was a fireable offense. Yokozuna would've been in his right to announce Harvey Wippleman as his new manager right then and there. Twitter is littered with sports fans who tweet, "I wouldn't even let Coach _____ on the plane" after their favorite team loses a meaningless regular season game. Could you imagine the backlash? Could you imagine if Yokozuna was your favorite wrestler, or you rostered Mr. Fuji in your Fantasy Manager League? (Lord knows the Slickster wasn't carrying his weight). Fuji's incompetence turned a title victory, an actual championship match win, into an unmitigated disaster. How do you recover from that? How could Yoko supporters ever show their face again?

@TeamYoko505

YOU'VE GOT TO BE KIDDING

8:58 PM · 4/4/93

57,813 Retweets 167,925 Likes

@BanzaiDripDrop

I'M IN HELL

9:04 PM · 4/4/93

64,244 Retweets 202,187 Likes

Every comment underneath these tweets would've been from little Hulkster trolls writing "cry" or "cope" or posting the gif of a weeping James Van Der Beek. Yokozuna fans would have had no choice but to delete their account and move off the grid.

"Anyone heard from Jim lately?"

"Nah, not since he threw his WrestleMania IX shirt in the fire pit. He took the Hogan loss pretty hard."

This was gross negligence. Bask in the victory. Break out the cigars. Fuji and Yoko should've been on the Strip, taking in all the vices Vegas had to offer. When the Eagles beat the Patriots in Super Bowl LII, you didn't see me putting the Lombardi Trophy on the line against the '85 Bears. And if I was stupid enough to challenge the '85 Bears, THEN I WOULD'VE MADE IT A NON-TITLE MATCH. Mr. Fuji had to stroke his own ego. He couldn't help himself. Leading his protégé to victory over Bret Hart AND destroying Hulkamania is not a bad day's work if you can get it, but sheesh, dude. Save some for the rest of us. Your legacy was already set. Yoko was gassed. You both were ill-prepared, and everyone knows that the Hulkster is lights out in odd-numbered WrestleManias. Look at his track record.

Good grief, Fuji.

The official time of the match was 0:22.

THE KID

> **Event:** *Monday Night Raw* (Manhattan, NY)
>
> **Match:** Razor Ramon vs. The Kid
>
> **Date:** May 17th, 1993
>
> **Attendance:** 1,000
>
> **Top Selling Super Nintendo Game in the U.S:** *Star Fox*

Randy Savage: *"I got a question for you, Vince McMahon. What's the kid's name this week?"*

Vince McMahon: *"Ah, he has been changing his name a bit."*

Malcolm Gladwell theorized that you could become an expert in anything if you practice for 10,000 hours. With all due respect, I don't think Mr. Gladwell ever played Nintendo's *Battletoads*.

Released in 1991, the game garnered critical acclaim for its cutting-edge graphics and creative gameplay. Today it's remembered for being a mountain that couldn't be climbed. I once read an article ranking the top-100 most difficult video games of all time, and *Battletoads* didn't come in second. 95% of you reading this have no idea what I'm talking about, and that's ok. I'm not talking to you. I'm talking to the 5%; The 5% who got stymied by *Battletoads* day after day, week after week. The 5% whose wills got broken, whose spirits got deflated, and who chucked their cartridge against their bedroom wall in a fit of rage.

"Hey, what's all that racket!?"

"Must be a family of raccoons inside the walls, mom."

The working theory is that *Battletoads* was so difficult in response to a surging video store rental market. If the game was too easy, players could beat it in a day or two. To master it, to defeat the evil Dark Queen, it took time, lots of time, and ideally, your or your parents' money. You couldn't rent this on a Friday and beat it by Saturday. You needed to dedicate your life to it, so best get your ass to K·B Toys and fork up that $39.99. I never beat *Battletoads*. Frankly, I didn't get close. The game wasn't intended to be beaten. It was Nintendo's version of Joe DiMaggio's 56-game hit streak. *Battletoads* was designed so you would fail. You were never meant to win.

~ ~ ~

The Kid was the smallest wrestler I saw in my re-watch. Even slighter than a young Duane Gill, who was propped up by his 25 lb mullet. Kid wrestled on three consecutive *Raws*, changing his identity each outing. His creativity waned with each appearance. A person only has so many good ideas after all. (If I was forced to write an 88th chapter, I would just list wrestlers alphabetically). On April 26th, he was the Kamikaze Kid, then the Cannonball Kid, and now simply 'The Kid.' To further complicate matters, the back of his tights read, "L. Kid," as if his first name was 'Larry' or 'Len.' In his prior two defeats against Doink the Clown and Mr. Hughes, respectively, Kid showed next to nothing. He was a non-prospect, a J.A.G (Just Another Guy), and given his own feathered mullet, it was fair to wonder if Kid and Barry Hardy had ever been seen in the same room together. The Kid, like so many guys before him, was there to lose.

His opponent on that May 17th *Raw* was a problem, and perhaps even more dangerous than Doink and Hughes. Razor Ramon was 6'7", almost 290 lb. He rocketed to the top of the rankings in short order. Razor had already teamed with Ric Flair at the '92 Survivor Series and dispatched the veteran Bob Backlund a month earlier at WrestleMania IX. He came within inches of defeating Bret Hart for the World Title at that year's Rumble. Kid was there to be a sparring partner for Ramon, a punching bag for Razor to iron out his mechanics.

Is the fallaway slam working properly?

Is the toe tucked in on the abdominal stretch?

Is the Razor's Edge clicking on all cylinders?

Nine days earlier, Ramon had defeated the crafty El Matador in a King of the Ring qualifying match. Vegas pegged him as one of the tournament favorites. Everything from here until the June pay-per-view was window dressing. Razor Ramon was merely here for a tune-up.

The Kid won with a moonsault at 2:12. He mounted zero offense before the pinfall. As far as shockers go, it ranks right up there with Farleigh Dickinson beating #1 seed Purdue in the NCAA tournament. Historians draw the comparison to Barry Horowitz' upset victory in '95, and I get it, but the savvy vet beat Bodydonna Skip, not a 4-time Intercontinental Champion. Even thirty years later, I'm scratching my head. How? How did Razor lose?

I wonder if the intimate atmosphere played a factor. The Manhattan Center only held 1,000 seats. It's hard to get up for a crowd that size. (While not nearly as romanticized as the Kid/Ramon match, the youngster P.J. Walker defeated I.R.S. with a roll-up on the September 20th, 1993 Manhattan Center *Raw*). Was Razor motivated? Did he care? I once saw the Spin Doctors phone in a free concert at a Six Flags, so I get it. You can't treat everything like Woodstock. Does the Kid pull the upset at the Alamo Dome or MetLife Stadium? You'd imagine Ramon's focus would be sharper on a bigger stage.

"You got beat brother. What happened?"

– Randy Savage.

When my Philadelphia 76ers choked away a series to a mediocre Atlanta Hawks team in the 2021 Eastern Conference semi-finals, I muted every NBA writer on Twitter and didn't watch ESPN for two weeks. Healthy, right? It was part of the grieving process. Ramon should've followed my script. He should've kept his head down and laid low – take the L. Don't make excuses or blame a fast count. Instead, Razor tweeted through it. He came back week after week, subjecting himself to a trolling tsunami. Bret Hart, his first-round opponent at the King of the Ring, gave him shit. So did the crowd. They chanted "1-2-3" at every turn. Razor reiterated that the loss was a fluke; that it would never happen again. He offered Kid $2,500 for a rematch, then $5K, then $7,500. The Kid capitalized on Ramon's desperation, getting him to up the prize to $10,000.

The rematch took place on the June 21st *Raw*. Lightning didn't strike twice, but Ramon didn't avenge his loss either. Mid-match, the rookie yanked the bag with the money and split. As Katharine Hepburn said, "Everyone is an opportunist if they have an opportunity." The Kid didn't have to win, only survive.

He hopped in a car outside the arena and sped away.

FUJI VICE

> Event: TNT (Tuesday Night Titans)
>
> Cop Drama: Fuji Vice
>
> Date: May 7th, 1986
>
> On This Date: MacGyver goes in disguise to foil the plans of a hired assassin

"You have exceeded the previous Fuji pieces. This, without a doubt, is definitely the worst one. There is no doubt. This is horrible."

– **Vince McMahon** (*Tuesday Night Titans*, May 7th, 1986).

Everyone's a critic. I didn't hate *Fuji Vice*. I even kinda liked it. Was it the best thing I ever saw? No, but it beats the Brawl for All. My pops plans his week around *The Good Doctor*. My wife's favorite *Karate Kid* movie is the one with Hilary Swank (how embarrassing), and I've seen *Bio-Dome* more times than I care to admit. Not everything we watch can be *Citizen Kane*. I think Muraco and the Devious One were rounding into form here, and it was a marked improvement from *Fuji General* and *Fuji Bandito*. The two showed guts. It's not easy putting yourself out there. Hell, I'm writing a book about wrestling from 35 years ago that I'm praying you don't shit on. Fuji and Muraco flexed their versatility in '85/'86. They had established and decorated wrestling careers and were now pursuing a new discipline. MJ didn't hit .400 for the Birmingham Barons, did he? I give the duo credit. They were actors. They dabbled in stand-up, and they found the time to explore these creative outlets when they weren't hanging Ricky

Steamboat by his *karate gi* belt on *Championship Wrestling*. Now, *that's* range.

(On *TNT*, February 14th, 1986, Muraco and Fuji traveled to Hollywood to secure representation for their budding acting careers. Two weeks later, the "Magnificent One" aided Bundy in breaking Hulk Hogan's ribs on *Saturday Night's Main Event*. Don's deplorable actions aside, you gotta admit the guy was burning the candle at both ends).

A quick *Fuji Vice* recap: Some kids are playing beach volleyball when they discover a dead body. The Lieutenant, who seems like a straight shooter, confirms it's the work of a drug dealer named Seahawk (presumably not Steve Largent, but another Seahawk). A bracelet on the victim is the giveaway, like how the Wet Bandits used to clog the sinks before running the faucet. A woman named Angelica then appears from nowhere and identifies the body. It's her brother Juan.

"*My Juan, my poor Juan.*"

Enter Muraco and Fuji. The Lieutenant gets the vice detectives up to speed, while expressing his doubts about the woman's story. He doesn't see the resemblance between Angelica and Juan, but we couldn't exactly 23andMe her in 1986. Fuji and Muraco promise to get the guy. The Lieutenant, almost ominously, warns them to not be so close-minded, to not assume gender. Suspect everybody. Rule out no one.

SPOILER ALERT

I hadn't seen *Fuji Vice* in at least thirty years, so I forgot who murdered Juan. I could only recall Muraco and the Devious One being tied up on the boat. When I re-watched the opening scene, I was like, "Oh, duh, the Lieutenant is Seahawk. He's this crooked cop running a drug ring in a position of authority." The line to Muraco and Fuji about not assuming gender was a classic bait and switch. He said it to keep his detectives at bay and give his men another bevy of suspects to consider.

I'm an idiot. The Lieutenant didn't kill Juan. Angelica did. Of course, she did. She was Seahawk and get this – her and Juan weren't even siblings. You couldn't put anything past the Lieutenant. The dude was sharp as a tack.

Fuji and Muraco showed their acting chops. It wasn't a riveting performance, but the effort was there. I saw improvement. McMahon's feedback, though, was harsh. The *Tuesday Night Titans* studio held an earned reputation as a glorified peanut gallery, a bunch of Statlers and Waldorfs heckling you from the cheap seats. That audience would boo their own mother if she made a disparaging comment about Sal Bellomo's cooking. Pay no mind to them, boys. You did a fine job.

I give *Fuji Vice* 3-stars. (Would've been 5, if they filmed at the Tokyo Dome).

What's the Story, Power and Glory

> Event: *Superstars* (Dayton, OH)
> Match: Paul Roma vs. Dino Bravo
> Date: July 21st, 1990
> Attendance: 7,500
> #1 Movie on This Date: *Die Hard 2*

Sean Mooney: *"I wasn't aware that Paul Roma was a close friend of Hercules."*

Lord Alfred Hayes: *"Oh, he is indeed."* Prime Time, June 18th, 1990 (Incredible Hulks 2020).

On the July 8th, 1990 *Wrestling Challenge*, the mighty Hercules hit rock bottom. With a singles career in a tailspin and prospects bleak, the powerhouse swallowed his pride and teamed with a youngster by the name of Jim McPherson.

It was hard to watch. Three and a half years earlier, Herc was a whisker away from defeating Hulk Hogan for the World Title on *Saturday Night's Main Event*. He was a hot commodity, a star on the rise; an asset so highly coveted by managers that his contract was purchased on three separate occasions. But that was then. Now, the only person in his corner was Jim McPherson. You wanted to shake Hercules and stage an intervention. Scare him straight like when the producers of *Maury* would send trouble teens to jail for a night.

You're the man who busted up that Billy Jerk Haynes at WrestleMania III! You pinned King Haku at WrestleMania V! You're the mighty Hercules, damnit! Now, look at you! Look at what you've become!

McPherson and Hercules got manhandled by the Orient Express. Afterwards, Tanaka and Sato laid the boots to Herc, both literally and figuratively kicking the man while he was down. In 2010, I saw the 90s band, Sister Hazel, play at a Best Buy. I watched them from the home appliances section, and I can't help but see the parallels.

> "You see, Hercules made another bad move. Picked another ham and egger for a partner. You never volunteer, dummy."
>
> **– Bobby Heenan (*Wrestling Challenge*, July 8th, 1990).**

It's difficult to write about Power and Glory objectively. It's like asking me to badmouth my grandmother. I loved these guys, and not just because Hercules and Roma were bad asses (They were). Or because their name was great (It was). Everyone loves a good comeback story. Discarded and left to rot, the two found common ground in their own cloudy futures. "Herc and Jerk," as Monsoon called them, clicked. Together, they rediscovered their swagger. The duo cut the sleeves off their t-shirts like a teenager after two sets of bicep curls. They rocked sunglasses that only 1% of the world's population could pull off. Hercules and Roma turned into shitheads, too, no doubt. They associated with bad company, and they were a bit too chummy with "The Model" Rick Martel for my tastes. But where had being nice gotten them? Sometimes you have to crack a few eggs. As a little kid, you were contractually obligated to root for their demise, but – BUT – there was a *tiny* part of you hoping to see that Power-Plex finisher. You just couldn't admit it out loud. Not with all these Rockers fanboys running around.

(I can compartmentalize. I admit that Hercules and Roma blindsiding Shawn Michaels with a chain before their 1990 SummerSlam match was fucked up, but I also didn't lose any sleep after Jannetty got obliterated with the Power-Plex).

Time has been kind to Power and Glory's legacy. You see terms like 'innovative' and 'underrated' flung around to describe the duo, and while the world slowly comes around on the team's greatness, the Slickster was ahead of the curve. He was the first to see something in these two. (July 1990 marked the second time Slick purchased Herc's contract). The team was a great buy low, guys fantasy football experts would've only mentioned for the deepest of leagues. They were castoffs, basically free for any manager, so save your #1 waiver wire claim for a Carolina Panthers wide receiver who you'll cut a week later.

Paul Roma, too, was in desperate need of a reset. His career had been stuck in mud since he and Jim Powers were co-victors with the Bees at the '87 Survivor Series tag team match. In fact, I don't even recall the Young Stallions disbanding. There was no announcement, no press release, not even a quick blurb on Gene Okerlund's studio update segment. It was the best kept secret in wrestling, even more tightlipped than where the Islanders were stashing Matilda. One day, Roma and Jim Powers were climbing up the ranks of the tag division. The next, the latter is teaming with a merry-go-round of randos.

"Tony, who's that teaming with Powers? That's not Roma."

"Oh, that's Rudy Boyd. A real up-and-comer."

(Judging by the August 6th *Prime Time* match between Power and Glory and Jim Brunzell and Jim Powers, we can assume the Young Stallions' break-up was not amicable. Powers and Roma did some jawing back and forth).

We've all had bad days. Everyone can relate. Heck, Daniel Powter wrote a terrible song about them. On July 21st, Roma had one. Losing to Dino Bravo was crappy enough, but getting belted post-match with Jimmy

Hart's megaphone was overkill. Roma was injured badly. So badly, in fact, that officials were still tending to him after the broadcast returned from Ronnie Garvin peddling WWF ice cream bars.

But we got a schedule to keep, folks. Keep the assembly line moving. The Rockers sprinted down the aisle for the next match, Paul Roma's injured back be damned. I guess they planned on working around him, like when I used to avoid my mom's clothesline in the backyard on crossing routes. The former Young Stallion shrugged Marty and Shawn off when they checked on him. When someone says, "Nothing is wrong," something is always wrong. You just don't know what. Roma was frustrated. He wanted space. He wanted them out of the ring for starters. So Paul shoved Marty, then Shawn.

Herc then sprinted down and joined the fray, siding with Paul as both teams shouted at the other. You saw that fire rekindled. The boys were back – the fight that was once lost had now been found. Speed and strength, Power and Glory. Roma and the mighty Hercules combined their powers like Planeteers. A week later, the Doctor of Style added his wisdom, putting the entire tag team division on notice.

They were pushovers no more. Thanks for everything, Jim McPherson, but your services are no longer needed.

The Coronation of King Haku

> **Event:** *Superstars* (Glens Falls, NY)
> **Date:** July 9th, 1988
> **Coronation Attendance:** 6,000
> **#1 Movie on This Date:** *Coming to America*

Heenan: *"The gentleman you are watching right now – sitting on the throne – qualifies to be King of the World Wrestling Federation for many, many reasons. His qualities are honesty …"*

McMahon (on commentary): *"Honesty?"*

Heenan: *"A keen sense of fair play …"*

McMahon (on commentary): *"You gotta be kidding. He's describing Haku?"*

Heenan: *"Loyalty … sportsmanship …"*

McMahon (on commentary): *"Huh?"*

Heenan: *"And a keen love for his fellow man."*

McMahon (on commentary): *"This is ridiculous …"* (Wrestling with Paul 2019).

The Heenan Family stood in mourning on the June 25th, 1988 *Superstars*. The reign of Harley Race, the grizzled and tatted World Wrestling Federation King, had uncermoniously ended. King Race had been out of commission after swan diving through a table in a *Saturday*

Night's Main Event match against the Hulkster. Fans took the king's demise in stride. In fact, they rejoiced in the streets – well, in the Oakland-Almeda County Coliseum Arena to be exact – and celebrated after Heenan acknowledged that their benevolent ruler had spent four hours in surgery. To be clear, Oakland residents didn't celebrate that Race underwent *successful* surgery. They were basking in the news that Harley had to go under the knife at all, which is pretty fucking sadistic, even for the king's biggest critics.

With Race handing over his crown, the World Wrestling Federation briefly operated without any checks and balances. President Jack Tunney surrounded himself with a bunch of suits and yes-men. Now void of additional leadership and oversight, there was no telling what special favors Tunney would dole out to the highest bidder. The situation was dire. Now, I admit. I haven't brushed up on the Wrestling King bylaws as it pertains to chain of succession, but I did see the first season of *The Crown*. With Race on the shelf, Heenan had it on good authority to anoint a new monarch.

Haku was a great choice. He was known as King Tonga in his past life, so he already had on-the-job experience. Also, his wrists were the size of my torso, so I damn sure wasn't protesting the coronation outside his quarters. What Haku wants, Haku gets. Sorry, excuse me. What King Haku wants, King Haku gets, my Benevolent One. He took his new role seriously. Ventura commented on his new haircut for the occasion, like how everyone dresses up for their first day of classes freshman year before settling into a routine of sweats and a hoodie.

"Bobby Heenan has out done himself. Take a look at this lavish display here."

– Vince McMahon.

Lavish indeed. The in-ring coronation was attended by Heenan Family members and other notable luminaries. Frenchy Martin, Dino Bravo, DiBiase, the Honky Tonk Man, Mike Sharpe, and others bore witness. (Even the little-known and scarcely seen Headbanger Butcher paid homage). Trusted and appointed adviser, Lord Littlebrook, ushered Haku down the aisle. It was nice to see a familiar face. (Littlebrook also presided over Harley Race's coronation in '86). His lordship wore glasses for the occasion, which caught me off-guard. Mr. Hughes wore shades. Adam Bomb wore goggles, but you rarely saw a wrestler in a pair of readers.

Despite a few hecklers and their "Weasel" chants, the ceremony concluded without a hitch. Andre the Giant gave his seal of approval, opening the middle rope for his king to exit. Haku's reign was prosperous, though his accomplishments weren't reflected in the polls. His approval rating hovered just north of Harley Race and King Mabel, but well below His Excellency (and successor), King "Hacksaw" Jim Duggan.

Haku ruled over the World Wrestling Federation for 308 days. The king is dead, long live the king.

You Sold Out! You Sold Out!

> Event: SummerSlam 1990 (Philadelphia, PA)
>
> Match: "The American Dream" Dusty Rhodes vs. "The Macho King" Randy Savage
>
> Date: August 27, 1990
>
> Attendance: 19,304
>
> #1 Song on This Date: "Vision of Love," by Mariah Carey

"My money can buy anybody, or anything, and tonight, Rhodes, it has bought your humiliation. And if there has ever been a doubt in your mind or in anybody's else's mind, that what I say isn't true ... then I want you to feast your eyes on my latest purchase – bought, lock, stock and barrel ... the sweet ... Sapphire!"

– Ted DiBiase (SummerSlam, August 27th, 1990).

We should've known. Throughout the summer months, Sweet Sapphire received lavish gifts such as a bracelet, a ring, and a cruise around the world from a mysterious benefactor. (Like, we *really* should've picked up on the mysterious gift giver, considering DiBiase was also Brother Love's benefactor. Jimmy Hart didn't have that kind of money). We knew something was up when she didn't show for her scheduled match against Queen Sherri, and it was cemented later that night when she aligned herself with that rich fuck and all his seasonal residences. Savage made quick work of "The American Dream," and I'm not surprised. Where was Rhodes' head at? How could he focus on Savage, when his #1 fan and biggest supporter had sold out?

I always laughed off DiBiase's mantra, "Everyone has a price," as a figure of speech. Like, not *everyone* has a price, right? I'm not going to pledge my allegiance to the Mets for a few grand. I got morals, and I'll be damned if you ever catch me in a José Reyes jersey. Maybe I'm wrong, though. Maybe Ted knew better. If he could buy Sapphire, then who didn't have a price tag? She believed in Rhodes. She believed in what he represented. She even wore polka dots like Dusty, and like my grandmother at my First Communion party.

Why, Sweet Sapphire, why? Was the money and gifts worth it? You mortgaged your principles for what? A ring? A fur coat? On the September 15th *Superstars*, she escorted DiBiase to the ring in her mink and "Million Dollar Man" Wrestling Buddy. It made me sick. I wanted to Garvin Stomp that Wrestling Buddy to kingdom come. Then finish it off with a camel clutch. Fur coats have long been these symbols of ostentatious wealth. It wasn't just Sapphire. It was the same in movies and television. It was Cruella de Vil. It was George Washington Duke in *Rocky V*. I never saw the appeal. If I got rich, the first thing I'd purchase would be a shuffleboard table, but I guess I'm just built different.

On the following week's *Superstars*, Sapphire was shown ironing DiBiase's money at a laundromat. Set aside the ironing – that was obnoxious – but why was "The Million Dollar Man" slumming it at a laundromat in the first place? Was your washer/dryer broke, Ted? I get that the DiBiase probably had about $10,000 in cash on hand there, but it was hard to take his wealth seriously when he was cleaning his clothes with the common folk. That's like rolling up to a Bob Evans in a Maserati. "The Million Dollar Man" didn't need Sapphire. He purchased her loyalty because he could. It was a game for him. In '88, he bought Hercules. (Herc didn't exactly greenlight the transaction, but still). Paying off Sapphire hurt

Dusty more than it helped DiBiase. It was like when Shooter McGavin purchased Happy's grandma's house. Ted was just being spiteful. He could've hired anyone to:

checks notes

Iron his money.

Sapphire's partnership with DiBiase didn't last long. Just a couple of months. Money can't buy happiness – only a necklace, a bracelet, a ring, a fur coat, a cruise around the world, and a Ted DiBiase Wrestling Buddy. Whether she realized her mistake or Ted no longer needed her services is anyone's guess. Sapphire was quietly removed from DiBiase's payroll without explanation and her new allegiance expedited her departure. It perhaps accelerated Rhodes' too (He was gone after the '91 Royal Rumble). One selfish decision unraveled a once great partnership. Once Sweet Sapphire chose not to stand beside Dusty, she didn't really stand for anything at all.

Captain Lou's Swan Song

> **Event:** *Wrestling Challenge* (Glens Falls, NY)
> **Match:** The British Bulldogs and Lou Albano vs. The Dream Team and Johnny V
> **Date:** November 16th, 1986
> **Attendance:** 8,500
> **#1 Movie on This Date:** *Crocodile Dundee*

Monsoon: *"Standing ovation by this capacity crowd for Captain Louis Albano and a final tribute ... this is his final match, not only as a professional wrestler, but his final appearance as a manager as well."*

Heenan: *"Well, I'm not standing, and I think it's way overdue. This guy should've retired in 1913."* (Wrestling Challenge, November 16th, 1986).

As a latchkey kid, Lou Albano practically raised me. Set aside his decorated managerial career or his LJN figure that I never pushed in my living room fed. Captain Lou starred in *The Super Mario Bros. Super Show!* which aired after school on the Family Channel.

(A goofy tidbit: Monday through Thursday, the program aired Super Mario Bros. cartoons, but on Fridays, they showed *Legend of Zelda*. I respected the way Mario and Luigi carved out a four-day work week for themselves).

The Super Mario Bros. Super Show! was fantastic. Was it *ThunderCats*? No, but what show was. Years ago, I rediscovered some episodes on YouTube. My wife walked in, and, at that moment, I would've rather her caught me watching porn.

"What are you watching?"

"Oh, nothing. It just came on."

"'It just came on?' Seriously, what is this?"

"That's Captain Lou Albano."

"Who?"

"The manager."

"Huh?"

"The guy from the Cyndi Lauper video."

"She-Bop?"

Well, yes, but whose go-to Cyndi Lauper song is "She-Bop?"

Albano's accomplishments within the tag team division are well-documented. The list of duos he guided to championship gold is a mile long: The Valiant Brothers, the Wild Samoans, the Yukon Lumberjacks, the Blackjacks, the Moondogs, and the Masked Executioners, among others. For decades, Lou found success through underhanded methods. He didn't *only* cheat. He was a compulsive liar, too. On the June 16th, 1984 *Piper's Pit*, he told Cyndi Lauper to "admit that he [Albano] wrote 'Time After Time.'" His devious behavior, we later learned, was actually the byproduct of a serious medical condition. Surgery was performed to remove a calcium deposit on the medulla of his oblongata, which, according to an article I found from *The New England Journal of Medicine*, checks out. Once that pesky calcium deposit was removed, Albano became a pillar of the community.

He twice led the U.S. Express to the titles, and then followed suit with the British Bulldogs at WrestleMania 2. After 40 years, though, he sought a new challenge. He had tenure. He had mastered his craft. What else did he have to prove? On the November 8th *Superstars*, Captain Lou was missing at a key contract signing between his Machines and Big John Studd and Bundy. Moments later, he announced his retirement (Albano intended to dedicate his time to philanthropical efforts, like fighting Multiple Sclerosis). Company man Derek Jeter played another 145 games after announcing his retirement, while *MY* Captain only gave eight days' notice.

Damn straight, Lou. Stick it to The Man.

His last appearance in a managerial role occurred on *Superstars* the following week, where his Machines lost a controversial contest to Heenan's men by pinfall. The next day, on *Challenge*, Albano wrestled his final match. You don't have to do much when you're teaming with Dynamite Kid and Davey Boy Smith, and Lou didn't. He entered the ring only to flop on Johnny V for the three count, and a celebratory champagne bath orchestrated by George Steele and Corporal Kirchner followed.

"Two men beat one man, and that big slob takes advantage of a beaten man. If you wanna call that a victory, Albano, you can have it. If you want to go out that way, you can have it. I think it stinks!"

– Bobby Heenan.

On the flip side, what a brutal 1986 for the Dream Team. Did anything go right? They rang in the New Year as World Champs and then nosedived into '87. Tag team wrestling is like the GMATs. Better or worse, things can snowball. The GMAT test's difficulty increases or falls in real time depending on your proficiency. So after I got one question that was like, "Hey Numbnuts, what is 8x7?" I knew my score was in the shitter.

Beefcake and Valentine lost the belts to the Bulldogs. They got beat in a two-out-of-three falls rematch on the October 4th *Saturday Night's Main Event* (after recording the first pin), and the Rougeaus upset them at The Big Event. Sure, defeating Rick Hunter and Serge Jodoin on *Championship Wrestling* lessens the sting a bit, but that win alone won't get you into a top-tier grad school. One loss leads to two, two leads to three. Soon your manager is getting pinned by Captain Lou, and you're staring up at Tiger Chung Lee and his partner *du jour* in the Championship Committee's rankings.

Brutus and "The Hammer" parted ways after WrestleMania III.

"This Is One of the Greatest Matches I've Ever Seen, Gorilla"

> Event: WrestleMania III (Pontiac, MI)
>
> Match: "Macho Man" Randy Savage (Champion) vs. Ricky "The Dragon" Steamboat (Challenger)
>
> Date: March 29th, 1987
>
> Attendance: 93,173
>
> #1 Arcade Game on This Date: *Out Run*

"Well, all I got to say is that Ricky 'The Dragon' Steamboat better cut that belt in half and give half of it to George 'The Animal' Steele."

– Jesse Ventura.

I was talking to this girl via the world's first ever known dating app: AOL's Instant Messenger. It was a real 'will they or won't they' type deal. The dialogue was breezy and flirty, littered with ellipses and the exchanging of hobbies and common interests like, "I like the onion rings at Red Robin too ..."

The future was bright, and plans were being discussed. She threw out a date later in the week, and I fired back in tow.

"My last opportunity. The day has finally come. The minutes, the seconds, we have reached our moment."

I think her exact reply was "lol." I didn't get the "LMFAO" approval I was seeking – the gold standard of Instant Messenger responses – but "lol" would suffice. Then I got greedy. I pushed the envelope.

"As you and I climb into the ring, we clash like two titans. But there will only be one winner. One winner, <redacted>. This dragon is breathing fire. This dragon will scorch your back. I will come away with the championship belt and see new horizons!"

She responded with, "Huh?"

I know, I know. Keep it simple, stupid. "Yeah, Thursday works. I'll hit up the cell" was the optimal play, not Ricky Steamboat's entire WrestleMania III promo, but I had to go down with my best material. I regret nothing.

There is no match I've seen more than Steamboat/Savage. If you gave me enough time and enough beer, I could probably write out the entire match dialogue between Monsoon and Ventura. Once a month or so, I catch myself mumbling, "I think the bell rammed Savage in the head," even though, no, Gorilla, the bell never rammed Savage in the head. It's not hyperbole to say I've watched this match a thousand times. In 2005, a website called YouTube, was created (ever hear of it?). Once I discovered that people uploaded old wrestling matches on to the site, I lost the need and desire for human interaction. Forget dusting off a VCR. All these OG YouTube uploads included Ricky's original entrance music: The incomparable "Sirius" by The Alan Parsons Project. Everyone has one match they can reference to explain why they love pro wrestling. This is mine. My brother once got me a gift card to the Cheesecake Factory. You could upload a photo with the certificate, and he chose a shirtless Steamboat. When I presented the printout to the hostess, she stared at it for a second before asking me, "Is that you?" No, ma'am, I am not a former

NWA World and Intercontinental Champion but thank you. Truly. I can't think of a higher compliment.

> *"They say he has a lot of heart. I personally say he has a lot of throat."*
>
> **– Jesse Ventura.**

If it wasn't for Steamboat/Savage, I wouldn't know what a 'larynx' was. Now, I'm acutely aware. I diagnose any sore throat as "a crushed larynx." (I'm no doctor, but I've also never had an issue giving my opinion). 'Wicky' the 'Dwagon' was my favorite wrestler. (I couldn't pronounce R's as a kid). It's because of Steamboat that I describe every arm drag as 'deep.' He could do no wrong, and no one deserved their comeuppance more than that piece of garbage, Randy Savage. I loathed the "Macho Man" – and this may sound dramatic – but if Steamboat didn't win the Intercontinental Championship at WrestleMania III, I was going to *literally* die. I was blood thirsty for revenge. On the November 22nd, 1986 *Superstars*, that motherfucker Savage grabbed the timekeeper's bell and rammed it into Ricky's throat. That attack was a declaration of war. It eliminated Steamboat's ability to talk! He had to see a speech specialist! Why am I screaming!

Monsoon: *"Look at the back of the cranium of 'The Animal.'"*

Ventura: *"It's disgusting. I prefer not to."*

In Steamboat's corner was George Steele. The "Animal," too, had his issues with the champion. George simped hard for Miss Elizabeth. In modern times, he could've just sent his winner's purses to Liz' Cash App accompanied with some note like, "A night out for my queen!!!," but you had to get a bit more creative in '86. His gestures ranged from flowers (like on the Valentine's Day episode of *Tuesday Night Titans*) to more drastic overtures. He kidnapped her on the January 3rd, 1987 *Saturday Night's Main Event*. (Though, to be fair, he did return her). Steele lost at

WrestleMania 2 to Randy, and the subsequent rematches thereafter. When Ventura asked what sort of advice the dim-witted Steele could provide, Gorilla suggested his presence was more for moral support. Little did we know the X-factor "The Animal" would become.

Ventura: *"Look it. Look, Hebner out of position!"*

Monsoon: *"How could you possibly get around any quicker than that?"*

Before the *alleged* plastic surgery, Dave Hebner was just another nameless, faceless official. That's a compliment. In '87, the referee spotlight was focused solely on the beleaguered Danny Davis. Referees are like children. If they're behaving, you don't notice them. The officials in the first eight matches of WrestleMania III did their job. I can't pinpoint one glaring mistake. Sure, I wished that "Angry Ref" Jack Kruger caught Danny Davis hitting Davey Boy Smith with Jimmy Hart's megaphone, but you can only call what you see.

Steamboat/Savage tested the skill and conditioning of Hebner, and Dave was up to the task. They moved at a lightning pace. Both combatants recorded near fall after near fall, but Hebner's aptitude, or lack thereof if you asked Ventura, became a talking point.

"This Hebner slow counting. He better stay consistent then."

Monsoon ran to Hebner's defense, and for good reason. There was a point in the match where Savage went for the cover after planting Steamboat with a *textbook* gutwrench suplex. Hebner flew around them both and seamlessly jumped into the count. He correctly spotted Randy's leg draped over the bottom rope on a "Dragon" pin attempt. It was a masterclass in officiating, but no one's immune from criticism. His detractors will point to the slow counts of Steamboat while Ricky laid outside the ring, and, of course, the match's most controversial moment: George Steele pushing the "Macho Man" off the top turnbuckle. (Steamboat won the Intercontinental Championship seconds later with a small package). I don't blame Hebner for missing Steele's interference. I can't. Dave was unconscious at the time.

You can only call what you see.

Ventura: *"I don't think there is a better talent in the world of professional wrestling than 'Macho Man.'"*

Monsoon: *"I'll tell you what. I have my doubts, and you've heard me express them many times, Jess, about how he got the title, but he faced everybody in these, what, 14, 15 months that he's been champion."*

There's a stark contract between the lengthy Intercontinental Championship reigns of the Honky Tonk Man and Randy Savage (In a pre-Gunther world, Savage held the third longest reign behind Pedro Morales at 414 days). While the Honky Tonk Man was perpetually lucky, Savage was just too damn good. Early in the match, "Macho Man" hurled Steamboat over the ropes, but the uber-athletic "Dragon" held on and skinned the cat. After Ricky flipped himself back over, Savage leveled him with a clothesline.

"You gotta wake up pretty early in the morning to outsmart the 'Macho Man.'"

– Jesse Ventura.

He emptied his arsenal on Steamboat: The flying double axhandle on the outside, the barrage of suplexes, perfectly measured elbows that would've knocked a common man out cold. Steamboat, though, was resilient, weathering maneuver after maneuver, digging deep to kick out of countless pinning combinations. Ricky recognized that winning was the ultimate revenge. The championship meant everything to Savage. Forget an eye for an eye, or a throat for a throat. Attacking the Macho Man's larynx wouldn't have given Steamboat the payback he craved. To stick it to Savage, to avenge the heinous attack he suffered in November of '86, Ricky had to beat Randy.

It wasn't easy.

"I'll give Savage credit where credit is due. A lesser man would've been put away a long time ago."

– Gorilla Monsoon.

Savage, too, kicked out of *everything*. It was like trying to finish off a floating Jigglypuff in *Super Smash Bros.* (Come down from there and fight me, Jigglypuff). The stars had to align to take the belt off Randy. You didn't have to necessarily be perfect, but you needed a few bounces to go your way and Steamboat got 'em in droves. Savage had the match won after landing a patented flying elbow drop, but Hebner wasn't conscious to make the count. Then came Steele's intervention. Ricky got the breaks, and while Ventura screamed from high above inside the Pontiac Silverdome about a "miscarriage of justice" and "flagrant interference," Hebner's decision was final.

History had been made, and I couldn't have been happier.

Good Riddance, Tunney

@HorowitzWins

With the breaking news from today's Wrestling Challenge that President Jack Tunney (and his administration) resigned yesterday, effective immediately, I thought it'd be an appropriate time to look back at ol' On the Take Tunney's disastrous reign. A THREAD: (1/19)

3:16 PM · 7/9/95

17,096 Retweets 38,202 Likes

@HorowitzWins

Tunney's tenure was tarnished by uneven decision making and preferential treatment. No one was above the law – well, unless you were Hogan – or you had enough money to line Jack's pockets. (2/19)

3:19 PM · 7/9/95

15,284 Retweets 32,725 Likes

@HorowitzWins

His 'pay for play' decisions were never confirmed, but where there's smoke, there's fire. Ex: Andre missed a few shows in '86 and was suspended indefinitely after Heenan's prodding. Then he was curiously AND suddenly reinstated at Bobby's behest? (3/19)

3:23 PM · 7/9/95

12,921 Retweets 26,043 Likes

@HorowitzWins

It has long been speculated that Heenan pulled the strings during this era; that Tunney just followed Bobby's orders. Or, as one colleague of mine once quipped, "To be in Jack's ear, make sure the check clears." (4/19)

3:27 PM · 7/9/95

11,087 Retweets 24,417 Likes

@HorowitzWins

"Suspended for life + 10 years?" Hardly. Just another one of Tunney's empty threats. Disgraced official Danny Davis was back officiating two years later, as if nothing had happened. Tell that to Tito Santana & the Bulldogs (not that Jack ever explained Davis' sudden leniency to the former champs) (5/19)

3:33 PM · 7/9/95

9,114 Retweets 22,552 Likes

@HorowitzWins

Rick Rude told a few Big Boss Man jokes and got suspended indefinitely. Jake Roberts coaxed his venomous cobra into biting Randy Savage and got a slap on the wrist. Got it? Good. (6/19)

3:40 PM · 7/9/95

8,662 Retweets 20,105 Likes

@HorowitzWins

The year is 1992. Tunney, who by this time was more checked out than a second semester high school senior, appoints Sgt. Slaughter as "Special Rules Enforcer." That's right. Pyromaniac and former Iraqi Sympathizer, Sgt. Slaughter. Guess it's hard to find good help nowadays (7/19)

3:44 PM · 7/9/95

7,662 Retweets 18,482 Likes

@HorowitzWins

Tunney declared that there would be no Hogan/Warrior rematch because ... reasons???? Imagine no Ali/Frazier trilogy, or if Coppola and Puzo called it quits after the first Godfather. Hulk kicked out of a Warrior splash an eyelash after the three count and had to wait another year for a title shot (8/19)

3:52 PM · 7/9/95

6,739 Retweets 15,234 Likes

@HorowitzWins

Don't shed a tear for Hogan, though. No wrestler benefited more from Tunney's nepotism. Despite coming in 3rd at the '92 Royal Rumble, Hulk was originally declared the #1 contender to Flair's World Title at WM8. No wonder Sid snapped ... (9/19)

4:02 PM · 7/9/95

6,140 Retweets 14,881 Likes

@HorowitzWins

"A championship has to be defended every 30 days." Wait, what's that? You didn't read the fine print? Here, I did the legwork for you. It should read, "A title has to be defended every 30 days ... unless Hulk Hogan is the champion." (10/19)

4:13 PM · 7/9/95

5,707 Retweets 14,055 Likes

@HorowitzWins

Between WM9 and King of the Ring, the Hulkster defended his title zero times. At least my absentee father once sent me $5 on my birthday. (11/19)

4:21 PM · 7/9/95

5,239 Retweets 12,892 Likes

@HorowitzWins

Tunney instituted a "gag order" after The Main Event in February '88. I suppose if one of my referees was corrupted, my title match fixed, and my World Championship was bought and sold, I wouldn't want people talking about it either. (12/19)

4:30 PM · 7/9/95

5,004 Retweets 10,621 Likes

@HorowitzWins

Not sure anyone got a longer leash than "Rugged" Ronnie Garvin, who was the worst, most combative official I'd ever seen. How many wrestlers was he allowed to knock out before Jack mercifully revoked his referee's license? (13/19)

4:43 PM · 7/9/95

4,820 Retweets 9,772 Likes

@HorowitzWins

GREASING THE WHEELS: In May '93, "Hacksaw" Jim Duggan defeated IC Champ, Shawn Michaels, by count out. Jim then calls Tunney on the phone and negotiates a Lumberjack Match rematch. Michaels: "I don't even have his home phone number, and I'm the Intercontinental Champion." (14/19)

5:02 PM · 7/9/95

4,233 Retweets 8,641 Likes

@HorowitzWins

FOLLOW THE MONEY: In Nov '88, Bad News Brown made some damning accusations on the Brother Love Show. Despite winning the WM IV battle royal, beating everyone put in front of him, AND sending countless letters to Tunney's office, he wasn't the #1 Contender. Why? Cont'd ... (15/19)

5:16 PM · 7/9/95

3,917 Retweets 8,158 Likes

@HorowitzWins

"Ever since 'Macho Man' Savage became the world champ, I notice you have a 35-room mansion in Beverly Hills. You have a 200-ft yacht in Florida, & you drive around in a brand-new Rolls-Royce."

The timeline checks out & the financial records back Bad News' claims. Did Savage pay off Jack to avoid Bad News? Tunney obvi could be bought (16/19)

5:22 PM · 7/9/95

3,629 Retweets 7,711 Likes

@HorowitzWins

Oh, and here's the obligatory mention of the ramped snake attacks and nonconsensual haircuts that were tolerated FOR YEARS (17/19)

5:30 PM · 7/9/95

2,947 Retweets 6,554 Likes

@HorowitzWins

Whoever takes over will be an immediate upgrade, but it's gonna take years to undo Tunney's reign of incompetence. We could play the 'What If game for hours, and we will ... later: What if Crooked Jack choose the righteous and fair path? Where would the World Wrestling Federation be? But that can wait ... (18/19)

5:52 PM · 7/9/95

2,625 Retweets 5,920 Likes

@HorowitzWins

It's dinner time here, and I'm hungry. Gonna wash my meal down with a celebratory drink. For the first time in years, I have hope. It's a new day & we *are all free from the shackles of Tunney's corruption. I think I speak for everyone, Jack, when I say ... good riddance.*

Don't let the door hit ya on the way out. (18/18)

6:01 PM · 7/9/95

1,627 Retweets 5,193 Likes

A LOVE STORY

> Event: WrestleMania VII (Los Angeles, CA)
>
> Match: "Macho Man" Randy Savage vs. The Ultimate Warrior (Retirement Match)
>
> Date: March 24th, 1991
>
> Attendance: 16,158
>
> #1 Movie on This Date: *Teenage Mutant Ninja Turtles II: The Secret of the Ooze*

Heenan: *"This may be Savage's greatest moment."*

Monsoon: *"Or his final one."*

I met this astronomer a while back. We talked shop for a bit and after a few beers, I drummed up the courage to ask him the one question on every layman's mind. No, not, 'Is there life on Mars?'

The other one.

"So, what's the deal with Pluto?"

In the late 1800s, folks had theorized that there was another planet in our Solar System. It was just a matter of 'where,' like one of those, "hang a left when you hit Neptune" type deals, and they were right. Astronomers discovered a moving object in February 1930, and a month later, Pluto, the 9th planet, was recognized by the American and the Royal Astronomical Society, respectively. As years passed, some folks expressed their doubts about the planet's validity – not about Pluto's existence, but of its classification. Planets belong to an exclusive club, you see. The scientific community doesn't hand out memberships liberally. It's not as easy as getting a library card. To gain acceptance, to ensure membership, a 2006 resolution from International Astronomical Union declared that a planet must adhere to the below criteria:

A) Orbit around the sun.
B) Be large enough to be rounded by its own gravity.

and

C) Must have cleared the neighborhood around its orbit.

I don't quite understand the last parameter, but Pluto's detractors believed this sham of a planet didn't pass that third test. I just figured Pluto was a homebody. This modern definition of a planet was formally recognized in '06, so Pluto, by proxy, was out. Think of the Solar System as English fútbol. In '06, Pluto got relegated to the 'Dwarf Planet' league. This resolution – shaping new uniformed standards for planets – went to a vote on the last day of a 2006 conference in Prague when most attendees had already departed. Astronomers were checking out of hotels, securing rides to the airport, or already halfway across the globe when the vote took place.

"Many planet scientists were disgruntled over the 2006 IAU decision, which they said involved a vote of just 424 astronomers out of some 10,000 professional astronomers around the globe." (Bryner 2008).

Most field members disregarded the vote. Their stance on Pluto hasn't wavered, and they still recognize our diminutive neighbor as the Solar System's 9th Planet. As my astronomer friend put it, "My colleagues don't acknowledge it. As far as they're concerned, it never happened."

~ ~ ~

The Title Match(es)

Randy Savage just wanted a world title shot. He had only received one opportunity since losing the belt at WrestleMania V, and here he was, now at Royal Rumble '91, sending Sensational Sherri to stump on his behalf. Though – and this is important – Sherri's request was a *bit* disingenuous. Randy Savage *did* receive world title matches after WrestleMania V. He got a ton of 'em. In fact, by my math, he received 90 title matches from April 1989 to January of '91, but only *one* of those title matches was televised. What's the adage? If a planet classification vote happens in Prague and no one is there to see it, etc, etc. The lone televised match occurred on the February 23rd, 1990 *Main Event*. Hogan seemed exasperated by another familiar championship defense and sent a cryptic message to President Jack Tunney in his pre-match promo with Gene Okerlund.

"This is probably the last time I'll ever face 'The Macho King' Randy Savage" in the ring."

ie: Find me a new #1 contender, brother.

(Enforcer, and newly crowned World Heavyweight Boxing Champion, James "Buster" Douglas, officiated on the outside, and had a quick trigger finger. He tossed Sherri from ringside in the opening minutes, which changed the complexion of the match).

So, about these other title matches. Did they *really* take place because Savage and Sherri never acknowledged the other 89 near misses? "The Macho King" wasn't 0-90, you see. He was just 0-1, and that loss occurred 11 months ago and was clouded in controversy. In their eyes, they were unfairly blackballed, victims of Tunney's preferential treatment and the champion's cowardice. Hogan had ducked Randy. So, too, was the Warrior. Sherri pleaded her case and appealed to the champ's humanity, but Warrior rejected her petition with an emphatic "NOOOOOO!" The career ending match at WrestleMania VII was unfortunate. These high stakes could've been avoided. The Ultimate Warrior could've deescalated the situation by granting Savage (yet another) title shot, but I understand the hesitation. Like, haven't you had enough, Randy? Save some for the Warlord.

Sgt. Slaughter, however, was more accommodating. If victorious at the Rumble, he agreed to give "Macho King" a shot at the belt*. So Savage and Sherri tipped the scales. Their interference on Sarge's behalf cost Warrior the gold, which set the stage for a Retirement Match at WrestleMania VII.

*Interestingly, Savage never did get that title opportunity from Slaughter. If you can't trust a traitor and a turncoat, who can you trust?

The Match

I lived with a few high school buddies in my early 20s. Tensions flared between two of them, so they settled their dispute the only way they knew how: They played *WCW/nWo Revenge* and had a "Loser Leaves Town Match." The loser had to LEAVE the house for three days (no joke), and you don't know pressure until you're fighting for the roof over your head. The quality of play, Scott Hall vs. Chris Jericho, was never higher. Both guys were crisp, cautious, and calculated in their approach. The embarrassment of a 23-year-old telling their mom and dad *why* they must crash at home for three days elevated their game to unprecedented heights. I watched in silence, a witness to something special. In the end, my friend Mike (Jericho) lost. There were no handshakes between the two combatants, no nods of mutual respect. Mike grabbed his car keys and returned the following Tuesday.

Warrior and Savage's epic encounter wasn't a match; it was survival. The two weren't fighting for a belt, or a winner's purse. They wrestled for their livelihood. Everything about the conflict *felt* different. Savage did less grandstanding. The Ultimate Warrior didn't stampede down the aisle – he needed to conserve that gas tank. What choice did they have? If not wrestling, what career awaited the Ultimate Warrior? Was Savage gonna take a desk job? They wrestled out of desperation. Warrior kicked out after five – FIVE – flying elbow drops. After the kick out, Randy flashed an incredulous glance towards referee Dave Hebner, like 'what do I have to do?' After the Warrior made his comeback, "The Macho King" kicked out of a big gorilla press and splash. The Ultimate Warrior then looked up to the gods in disbelief, as if to ask them if retirement was his destiny. When you're fighting for something more than just accolades, the human body can achieve something extraordinary. Both gladiators ran on adrenaline, like how you hear stories of people lifting cars off the ground to save a trapped child. You don't know what you're truly capable of until the consequences are dire.

The Ultimate Warrior survived after administering three massive shoulder blocks. He outlasted his arch nemesis. After the pinfall, it wasn't so much a party, but a sigh of relief. His celebration was subdued, as subdued as an Ultimate Warrior celebration could be anyway. He put back on his duster (naturally), raised his arms from the middle turnbuckle, and departed.

The Happily Ever After

I feel for Sherri. I do. I won't defend her actions, however. She interjected herself into more matches than any other manager – I think 90% of the roster got hit with her high heel or (loaded?) purse at one time or the other – but seeing your boyfriend's ex every time you look up would drive anyone mad. Liz appeared at SummerSlam '89. She then crossed the border into Canada for WrestleMania VI. Now, here was Miss Elizabeth a year later sitting in the stands. Heenan first spotted Liz before Howard Finkel's pre-match introductions, and he was skeptical.

"How low could a woman get? She's hoping Savage – she's here to see him lose and rub it in!"

"The Brain" had a point. Liz' track record was spotty. Her past appearances were in an antagonizing role. She was hurt and she was angry, and I think she wanted to see Savage and Sherri suffer. Liz didn't interject when that lowlife Beefcake cut a fellow woman's hair, and she played a vital role in Dusty and Sapphire's victory at WrestleMania VI. This time, though, she was a bystander, observing out of curiosity, or nostalgia, or as someone who was still deeply in love.

Sherri didn't take the loss well. She didn't have a stable of wrestlers under her tutelage. If Heenan watched Barbarian lose a career-ending match, Bobby could just allocate more time to Mr. Perfect and Haku. It's not ideal, but it's a backup plan. Sherri didn't have a safety net. She only had one client. When Savage's career ended, so did hers. She abused a beaten and exhausted "Macho King" after the match, kicking him repeatedly in the ribs. Monsoon took exception, calling her an "ingrate," an insult my father reserved for only the shittiest of people. Liz had seen enough. She jumped the barricade and charged the ring. She grabbed Sherri by the hair and hurled her outside.

(It should be noted that security did not apprehend Miss Elizabeth when she jumped the guardrail. Four years prior, however, a fan climbed into the ring while Roddy Piper celebrated his farewell victory, and half the cops in Michigan tackled him).

Savage slowly collected himself. He didn't even know Liz was inside the arena, and now she was standing right in front of him. Fans and Hebner helped Randy piece the puzzle together.

Sherri had put the boots to him ... Miss Elizabeth had saved him ...

Liz, it had to be Liz. It was always Liz. Years of running, years of being someone he wasn't. Randy wasn't a King. That wasn't him. He reached great heights – a former Intercontinental Champ, a former World Champ

– *because* of her, *because* of the woman who stood beside him. Tears rolled down Miss Elizabeth's face.

Heenan: *"She loves him. She's in love with 'The Macho King.'"*

Monsoon: *"She's loved him from the beginning."*

Randy and Liz then embraced, and I'm not crying, you're crying. Fans erupted; thousands were in tears. The gauntlet Savage had gone through just ten minutes ago a distant memory. Miss Elizabeth then moved to hold the second rope for her man, but, no, not this time. This time was different. Savage reversed course. To a thunderous roar, he held the rope up for Liz, a simple, yet powerful gesture that let the world know Randy was a changed man.

It was perfect, the perfect love story.

Monsoon: *"He certainly lost the match, but he got something much more valuable – his woman."*

Heenan: *"I'd rather have the match."*

Oh, Bobby, will you stop?

Bibliography

Adorable Adrian 2009. "Bobby Heenan 1985 San Francisco Promo." *YouTube*. 2009. Accessed May 17, 2022. https://www.youtube.com/watch?v=S5zo3EAGGN8.

All Out of Bubblegum. "Piper's Pit with Big John Studd (04-06-1985)." *YouTube*. 2017. Accessed July 20, 2023. https://www.youtube.com/watch?v=wtA576K5n2M.

All Out of Bubblegum. "Piper's Pit with doctor to discuss Orton's injury (12-21-1985)." *YouTube*. 2016. Accessed February 13, 2022. https://www.youtube.com/watch?v=zNbNhO4rBr4.

All Out of Bubblegum. "Piper's Pit with Paul Orndorff (05-11-1985)." *YouTube*. 2022. Accessed February 14, 2002. https://www.youtube.com/watch?v=IFNHsAGWeLs.

All Out of Bubblegum. "The Flower Shop with Roddy Piper (08-16-1986)." *YouTube*. 2015. Accessed April 7, 2023. https://www.youtube.com/watch?v=4gTdtV0XmBI&t=4s.

Bryner, Jeanna. "Pluto's Identity Crisis Hits the Classroom." *NBC News*. 2008. Accessed July 16, 2023. nbcnews.com/id/wnba26041012.

Championship Central. "MSG Battle Royal." *YouTube*. 2021. Accessed May 3, 2022. https://youtu.be/k8Vl9NUIoFE.

Fabulous One. "The Fabulous Spider, errr Moolah vs. Wendi Richter, 11-25-1985." *YouTube*. 2017. Accessed August 4, 2022. https://www.youtube.com/watch?v=JW36ll-hyT0.

Feldman, Dan. "How Michael Jordan Once Shut Down Bulls Teammate Scott Burrell with One-Liner." *NBC Sports*. 2020. Accessed August 5, 2022. https://www.nbcsports.com/nba/news/how-michael-jordan-once-shut-down-bulls-teammate.

H, Christian. "Kim Peek Documentary." *YouTube*. 2013. Accessed June 19, 2023. https://youtu.be/k8VI9NUIofe.

Incredible Hulks. "Hercules vs. Rick Martel." *YouTube*. 2020. Accessed June 27, 2023. https://www.youtube.com/watch?v=UHsPidXifOA.

Jake JP. "Chris Curtis vs Brutus the barber Beefcake hair vs hair match." *YouTube*. 2019. Accessed March 11. 2022. https://www.youtube.com/watch?v=jeC2HmAm9KE.

Kidd, Patrick. "The Top 50 Sporting Scandals." *The* Times. August 22, 2007. Accessed December 3, 2022.https://www.timesonline.co.uk/tol/sport/more_sport/article2304891.ece

Korderas, Jimmy. @JimmyKorderas. *X*. March 4, 2019. Accessed March 13, 2022.https://twitter.com/jimmykorderas/status/1102706278130839552?s=11

Love, John Arthur. "Killer Bees in Puerto Rico – 1985." *YouTube*. 2013. Accessed February 5, 2023. https://www.youtube.com/watch?v=ilqBhdJAbx8.

"Monday Night Raw February 22nd, 1993." *Monday Night Raw*. Created by Vince McMahon. WWE, 1993.

"Monday Night Raw May 17th, 1993." *Monday Night Raw*. Created by Vince McMahon. WWE, 1993.

Monsoon Classic. "British Bulldog vs Repo Man: May 3, 1992, Wrestling Challenge." *YouTube*. 2022. Accessed March 23, 2023. https://www.youtube.com/watch?v=RWWRoQ0r8bY.

Monsoon Classic. "El Matador Tito Santana vs Tanaka Wrestling Challenge Nov 3rd, 1991." *YouTube*. 2021. Accessed March 3, 2023. https://www.youtube.com/watch?v=dZnGiuhZDNA.

Monsoon Classic. "Honky Tonk Man vs. Hillbilly Jim." *YouTube*. 2022. Accessed January 8, 2023. https://www.youtube.com/watch?v=63sUL5-lsbk.

Old School Wresting TV. "El Matador Vignette [1991-09-22]." *YouTube*. 2019. Accessed September 14, 2022. https://www.youtube.com/watch?v=-wijYAPjqXk.

Old School Wrestling TV. "Heenan Buys Hercules from Slick [1986-11-08]." *YouTube*. 2019. Accessed June 27, 2022. https://www.youtube.com/watch?v=pV2XUMN7_e0.

Old School Wrestling TV. "Mr. Fuji Sells the Power of Pain [1990-03-10]." *YouTube.* 2019. Accessed April 3, 2023. https://www.youtube.com/watch?v=gdS4BiQ1yro.

Randall G. "David Sammartino vs Ron Shaw (The Phantom Submission Match)." *YouTube.* 2016. Accessed September 5, 2022. https://www.youtube.com/watch?v=3kBectvqEYY.

"Prime Time August 14th, 1989." *Prime Time Wrestling.* Created by Vince McMahon. Titan Sports, Inc., 1989.

"Prime Time August 21st, 1989." *Prime Time Wrestling.* Created by Vince McMahon. Titan Sports, Inc., 1989.

"Prime Time July 28th, 1986." *Prime Time Wrestling.* Created by Vince McMahon. Titan Sports, Inc., 1986.

"Prime Time June 16th, 1986." *Prime Time Wrestling.* Created by Vince McMahon. Titan Sports, Inc.,1986.

"Prime Time March 6th, 1989." *Prime Time Wrestling.* Created by Vince McMahon. Titan Sports, Inc.,1989.

"Prime Time, February 11th, 1988." *Prime Time Wrestling.* Created by Vince McMahon. Titan Sports, Inc.,1988.

"Prime Time, January 16th, 1989." *Prime Time Wrestling.* Created by Vince McMahon. Titan Sports, Inc., 1989.

"Prime Time, January 23rd, 1989." *Prime Time Wrestling.* Created by Vince McMahon. Titan Sports, Inc., 1989.

"Prime Time, June 23rd, 1986." *Prime Time Wrestling.* Created by Vince McMahon. Titan Sports, Inc.,1986.

"Prime Time, November 19th, 1987." *Prime Time Wrestling.* Created by Vince McMahon. Titan Sports, Inc., 1987.

"Saturday Night's Main Event II." *Saturday Night's Main Event.* Created by Vince McMahon. Titan Sports, Inc., 1985.

"Saturday Night's Main Event VIII." *Saturday Night's Main Event.* Created by Vince McMahon. Titan Sports, Inc., 1986.

"Saturday Night's Main Event XVI." *Saturday Night's Main Event.* Created by Vince McMahon. Titan Sport, Inc., 1988.

"Saturday Night's Main Event XVIII." *Saturday Night's Main Event*. Created by Vince McMahon. Titan Sports, Inc., 1988.

"Saturday Night's Main Event XXI." *Saturday Night's Main Event*. Created by Vince McMahon. Titan Sports, Inc., 1989.

"Saturday Night's Main Event XXIV." *Saturday Night's Main Event*. Created by Vince McMahon. Titan Sports, Inc., 1989.

"SummerSlam 1989." *SummerSlam*. Created by Vince McMahon. Titan Sports, Inc., 1989.

"SummerSlam 1990." *SummerSlam*. Created by Vince McMahon. Titan Sports, Inc., 1990.

"SummerSlam 1991." *SummerSlam*. Created by Vince McMahon. Titan Sports, Inc., 1991.

"SummerSlam 1992." *SummerSlam*. Created by Vince McMahon. Titan Sports, Inc., 1992.

"Superstars April 25th, 1992." *Superstars*. Created by Vince McMahon. Titan Sports, Inc., 1992.

"Superstars February 15th, 1992." *Superstars*. Created by Vince McMahon. Titan Sports, Inc., 1992.

"Superstars January 30th, 1993." *Superstars*. Created by Vince McMahon. Titan Sports, Inc., 1993.

"Superstars January 31st, 1987." *Superstars*. Created by Vince McMahon. Titan Sports, Inc., 1987.

"Superstars July 3rd, 1993." *Superstars*. Created by Vince McMahon. Titan Sports, Inc., 1993.

"Superstars June 12th, 1993." *Superstars*. Created by Vince McMahon. Titan Sports, Inc., 1993.

"Superstars June 25th, 1988." *Superstars*. Created by Vince McMahon. Titan Sports, Inc., 1988.

"Superstars June 27th, 1992." *Superstars*. Created by Vince McMahon. Titan Sports, Inc., 1992.

"Superstars June 9th, 1990." *Superstars*. Created by Vince McMahon. Titan Sports, Inc., 1990.

"Superstars June 9th, 1990." *Superstars*. Created by Vince McMahon. Titan Sports, Inc., 1992.

"Superstars March 10th, 1990." *Superstars*. Created by Vince McMahon. Titan Sports, Inc., 1990.

"Superstars March 4th, 1989." *Superstars*. Created by Vince McMahon. Titan Sports, Inc., 1989.

"Superstars May 16th, 1992." *Superstars*. Created by Vince McMahon. Titan Sports, Inc., 1992.

"Superstars May 2nd, 1987." *Superstars*. Created by Vince McMahon. Titan Sports, Inc., 1987.

"Superstars May 30th, 1992." *Superstars*. Created by Vince McMahon. Titan Sports, Inc., 1992.

"Superstars November 14th, 1987." *Superstars*. Created by Vince McMahon. Titan Sports, Inc., 1987.

"Superstars November 8th, 1986." *Superstars*. Created by Vince McMahon. Titan Sports, Inc., 1986.

"Superstars October 13th, 1991." *Superstars*. Created by Vince McMahon. Titan Sports, Inc., 1991.

"Superstars September 28th, 1991." *Superstars*. Created by Vince McMahon. Titan Sports, Inc., 1991.

"Survivor Series 1987." *Survivor Series*. Created by Vince McMahon. Titan Sports, Inc., 1987.

"Survivor Series 1988." *Survivor Series*. Created by Vince McMahon. Titan Sports, Inc., 1988.

"Survivor Series 1990." *Survivor Series*. Created by Vince McMahon. Titan Sports, Inc., 1990.

"Survivor Series 1991." *Survivor Series*. Created by Vince McMahon. Titan Sports, Inc., 1991.

The Hulk Hogan Archive. "Hogan and Orndorff vs. Studd and Bundy." *YouTube*. 2019. Accessed April 12, 2022. https://www.youtube.com/watch?v=vQ7KqWx6vhu.

The Statutes Project. "1835 Cruelty to Animals Act." 2023. Accessed May 1, 2023. https://statues.org.uk/site-the-statues-nineteeth-century-1835-5-6-william-4-c-cruelty-to-animals-act/.

"The Main Event." Created by Vince McMahon. Once a Month Productions and Titan Sports, Inc., 1988.

"The Wrestling Classic." *The Wrestling Classic*. Created by Vince McMahon. Titan Sports, Inc., 1985.

This Tuesday in Texas. Created by Vince McMahon. Titan Sports, Inc., 1991.

"*Tuesday Night Titans*, July 23rd, 1986." *Tuesday Night Titans*. Created by Vince McMahon. Titan Sports Inc., 1986.

"*Tuesday Night Titans*, May 21st, 1986." *Tuesday Night Titans*. Created by Vince McMahon. Titan Sports Inc., 1986.

"*Tuesday Night Titans*, May 7th, 1986." *Tuesday Night Titans*. Created by Vince McMahon. Titan Sports Inc., 1986.

"WrestleMania I." *WrestleMania*. Created by Vince McMahon. Titan Sports, Inc., 1985.

"WrestleMania III." *WrestleMania*. Created by Vince McMahon. Titan Sports, Inc., 1987.

"WrestleMania IV." *WrestleMania*. Created by Vince McMahon. Titan Sports, Inc., 1988.

"WrestleMania VI." *WrestleMania*. Created by Vince McMahon. Titan Sports, Inc., 1990.

"Wrestling Challenge January 12th, 1992." *Wrestling Challenge*. Created by Vince McMahon. Titan Sports, Inc., 1992.

"Wrestling Challenge November 16th, 1986." *Wrestling Challenge*. Created by Vince McMahon. Titan Sports, Inc., 1986.

"Wrestling Challenge November 1st, 1986." *Wrestling Challenge*. Created by Vince McMahon. Titan Sports, Inc., 1986.

"Wrestling Challenge September 30th, 1990." *Wrestling Challenge*. Created by Vince McMahon. Titan Sports, Inc., 1990. https://www.youtube.com/watch?v=DlpCfHH10VU.

Wrestling with Paul. "WWF Wrestling January 1989." *YouTube*. 2020. Accessed January 28, 2022. https://www.youtube.com/watch?v=7eXFaByF7dw.

Wrestling with Paul. "WWF Wrestling July 1988." *YouTube*. 2019. Accessed February 12, 2023. https://www.youtube.com/watch?v=9XLh3G1q4sw.

WWE. ""Macho Man" Randy Savage WWE Debut." *YouTube*. 2014. Accessed October 7, 2022. https://www.youtube.com/watch?v=cBIXztSSNr0.

WWE. "Bunkhouse Stampede Battle Royal: Jan. 3, 1987." *WWE*. 2023. Accessed March 28, 2023. https://www.wwe.com/videos/bunkhouse-stampede-battle-royal-jan-3-1987.

WWE. "Hulk Hogan and Andre the Giant square off at WrestleMania III press conference in rare Hidden Gem." *YouTube*. 2020. Accessed January 8, 2023.https://www.youtube.com/watch?v=Vmu6XCVE4jk.

WWE. "Jake "The Snake" Roberts attacks Randy Savage with a cobra." *YouTube*. 2010. Accessed April 12, 2022. https://www.youtube.com/watch?v=Sbv54NTqEmo.

WWE. "Slick buys half-interest in the contracts of Freddie Blassie's talent: All Star Wrestling, Aug. 16." *YouTube*. 2013. Accessed June 14, 2022. https://www.youtube.com/watch?v=YTPw01D475s.

WWF the 80's. "This Day in WWF History!" *YouTube*. 2020. Accessed June 2, 2022. https://www.youtube.com/watch?v=ncj6dw-hme4.

www.ingramcontent.com/pod-product-compliance
Lightning Source LLC
Chambersburg PA
CBHW070136100426
42743CB00013B/2723